D0424745

GHOSTS OF LONDON

by J. A. Brooks

JARROLD

Jarrold Publishing, Norwich

ISBN 0-7117-0557-7

© 1982, 1991 Jarrold Publishing
First published 1982; second edition 1991; reprinted 1993

Printed in Great Britain by Jarrold Printing, Norwich. 3/93

Introduction

'... suppose I see the Apparition of one deceas'd, according to the *common Notion* the Soul of that Person went immediately to Heaven or Hell at the Moment it left the Body: if so, and it was the Soul of that Person I saw, it follows, that either the Souls of Men can revisit the Earth after they have received their Doom for another State, or they can be in more than one *Place at once;* neither of which Cases seems reasonable.'
(From a letter to the Gentleman's Magazine, *Volume IX, 1738–39, from Benjamin Martin.)*

The debate on whether or not it is reasonable to believe in ghosts has raged throughout history. London is a city particularly rich in episodes which would seem to support the proposition: over the centuries many accounts have appeared in print, and in this volume some of the stories are told again, generally from as close to the original source as possible. These old accounts are often not only good tales of the supernatural, but also shed valuable light on the ways of life and beliefs of the people involved. Some stories are sinister and chilling, others may seem hilarious, but few fail to add to the atmosphere and romance of our capital.

The modern stories are hardly less interesting. I remember finding a report in the files of the Society for Psychical Research which involved the haunting of a modern house built on the site of a wartime fighter station. A pilot in full combat uniform regularly appeared in the house. The householder complained that it would not be so bad if the ghost were not so clumsy. He always seemed to make a point of knocking over the tailor's dummy which the owner of the house had dressed in Nazi uniform.

Finally, the book contains a few episodes that would seem to have little to do with any sort of ghost, but since they pleased my ghoulish sense of humour I included them. I apologise to all those who do not share my delight in the misfortunes of those such as the beadle of the Royal College of Surgeons, who died of shock after seeing a corpse appear to come to life during an early experiment with electricity!

Contents

The East End

Bow is at the heart of the Cockney's London, for only those born within hearing of its church bells can truly be called Cockney. The ghosts of Bow are wise in their choice of haunts – nearly all of them are pubs.

Most famous of these is the Bow Bells – an article in the *East London Advertiser* in 1974 spoke of the 'phantom flusher' that made going to the loo a nightmare for ladies at the pub. Customers seated on the toilet would be startled by the locked door being thrown open, and the cistern emptied by an unseen hand. The landlord once felt an icy wind when all the doors were closed, and saw an inexplicable mist rise from the floor. When a seance was held to solve the mystery the toilet door crashed open, shattering the glass of its windows.

Another Bow Road pub with a ghost is the Black Swan. On the night of 23 September 1916, the original pub was completely destroyed by a bomb dropped by a Zeppelin in one of the first aerial attacks on London. Four people were killed – the landlord's two young daughters (aged twenty and twenty-one), the baby girl of the elder daughter, and his mother. The pub was subsequently rebuilt, but the ghosts of Cissie and Sylvia Reynolds, the two pretty daughters, remain and have been seen in several of the rooms, particularly the cellar, where there have been many strange incidents. Beer taps have seemingly turned themselves off, and barrels which were lifted on to the racks full have been found empty the next day, without having a pint pulled from them. On one occasion beer taps were turned on in the middle of the night in the bar, causing a flood of bitter. The German Shepherd dog kept by the landlord in 1974, when the *Essex and East London News* wrote of the pub, refused to go down the cellar. Many of the customers believe that the strange happenings are connected with the funeral parlour next door, but it seems more likely the terrible events of that night in 1916 caused a disturbance that still has echoes in the psychic world.

The Bow Bells, in Bow Road.

Similar disturbances (taps being turned on, etc.) were experienced in the late 1960s in the Nag's Head, Hackney Road. A series of strange, unaccountable mishaps culminated in a cellarman actually seeing the ghost in the cellar. He described it as being a very old woman wearing a grey shawl over a long Victorian dress. Seances were held at the pub, and they seemed to put the ghost to rest.

POLICE *THE ILLUSTRATED* NEWS

LAW COURTS AND WEEKLY RECORD

SISTER OF VICTIM

FIFTH VICTIM

MORTUARY

THE BERNER S! VICTIM.

INSPECTOR REID

INQUEST ON FIFTH VICTIM AT S! GEORES IN THE EAST

TWO MORE WHITECHAPEL HORRORS. WHEN WILL THE MURDERER BE CAPTURED ?

BACK OF BERNER STREET

FIRST DISCOVERY OF THE CRIME

GOING TO HER DOOM

POLICE CONSTABLE WATKINS SIGNALLING FOR ASSISTANCE

FINDING THE BODY IN MITRE SQUARE

MITRE SQUARE ALDGATE

THE FATAL SPOT

THE SCENE ON SUNDAY IN BERNER STREET

DISCOVERY OF THE GATE

THE FIFTH VICTIM OF THE WHITECHAPEL FIEND.

FINDING THE MUTILATED BODY

East Enders have always been quick to cash in on slender opportunities and when the landlord of the Ten Bells in Commercial Street, Whitechapel (on the corner with Fournier Street) discovered that the body of the fourth of Jack the Ripper's eight victims had been found close to the back of the pub in Hanbury Street, he changed its name to 'Jack the Ripper'. The walls were decorated with contemporary accounts from the *Police Gazette* and other chronicles of the time, and with a facsimile copy of the original police file on the case. Then they discovered that the name of the Ripper's victim found behind the pub was Emily Annie Chapman – the maiden name of the landlord's wife!

The police never found the Ripper. He committed eight savage murders in the Whitechapel/Hackney area between April 1888 and July 1889. The district was then notorious for its prostitutes, who were far removed from their higher-class sisters who worked the West End. The East End ladies of the street were content to receive the price of a bed in a common boarding-house in exchange for their favours, and Emily Chapman was returning to just such a house when she was attacked. A witness who discovered her body described the horror of the sight:

> Her clothes were thrown back, but her face was visible. Her apron seemed to be thrown back over her clothing. I could see from the feet up to the knees. She had a handkerchief of some kind round her throat . . . it seemed as if her inside had been pulled from her, and thrown at her. It was lying over her left shoulder.

At first, when it was discovered that the woman had been disembowelled, it was thought that the murderer had intended to take away the womb, for which an American university would pay £20. However the injuries of the later victims were not consistent with this pattern, and the police abandoned their theory that the murders were done for gain. The enduring feeling of the local population was that the culprit was a member of the high aristocracy, Royal Family, or Government who was safe from the attentions of the police: after all, what were the deaths of a few ageing prostitutes against the mighty edifice of Victorian respectability?

There is no escaping that the sudden, horrific demise of the Ripper's victims should give rise to ghosts in the dark alleys of Whitechapel, and there were many reports of ghosts here after the murder. The most famous is that immortalised by Elliott O'Donnell –

The Illustrated Police News on 13 October 1888, reflected the public's growing fascination with the activities of the Ripper. (BRITISH LIBRARY, COLINDALE)

the 'huddled figure, like that of a woman, emitting from all over it a ghostly light, frequently to be seen lying in the gutter.' This was often seen in Durward Street where the Ripper's first kill, Polly Nicholls, was found. Furthermore the landlord of the 'Jack the Ripper' was quite certain that it was the ghost of Emily Chapman which haunted his pub. Anyway, he managed to get a good mention in the *Hackney Gazette* in August 1975, when he claimed the ghost for his pub, complaining of the strange gusts of cold wind that came from nowhere, and the radio that would switch itself on and off, and other more or less unaccountable happenings that took place there.

In 1979 the *Essex and East London News* reported on a disapproving ghost which haunted the Drivers' Arms, Mile End. The landlady was justifiably upset when her drinks completely vanished (at first she suspected that there was a practical joker among her customers). Then heavy objects began to be dislodged mysteriously, and were seen to move of their own accord. She called in a medium who was able to explain that there was a ghost of a previous, Victorian, tenant who disapproved of women drinking, and because of this caused the trouble.

Another Mile End ghost was unusual in being that of a person still alive. The same newspaper reported on a strange haunting at the Ancient Briton, Glaucas Street. The ghost was again that of a former tenant of the pub who was still alive and well and living in Goodmayes. She had had to leave the pub when her husband died, having spent fourteen enjoyable years there. She was seen in the cellar by the new manager who described the figure in detail to a former barmaid who was able to identify it as being that of the previous landlady.

You would expect the pubs of Dockland to be too busy with drinkers to have time for ghosts, yet both the Connaught Tavern in West Ham, and London's oldest riverside pub – the Gun Tavern at Coldharbour on the Isle of Dogs – are reputed to be haunted.

The Connaught has the ghost of a madwoman who committed suicide there. She was the aunt of the landlord, and after she died the bedroom on the second floor was abandoned as she had left it. Gradually over the years the rumpled sheets on the bed became grey with dirt, and layers of dust covered the entire room. If any room should have a ghost it was this one, and sure enough when three members of the staff did manage to pluck up enough courage to look inside, they saw the old mad woman there, her eyes lit by the wild

The sinister sign of the Jack the Ripper pub.

light of insanity, and her mouth twisted into a leering, wicked shape. All three dashed down the stairs to safety. The ghost has not been seen recently, and the Connaught has had many landlords since the death of the old lady.

In 1965 the *Stratford Express* gave a brief mention to the ghost that haunts one of the bedrooms of the Gun Tavern at Coldharbour. Since Lord Nelson had clandestine meetings with Lady Hamilton here when he returned to land, it is always assumed that his is the ghost that is seen.

On the opposite side of the Isle of Dogs, upriver on Limehouse Reach, passengers on the trip-boats voyaging to Greenwich will see an ancient inscription: 'Site of the building and launching of Steamship "Great Eastern" 1853–8'. Because of the enormous size of the vessel (22,500 tons), Brunel had it built side-on to the river – its passage to the river and launching being controlled by hydraulic rams. Disasters regularly befell the ship during its construction. Four workmen were killed before the launching: one was crushed to death inside the superstructure; another fell to his death on the steel plates of the keel; a young boy working as a riveter's mate also fell and was impaled on a scaffolding support; and one of the 200 riveters disappeared without trace while working on the 3,000,000 hand-driven rivets which held the plates of the hull together – the hull was built with two thicknesses. A sightseer who came to Millwall to stand amazed and in awe at the enormous size of the *Great Eastern* was struck dead by a monkey-wrench which fell from the hand of a workman far above.

The launching of this 'Wonder of the Seas', six times larger than any ship built previously, was scheduled to take place on 3 November 1857, at high tide, which was at midday. Against Brunel's wishes a great crowd assembled to watch the spectacular event. The fastenings at bow and stern were slackened, and a great creaking, groaning sound came from the hull, but though the noise continued for ten minutes the ship failed to move. Then suddenly the slipway shook as she began to slide, taking by surprise the gang of men operating the giant windlass which was meant to control the rate of her descent into the water. Its enormous handles spun madly as the chain ran out, and the inattentive men were flung high into the air by the tremendous force unleashed. One was killed outright and others suffered terrible injury. Spectators on board barges in the river, seeing the monster begin its uncontrolled slide towards them, jumped

The SS Great Eastern. (BRUNEL UNIVERSITY)

into the water in desperate efforts to escape: two were drowned. In fact there was no need for such panic for the great hull came to a standstill before reaching the water, in a great welter of noxious Thames mud.

It took many more months before the gigantic, jinxed ship could be got afloat, and the worries and recriminations finally broke Brunel's failing health. However, early on the morning of 5 September 1859, he came on board the ship in order to select cabins for himself and his family on the maiden voyage. He undertook a final tour of inspection, and having completed this was photographed on board the ship. Within minutes he collapsed with a stroke and was carried ashore to his home; he never arose from his bed again.

The *Great Eastern* put to sea attended by a host of small boats carrying cheering crowds. At six o'clock on the evening of 9 September she was in the Channel abreast of the Dungeness Light, steaming at thirteen knots, when the paddle-wheel boilers blew up, killing six stokers and wrecking much of the superstructure and all of the Grand Saloon. The explosion had been caused by an engineer's negligence in allowing too much steam into the feedwater heaters, but the day before the captain had complained of a constant

hammering that seemed to come from below. The cause of this was never found, yet the hammering always recurred when a mishap was about to hit the vessel. In this instance the hammering heralded not only disaster to the *Great Eastern* but the death of Brunel: he died shortly after being told of the explosion, on 15 September.

The *Great Eastern*'s career was comparatively short. She had been designed to carry a great number of passengers cheaply on lengthy voyages. She would have made an ideal carrier for the thousands of emigrants who were at the time leaving Europe for America and Australia. Brunel had intended her to steam non-stop to Australia. Her owners never used her on this run, persisting in using her as a luxury vessel on the Atlantic – in this role she was an economic disaster, and in the 1860s her luxurious fittings were taken out and she was converted to cable-laying, putting down the first transatlantic telegraph cable between 1865 and 1866. After this her useful life was virtually at an end, and she was scrapped in 1888. On the way to the breaker's yard the unaccountable hammering was heard once more, as it had been before each untoward incident in the past. Shortly afterwards the tow-lines parted and the *Great Eastern* was almost wrecked. When the breakers came to dismantle the mighty hull they found a sealed compartment in the space between the outer and inner shells. In it was a skeleton with an old carpet-bag containing rusty tools. Presumably this was the missing 'rivet-basher' whose ghostly knocking had presaged the disasters which befell the mammoth ship so frequently.

Ten years before the demise of the *Great Eastern* a more tragic accident had occured on the Thames on Barking Reach, a little way downstream from her launching site. In September 1878 the pleasure-steamer *Princess Alice* was rammed by a collier. Cut in two, the *Princess Alice* sank almost immediately and 640 day-trippers died. Many of them were later found not to have drowned but to have been poisoned by the horribly polluted waters (the collision took place close to the outfall of the London drainage system, and in those days sewerage was released untreated into the Thames). The victims' pathetic cries may be heard echoing over the marshes on the anniversary of the incident.

Limehouse, upstream again, was once the roughest area of Dockland. Whores would sell themselves to newly landed sailors for the price of a drink or a 'doss' in a boarding-house. There were lodging-houses for the sailors too, and it is said that one of them was

The last photograph of Isambard Kingdom Brunel taken on board the Great Eastern *minutes before he suffered the stroke that proved fatal.* (BRUNEL UNIVERSITY)

15

The sinking of the Princess Alice *in September 1878.* (MARY EVANS PICTURE LIBRARY)

run by a clergyman, the Vicar of Ratcliff-Cross. Two hundred years ago he became notorious for murdering his wealthier clients during the night, and dumping their bodies in the river. Many of the old lightermen who used to work this stretch of the river would be reluctant to linger alone on Ratcliff Wharf, even in daylight (for this reason the wharf was always closed at five in the evenings).

In 1971 a building contractor engaged on construction work at the wharf became aware of a little old gentleman watching him at work from about twenty yards away. He was dressed in a strange black costume with a high collar, wore gaiters, and leaned on a cane. His long white hair was blown by the wind and his attention seemed to have been caught by something beyond the builder. The latter looked behind him to see what it was that the old man found so interesting, found nothing, and turned back to the old man. He was no longer there! Yet there was nowhere on that wharf that he could have hidden in those few seconds. He checked the dock, the river, and all around without success. When his three colleagues returned he told them of the mystery and they enjoyed his embarrassment when they started pulling his leg about it. Yet within the next few days all three were witness to a similar apparition, and none of them knew the story of the Vicar of Ratcliff. They were all pleased when their work at the wharf was finished. Locally it is said that the ghost usually appears on summer evenings, though all the 1971 sightings were on Sunday mornings in July.

Sadly this story is, in fact, a hoax dreamed up by Frank Smyth, an Assistant Editor of the part-work *Man, Myth & Magic*. First published in the part-work, it was later faithfully recorded in two books on the ghosts of London before the hoax was revealed in 1978 by Daniel Farson in the *Hamlyn Book of Ghosts*. However even before the tale was printed Smyth was startled to meet a lighterman who told him that the story of a ghostly Vicar of Ratcliff had been known to his family for generations. Was the invented story a residual memory that lurked in his unconscious mind? Fortunately the ghost of the murderous Vicar does not seem to have caught up with its creator, so far. . . .

In this chapter we have already dealt with East End pubs, but not with the haunted brewery office. This is the Bass Sales Office at Cephas Street in Stepney, and the *East London Advertiser* told the story in 1980:

> Staff at a brewery office are getting a terrific draught from the spirit world – and they want to find out why.
>
> For the workers at Bass Sales have been getting a cold sensation at their offices, a former doctor's surgery in Cephas Street, Stepney.
>
> And besides the cold shoulder the sweet sickly smell of embalming fluid has been sending cold shivers up and down their spines.
>
> One of the workers said: 'For the past year the smell has become so apparent it's unnatural.
>
> 'We can be talking about something and then there is a strange cold sensation, which makes the hair on your arms stand on end.'

The only explanation for this put forward was that the office was built on the site of a doctor's surgery, and about forty years ago a pregnant woman had been knocked down outside, and then brought in for medical attention. She had died there, though her baby was saved.

In July 1976, the same newspaper, worthy for the attention it gives the supernatural, reported on strange goings-on in the matron's room at the magistrates' court at Stepney. All sorts of incidents upset the day-to-day routine, caused, the Matron believed, by the old lady who had been her predecessor. This was old Mrs Browne who had worked there for twenty-five years, until she was seventy-seven. She was then taken ill with thrombosis and so had to retire, dying soon after. That had been five years previously, and since then a series of events had led her successor as matron, Mrs Gumbrill, to believe that the place was haunted. Articles often floated across the room, and food trays were sometimes snatched from Mrs Gumbrill's hands and dashed to the floor. Witnesses backed up Mrs Gumbrill's account, but as no sequel to the original account appeared it is not known for how long the ghost remained troublesome.

An unidentified ghost haunted the London Jewish Hospital, Stepney, in 1977. He was taken to be an ex-patient and his 'hazy figure' often visited a day-room used by nurses on night duty when they rest. Nurses were particularly frightened by the ghost brushing past them, and one positively identified him as a patient she had known. Although the Jewish religion has no service of exorcism it was suggested that a rabbi should be invited in to say prayers. Presumably this put the spirit to rest, for there have been no further reports of a sighting from the hospital.

Housing officers on local councils are accustomed to complaints of ghosts, and are generally sceptical when they are accompanied by requests for different accommodation. However not all such complaints are bogus, and undoubtedly many people leading normal untroubled lives can become seriously disturbed by paranormal happenings.

Barton House, Bow, is an ordinary-looking block of flats owned by the GLC. In February 1977, the *East Ender* told how the Ussher family had suffered from the appearance of the ghost of a little old lady wearing carpet slippers and a white apron. She proved to be a mischievous or even malevolent ghost, knocking items from shelves and tampering with electrical fittings. A favourite trick was to plunge the flat into darkness by throwing the mains switch. Exorcism by an Anglican vicar and by a Catholic priest failed to bring release from the old lady: a medium was called in but could only confirm the ghost's hostility to the family. The local librarian found that the flats were built on the site of an ancient convent – but the ghost was never described as being nun-like. The Housing Officer found that the flat had never been occupied by an old lady, but promised to move the Usshers elsewhere when an alternative became available. This story is typical of many, and researchers are always wary of people's motives in reporting seeing a ghost.

North London

The Ghosts of Islington

Pride of place must go to the Islington Ghost itself – Mr Richard Cloudesley. The account is taken from a booklet bearing that title in Islington Library: '. . . being a short account of the burial of a gentleman at Islington with a relation of several strange appearances which followed.' (Muggins & Co., Clerkenwell, 1842.)

> Thus far concerning ghosts in general: we now proceed to speak of the ISLINGTON GHOST. When we consider that this was in our own immediate neighbourhood, we might well be filled with horror, consternation, and dismay, were it not for the assurance that this ghost is now laid. The name of the gentleman whose ghost caused such alarm, was Richard Cloudesley. He was probably of the same family as William Cloudesley, an early benefactor to the parish,

Trinity Church, Cloudesley Square, Islington (it is now the 'Celestial Church of Christ' – a hot-gospel church of the pentecostal variety). (ISLINGTON LIBRARY)

Collins' Music Hall c. 1910. (ISLINGTON LIBRARY)

and possibly descended from, or in some way connected with William of Cloudesley, a famous archer and outlaw, who at an early period infested the northern counties of England. The aforesaid Mr Richard Cloudesley was an inhabitant of the parish of Saint Mary, Islington, and a considerable landed proprietor. He died in the year 1517, bequeathing to the parish an estate of fourteen acres (commonly called the Stonefield estate) which is situated in the Liverpool Road, Trinity Church standing upon a part of it. A window of this Church contains the portrait of Mr Cloudesley in painted glass, which we would respectfully urge our readers to examine upon the first opportunity. But we are imperceptibly diverging from our subject. Mr Cloudesley pursuant to the directions given in his last will was buried in the yard of the parish church. The passage in which these directions are given reads thus:– 'I bequeath . . . my body after I am passed this present and transitory life to be buried within the church-yard of the parish Church of Islington, near unto the grave of my father and mother.' The following epitaph was placed upon his tomb:

'HERE LYES THE BODY OF RICHARD CLOUDESLEY, A GOOD BENEFACTOR TO THIS PARISH, WHO DIED 9 HENRY VIII. ANNO DOMINI, 1517.'

20

All the provisions made by Mr Cloudesley for his repose would seem from the testimony of a respectable writer to have proved ineffectual. This author, after speaking of certain earthquakes, proceeds as follows:– 'and as to the same heavings, or *tremblements de terre*, it is said that in a certain field, near unto the parish church of Islington, in like manner did take place a wondrous commotion in various parts, the earth swelling, and turning up every side towards the midst of the said field, and by tradition of this, it is observed that one Richard Cloudesley lay buried in or near that place, and that his body being restless, on the score of some sin by him peradventure committed, did shew, or seem to signify, that religious observance should there take place, to quiet his departed spirit; whereupon certain exorcisers (if we may so term them) did at dead of night, nothing loth, using divers exercises at torchlight, set to rest the unruly spirit of the said Cloudesley, and the earth did return to its pristine shape, nevermore commotion proceeding therefrom to this day, and this I know of a very certainty.'

Elsewhere we are told that Richard Cloudesley's ghost was only laid after a thousand Masses were said for his soul. Moreover in 1813 his remains were moved (though without dire consequences apparently) as the inscription shows:

This tomb was erected by an order of Vestry held on Easter Tuesday the 20th Day of April 1813, to perpetuate the memory of Richard Cloudesley, a very considerable benefactor to this parish who was interred AD 1517, whose remains were found and deposited in a leaden coffin underneath on the 10th of June 1813.

Other ghosts of Islington include that of the impresario Sam Collins which used to haunt the Music Hall he once owned on the Green. Sam always used the same seat (Row B, No. 6) and the cleaning women got so used to his being there that they would clean round him. In 1960 he was seen to walk through the wall of the cellar, but there are no accounts of his ghost having appeared since the old building was knocked down, soon afterwards.

No. 113 Bride Street is now a telephone exchange, but once it was a chapel of the Sandemanian sect. Michael Faraday (who discovered the principle of electro-magnetic induction upon which Bell's telephone was dependent) was an elder of this sect, and a plate in the floor of the exchange marks the position of his pew when it was a

Michael Faraday by T. Phillips, 1841–2. (NATIONAL PORTRAIT GALLERY)

chapel. Faraday's ghost has been seen in the building.

The Old Queen's Head on Essex Road has several ghosts. The original pub, whose licence was granted by Sir Walter Raleigh and which was used by Queen Elizabeth herself, was pulled down in 1829. Even then strange stories were told of it: one of its upper rooms was sealed off because children, victims of the Plague, died there in 1665. Landlords of the rebuilt pub have often been troubled by ghosts – some described an Elizabethan lady, others swear that they have seen the sad figure of a little girl. On the first Sunday of every month doors open and close and footsteps are heard coming down the stairs. Legend says that Queen Elizabeth had a tunnel built from the Queen's Head to Canonbury Tower so that she could discreetly visit her lover, the Earl of Essex, there. An enduring theme of the haunting is the sound of a lady's footsteps with the swish of a full-skirted dress.

The Old Queen's Head, Islington. (ISLINGTON LIBRARY)

London North-West

In April 1980 the *St Pancras Chronicle* printed the report of a most curious episode. It concerned an ancient suit of armour that an antique-dealer had in his shop in Grafton Road. He obtained it from a house in Hackney which he had cleared out. After repair the armour (which he discovered was originally from Spain) stood in his shop for several months. Then one day it was spotted by an Arab gentleman who stopped his Rolls-Royce outside and paid the dealer the price he was asking without a quibble.

Soon afterwards the haunting began. A tall, bearded, noble-looking figure began to haunt the shop, a sad expression on his face. His dignity was in no way diminished by the fact that he only wore strange, scanty undergarments. After several meetings with the figure the proprietor decided that the ghost was restless because his armour had been removed. Unfortunately he found that it had already been shipped to the Middle East and so the sad knight continued to walk in the shop in Kentish Town.

Dr Hawley Harvey Crippen was hanged on 23 November 1910 for the savage murder of his wife. The fame of this murder owed more to the manner of the culprit's capture than to the deed itself – he was apprehended on a transatlantic liner with his mistress, the message having been transmitted by 'wireless'. Before the murder he spent many late nights wandering deep in thought around a piece of waste ground close to his house at Hilldrop Crescent, Kentish Town – presumably plotting the way to kill his wife. An investigator of the supernatural thought it worth while to watch here on the night before Crippen's execution. He was rewarded by seeing a phantom figure bearing a strange-looking parcel cross the ground, going towards ancient junk-strewn ponds near by. After a few minutes the ghost returned – without its burden. Mrs Crippen's head and some other portions of her anatomy were never found.

There are reports from other parts of the country of body-snatchers fabricating ghosts so that their own activities might continue undisturbed. This seems not to have happened so much in Central London, though the gang of 'resurrectionists' from St Pancras was probably the busiest of any operating in England. Furthermore one of their company even kept a diary between 1811 and 1812 which was published by the Librarian of the Royal College of Surgeons in 1896.

'Resurrectionists' at work.

These are the entries relating to the old churchyard of St Pancras (which was formerly in Pancras Road):

Feb. 20, 1812. Thursday.
'Met, and went to Pancras, and got 15 large, & 1 small. Took them to Bartholw.'
Mar. 3, 1812. Tuesday.
'Went to St Thomas's, at night went to Pencress, and got 8 adults, 2 small, and 2 foetus.'
Mar. 25, 1812. Wednesday.
'Went to Pencress got 5 adult, Took them to Bartholomew.'
Mar. 31, 1812. Tuesday.
'Went to Pencress, got 5 adults Bill, Ben & me. Dan'l, Jack and Tom went to Harps, missed.'
Nov. 25, 1812. Wednesday.
'Met at Jack at 2 p.m. Butler & myself went to the B. Ln. got 1 adt. Jack, Ben & Bill went to Pancs. got 5 adult, & 1 small. Took them to Bartholw. Removed 3 to Cline, got 2 sets of "cans" [canine teeth].'

Dec. 1, 1812. Tuesday.
'Met at Tottenham Court Road had a dispute in St Ts. Crib. Came home did not do anything, came to the Rockingham Arms, got Drunk.'
Dec. 2, 1812. Wednesday.
'Met at Vickers rectifyd our last account, the party sent out me & Ben to St Thos. Cb. got 1 adt., Bill and Jack Guys Crib 2 adt. but one of them opd. Butler look out for us, took them to St Thos. came home. Met at St Thos. Me & Jack went to Tootm. got 4 adts. Ben and Bill got 6 ad. 1 s. 1 f. at Pancrass took Tootenm. to Wilson, Pans. to Barthol.' (i.e. got 6 adults, 1 small, and 1 foetus from St Pancras: these were taken to St Bartholomew's; the four from Tottenham went to Mr Wilson).

The editor of the diary comments that the gang worked all the public and private graveyards in and around London. They supplied not only hospitals and doctors, but also teeth for use by dentists 'which they drew from bodies that were too decomposed for anatomical investigation'. The teeth, incidentally, were then used for dentures since artificial teeth were not then made.

Stories of the supernatural often embrace witchcraft but this is less common in London where the people have always had a reputation for being less gullible than their country counterparts. An exception is the story of Mother Red Cap of Camden Town, quoted verbatim here from *History of St Pancras*, written in 1870 by Samuel Palmer:

LIFE OF MOTHER DAMNABLE,
THE ORIGINAL MOTHER RED CAP OF CAMDEN TOWN.

This singular character, known as Mother Damnable, is also called Mother Red Cap, and sometimes the Shrew of Kentish Town. Her father's name was Jacob Bingham, by trade a brickmaker in the neighbourhood of Kentish Town. He enlisted in the army, and went with it to Scotland, where he married a Scotch pedlar's daughter. They had one daughter, this Mother Damnable. This daughter they named Jinney. Her father on leaving the army took again to his old trade of brickmaking, occasionally travelling with his wife and child as a pedlar. When the girl had reached her sixteenth year, she had a child by one Coulter, who was better known as Gipsy George. This man lived no one knew how; but he was a great trouble to the

The old 'Mother Red Cap' Inn, 1746. (MANSELL COLLECTION)

magistrates. Jinney and Coulter after this lived together; but stealing a sheep from some lands near Holloway, Coulter was sent to Newgate, tried at the Old Bailey, and hung at Tyburn. Jinney then associated with one Darby; but this union produced a cat and dog life, for Darby was constantly drunk; so Jinney and her mother consulted together, Darby was suddenly missed, and no one knew whither he went. About this time her parents were carried before the justices for practising the black art, and therewith causing the death of a maiden, for which they were both hung. Jinney then associated herself with one Pitcher, though who or what he was, was never known; but after a time his body was found crouched up in the oven, burnt to a cinder. Jinney was tried for the murder, but acquitted because one of her associates proved he had "often got into the oven to hide himself from her tongue."

Jinney was now a lone woman; for her former companions were afraid of her. She was scarcely ever seen, or if she were, it was at nightfall, under the hedges or in the lanes; but how she subsisted was a miracle to her neighbours. It happened during the Commonwealth troubles that a man, sorely pressed by his pursuers, got into her house by the back door, and begged on his knees for a night's lodging. He was haggard in his countenance, and full of trouble. He offered Jinney money, of which he had

27

Mother Damnable

of KENTISH TOWN

—— Anno 1676. ——

From a Unique Print in the Collection of I. Bindley Esq.ʳ

Publish'd by I. Caulfield 1793.

plenty, and she gave him a lodging. This man, it is said, lived with her many years, during which time she wanted for nothing, though hard words and sometimes blows were heard from her cottage. The man at length died, and an inquest was held on the body; but though every one thought him poisoned, no proof could be found, and so she escaped harmless.

After this Jinney never wanted money, as the cottage she lived in was her own, built on waste land by her father.

Years thus passed, Jinney using her foul tongue against every one, and the rabble in return baiting her as if she were a wild beast. The occasion of this arose principally from Jinney being reputed a practiser of the black art—a very witch. She was resorted to by numbers as a fortune-teller and healer of strange diseases; and when any mishap occurred, then the old crone was set upon by the mob and hooted without mercy. The old, ill-favoured creature would at such times lean out of her hatch-door, with a grotesque red cap on her head. She had a large broad nose, heavy, shaggy eyebrows, sunken eyes, and lank and leathern cheeks; her forehead wrinkled, her mouth wide, and her looks sullen and unmoved. On her shoulders was thrown a dark grey striped frieze, with black patches, which looked at a distance like flying bats. Suddenly she would let her huge black cat jump upon the hatch by her side, when the mob instantly retreated from a superstitious dread of the double foe.

The extraordinary death of this singular character is given in an old pamphlet—"Hundreds of men, women, and children were witnesses of the devil entering her house in his very appearance and state, and that, although his return was narrowly watched for, he was not seen again; and that Mother Damnable was found dead on the following morning, sitting before the fire-place, holding a crutch over it, with a tea-pot full of herbs, drugs, and liquid, part of which being given to the cat, the hair fell off in two hours, and the cat soon after died; that the body was stiff when found, and that the undertaker was obliged to break her limbs before he could place them in the coffin, and that the justices have put men in possession of the house to examine its contents."

Such is the history of this strange being, whose name will ever be associated with Camden Town, and whose reminiscence will ever be revived by the old wayside house, which, built on the site of the old beldame's cottage, wears her head as the sign of the tavern.

Highgate

A featherless chicken would seem to make an unlikely ghost, yet it is this that has haunted Pond Square for hundreds of years, since Francis Bacon, a Lord Chancellor of England and extraordinary man of science, undertook his final experiment in 1626. The account is from John Aubrey's *Anecdotes*:

> His lordship was trying an experiment, as he was taking the aire with Doctor Witherborne, a Scotchman, physitian to the king, towards Highgate. Snow lay upon the ground; and it came into my Lord's thoughts why flesh might not be preserved in Snow as in salt. They were resolved they would try the experiment presently; they alighted out of the Coach, and went into a poor woman's House, at the bottom of Highgate Hill, and bought a hen, and made the woman exenterate it, and then stuffed the bodie with snow; and my lord did help to do it himself. The snow so chilled him, he immediately fell so ill that he could not return to his lodging (I suppose then at Gray's Inn), but went to the Earl of Arundel's house at Highgate, where they put him into a good bed warmed with a panne; but it was a damp bed, that had not been layn about a yeare before, which gave him such a cold, that in two or three days he died of suffocation.

The following is a copy of Lord Bacon's last letter to the Earl of Arundel and Surrey:—

> 'MY VERY GOOD LORD,—I was likely to have had the fortune of Caius Plinius the elder, who lost his life by trying an experiment about the burning of Mount Vesuvius; for I was also desirous to try an experiment or two touching the conservation and induration of bodies. As for the experiment itself, it succeeded excellently well; but in the journey between London and Highgate, I was taken with such a fit of casting as I know not whether it were the Stone, or some surfeit or cold, or indeed a touch of them all three. But when I came to your Lordship's House, I was not able to go back, and therefore was forced to take up my lodging here, where your housekeeper is very careful and diligent about me, which I assure myself your Lordship will not only pardon towards him, but think the better of him for it. For indeed your Lordship's House was happy to me, and I kiss your noble hands for the welcome which I am sure you give me to it, etc.

'I know how unfit it is for me to write with any other hand than mine own, but by my troth my fingers are so disjointed with sickness that I cannot steadily hold a pen.'

Perhaps the poor bird knew that in the twentieth century millions of its kind would be bred to meet their ends in a similar way without ever experiencing a natural life. The macabre carcass, flapping stumpy wings, has appeared far less frequently in recent years, and its frantic squawks are no longer heard.

Ye Olde Gate House pub is at the top of Highgate Hill: in the days of the cattle-drovers it would be the last resting-place for men and beasts before they reached Smithfield the next day. Its history goes back to 1310 when it received its first licence. The ghost is that of an old lady, Mother Marnes, who was killed here (with her pet cat) for her money. The black-robed figure still haunts the pub, though it never appears if children or animals are in the building.

Elthorne Road is at the bottom of Highgate Hill, and the occupants of a three-year-old GLC flat in Beechcroft Way close by were greatly troubled by poltergeist activity in 1978. Heavy objects were seen to be moved by invisible means, and the vague outline of a figure was seen, not only by the couple living in the flat but by several of their neighbours as well. In this case the occupants stressed that they had no wish to move, as they had spent a lot decorating and furnishing the flat. Things quietened down after a service of blessing was held.

Highgate Cemetery has long had the reputation of being one of the most haunted, evil places in London. Its array of ornate sarcophagi, monuments and dark vaults evoke the feeling of a menacing presence which waits to envelop the unwary soul.

One of the earliest of the strange incidents that have taken place her was the disinterment of Elizabeth Siddal, a woman of distinctive beauty who was the favourite model for the Pre-Raphaelite painter, Dante Gabriel Rossetti. Later he married her and was heart-broken when she died in 1862 at the age of twenty-nine. As a gesture of love, he placed a manuscript volume of poems in her coffin. The death of Elizabeth marked a watershed in Rossetti's life – from then on his reputation was in decline, both as an artist (he believed that he was going blind) and as a writer.

He had engaged a ruthless entrepreneur, Charles Augustus Howell, as his literary agent. Howell also handled the work of Ruskin and Swinburne (the latter calling him 'the vilest wretch I ever came

Elizabeth Siddal (MANSELL COLLECTION)

across'), and after years of persuasion he managed to get Rossetti to agree to the opening of Elizabeth Siddal's grave at Highgate in order to retrieve the unpublished poems – 'The Book from the Grave'. This was done on a cold, damp autumn night – 5 October 1869 – by the light of a huge bonfire which soon disclosed that in death Elizabeth's hair was as golden and glorious as it had been when she was alive (it was also considerably longer). The poems were retrieved, disinfected and published soon afterwards. Before the opening of the grave, Rossetti had taken himself off to Scotland where he began to drink the terrible mixture of chloral and whisky which ensured that none of his later work showed the genius of his youth, and brought about an early death.

Neither did Howell fare much better. In 1890 his body was found in the gutter outside a Chelsea public house. His throat had been cut

The Gatehouse and Highgate Village (GUILDHALL LIBRARY)

and a gold coin was between his clenched teeth. The murderer was never found, though for many years Howell's financial affairs had been so disastrous that he had been forced to make a premature announcement of his own death!

Access to Highgate Cemetery is now difficult, due partly to the activities of a self-styled vampire-hunter, Allan Farrant, and his followers in the early 1970s. In August 1970 the *North London Press* reported the first of many disturbances at the cemetery:

> Police are investigating the possibility that the headless body found in Highgate Cemetery last week may have been used in Black Magic rites. Two young girls made the gruesome discovery of a charred woman's body – minus head – as they walked through the cemetery on Friday last week. The body, which had been buried in 1926, came from a family vault in the catacombs of the old cemetery.
>
> 'The body had been charred. It was very well preserved, like a fossil', a police spokesman said.

Two weeks later the *Islington Gazette* carried the story of Farrant's appearance in court, where a large wooden cross, a piece of rope and a crucifix were produced in evidence. He was found guilty of being in St Michael's churchyard for an unlawful purpose, but this seems not to have deterred him, as in the following October he was interviewed by the same newspaper and told them how he and his colleagues of the British Occult Society kept watch over the cemetery at night as they were convinced of a vampire's presence there. Many graves had been smashed and corpses dispersed. In 1973 the *Hornsey Journal* carried an account of more weird goings-on:

> A cat was sacrificed to a horned god in a macabre night-ritual at Highgate Woods during the weekend involving eight hooded coven members and a naked High Priestess who left at the scene a bloodstained carving knife, blood-spattered stockings, and offal. . . .

Farrant's downfall came in the following year: the trial received great publicity at the time. He was sent to gaol for four years and eight months after being found guilty on the following counts: unlawfully and maliciously damaging a memorial to the dead; unlawfully entering a place of interment and interfering with a body; threatening two detectives by sending them voodoo death-spell dolls to prevent or dissuade them from giving evidence in criminal proceedings against fellow occultists, etc. He was also alleged to have conducted Black Magic ceremonies in a vault in which a pretty French girl danced naked over desecrated coffins. The Judge, Michael Argyle, spoke of the horror of the case in his summing-up: 'We were unfortunate enough to have to look at a corpse which had been horribly interfered with on the previous evening. The body had been laying in her coffin since 1884. The tomb had been smashed open and the corpse mutilated.'

The *Islington Gazette* of 2 August 1974, carried an amusing postscript to the story concerning the dolls that had been sent to intimidate the police:

> The dolls had been carefully made in the shape of a grown man – each with an outsize phallus. During their journey through the post, however, the phallic symbols had fallen off.
>
> For weeks leading up to the trial the two detectives had to endure certain embarrassing questions from their colleagues. Word quickly got around the office and even blushing typists and wives were let in on the leg-pull.
>
> The two detectives are happy to report that they are fit and well and that they have nothing amiss to report.

Highgate Cemetery today.

There are more orthodox supernatural activities that occur in the cemetery apart from those involving voodoos and vampires. An old madwoman distractedly searches among the tombs for the children she once murdered; a tall man with a black hat mysteriously fades into the walls of the cemetery at Swain's Lane; and a ghost with bony fingers lurks near the main entrance.

A classic Victorian ghost story was printed in the short-lived *Mother Shipton's Miscellany* on 2 December 1878. Since it concerns Highgate it is reprinted here:

THE SPECTRAL VISITANT,
Or, THE STUDENT'S DEATH BED.

A Narrative founded on facts.
"Truth is strange, stranger than fiction."

HIGHGATE still rejoices in many quaint old mansions, any one of which might possess its own peculiar ghost; rambling red-brick houses, with moss-grown courtyards in front, and spacious yet gloomy apartments, and with gardens stretching far and wide, which with their wealth of sombrous trees and thick plantations, have a stately and mournful aspect. But the house in which the scene of this narrative is laid has gone the way of many a fine suburban residence. The ivy covered walls, worthy of a medieval castle; the massive gates, rust-eaten by age; the broad flight of steps, the richly carved doorway; the spacious marble staircase; the rambling out-houses, each larger than a modern villa; the great bell that clanged the announcement of a new arrival; the terrace walks, with their curiously clipt yews and gardening of a by-gone age; the thatched summer-house, with geometric floor and seats and tables, from which far-reaching views over a smiling landscape were obtained—all, all have gone. But the memory of the strange history now to be related still remains; and "I tell the tale as 'twas told to me."

Wild and reckless had been the youth of the only son and heir of Mr. ——, who lived at the Big House at Highgate—as I shall prefer to call it. He had been away for nearly two years; his name was never mentioned by his stern and high-minded father, and but in hushed whispers by his broken-hearted mother and sisters. But as the Christmas of 1790 approached he came home—as people said, to die.

A nurse was engaged—one of a trusty nature; and one evening a rickety hackney coach toiled up the steep hill, and deposited the worthy woman at the Big House, much agitated by an adventure in the Hollow Way, not unfrequent in those days—the stoppage of the coach by a highwayman near what is now known as Red Cap lane. But the highwayman was in good humour, and after frightening Nurse terribly by strange oaths, let the jarvie drive on, with a warning to have a richer fare next time he ventured on the great North road. As Nurse was shown into the room she shuddered involuntarily: the oak panelling was black with age; the fireplace was supported by massive buttresses, the bed seemed as large as a moderate-sized room. There was but the glimmer of a single lamp in the fireplace, which served only to make darkness visible. The Doctor was just leaving as the good woman arrived, and as he left he enjoined absolute silence. Nurse sat down, replenished the fire, and commenced reading a book of devotion. Now and again, a blast of wind shook the leafless branches of the great elms, while the snow—which had begun to fall—spluttered on the embers as it was wafted down the wide chimney, and gradually wrapt the gardens in a shroud. Curious to see her patient, Nurse gently opened the curtains: contrary to her expectations, he was not asleep, but lay motionless on his back, his bright blue eyes glaring fixedly upon her, his under-lip fallen, and his mouth apart, his cheek a perfect hollow, and his long white teeth projecting fearfully from his shrunken lips, whilst his bony hand, covered with wiry sinews, was stretched upon the bedclothes, and looked more like the claw of a bird than the fingers of a human being. Nurse quietly retired, and two hours passed heavily away. About midnight the patient began to breathe heavily, and appeared very uneasy; turning to look towards him, she was surprised to see a lady closely veiled, seated on a chair near the head of the bed beside him. Nurse though startled was about moving to the bed when the lady with her gloved hand motioned her to keep her seat. Nurse obeyed, but the more she reflected as to how the strange visitor had entered, the more perplexed she became. The shape and turn of her head and neck were graceful in the extreme; the rest of her person she could not so well discern. She at length concluded that the visitor must be some relative of the young man's, although she had been told that the apartment was some distance from the other living rooms. With the curiosity inherent in her sex, she determined to watch the stranger, who continued gazing on the patient, who heaved and sighed and breathed in agony, as if a night-mare were upon him. Nurse again moved towards the bedside, but was again motioned off. Strangely fascinated, she complied, though against her will; and her eyes closing for a moment (for she was fatigued by her journey) she opened them to find the lady gone, and the young man breathing more freely.

Nurse was at her post the next night, but was naturally somewhat nervous. The same scene was enacted. The strange lady entered, how she knew not. As Nurse advanced towards the

Highgate Cemetery (GUILDHALL LIBRARY)

bedside—undeterred by the repellent action of the stranger, the latter withdrew to the table. The thundering clap of a distant door alarmed poor Nurse, more terrified still by the countenance of the patient; big drops of cold sweat were rolling down his pale brow; his livid lips were quivering with agony; and as he motioned her aside, his glaring eyes followed the retreating figure of the lady. Piqued at the young man's refusal of her attentions, she retired in dudgeon; again determined to watch the departure of her mysterious companion, again was she baffled. Sinking to slumber, she was only awoke by the female who had come to relieve her watch. If the room had looked dismal as the flickering fire-light filled it with fantastic shadows, it looked miserable as the dazzling whiteness of the reflected snow outside showed its dirty and dilapidated condition.

The next night was Christmas Eve. Nurse had made up her mind to leave; but the medical man represented how much inconvenience such a course would cause, and pooh-poohed the idea of the occurrence being supernatural in its character, which the old woman began now—with all her piety—to suspect. Nurse accordingly consented to remain; and commenced to watch—not merely the departure but the arrival of her fair friend. The night was stormy, the dry crisp sleet hissed on the window, whilst the wind soughed among the trees like the agonizing wails of lost spirits, and the rattling of ill-secured shutters echoed fearsomely along the dismal passages of the Great House. But as the strange visitant had not appeared on former occasions till the night was far advanced, she now did not expect her sooner, and endeavoured to occupy her attention till that time by some other means. The

occasional ticking of the death-watch; the dull falling of masses of snow from the branches to the ground, all the slight sounds of the sick room, were intensified to Nurse's imagination. She closed her eyes with a feeling of pain; when she opened them, the singular being was there! Again the same distressing scene ensued, her suffering charge gasped and heaved till the noise of his agony made her heart sicken within her; when she drew near the bed his corpse-like features were horribly convulsed and his ghastly eyes straining from their sunken sockets. She spoke, but he answered not; she touched him, but he was cold with terror, and unconscious of any object save the one mysterious being whom his glance followed with a fixed intensity, and who had moved silently away towards the table. Thinking the young man was about expiring, Nurse prepared to leave the room for further assistance, when she saw the lady again move towards the bed of the dying man: she bent over him for a moment, whilst his writhings were indescribable; she then moved statelily towards the door. Now was the moment! Nurse advanced at the same time, laid her one hand on the lock, whilst with the other she attempted to raise the veil of the stranger. The next instant she fell lifeless on the floor. As she glanced on the face of the lady, she saw that a lifeless head filled the bonnet; its vacànt sockets and ghastly teeth were all that could be seen beneath the folds of the veil.

Daylight was breaking on the Christmas morning, when the poor old woman, cold and benumbed, was found stretched on the floor of the passage. The invalid lay stiffened and lifeless: one hand thrown across his eyes, as if to shade them from some object on which he feared to look; the other grasping the coverlet with convulsive firmness.

That Christmas morning the body of a woman—young and beautiful—was washed ashore hard by Queenhithe. It had apparently been in the water three or four days. Letters found in her pocket showed conclusively her connection with the young man at the Big House. The family soon deserted the mansion, after pensioning the old Nurse, who, however, never recovered from the shock.

This is the tale; we repeat, a true one, if the solemn asservations of a Christian woman drawing near her end have any weight. The exact measure of that young man's sin was never known. That its punishment was terrible, this narrative at least has demonstrated.

'. . . a lifeless head filled the bonnet; its vacant sockets and ghastly teeth were all that could be seen beneath the folds of the veil.' (LONDON DUNGEON)

Hampstead

The following appeared in the *St James's Gazette*, January 1889:

EXORCISING A GHOST AT HAMPSTEAD.

Miss Frith, daughter of the well-known artist, who writes under the signature "Walter Powell" in a Canadian paper, tells in a recent letter the following version of the ghosts at Hampstead:—

There are two rows of old red brick houses at Hampstead, forming an avenue to the church, which houses, built on ground which once belonged to a monastery, are continually troubled by the most unaccountable noises, in one or two cases the inhabitants declaring that the noises, which they *can* bear, have been further supplemented by the appearance of apparitions, which they *cannot*. Not long ago one of those possessing the worst of reputations was taken in all innocence by some people who, till they had been in the place sometime, were left unmolested. But very soon steps pattered up and down stairs in the dead of night; doors, previously locked, unaccountably flew open; often there was a feeling, even in the broad daylight, that one was being watched (said my informant) by invisible eyes, touched by invisible fingers. The maids gave warning continually, the children occasionally were frightened, but as months went on without anything actually being seen, the footsteps and rustlings, growing monotonous, were at last almost

Church Row, Hampstead.

unheeded, and the household settled down with the firm determination, annoying enough to the ghost, to ignore its presence altogether, a resolution not always strictly kept. One afternoon a November or two ago, the lady of the house sat by the fire in a small drawing-room, shut off from a larger one by folding doors, reading fairy tales to her little daughter, and as she read she heard some one walking overhead, in a room from which the ghost always started on its peregrinations. She glanced at the child, who was staring at the flames absorbed in the history of "The Snow Queen" and who, wisely enough, had no ears for anything else, and continued the story without a pause. Soon on each of the shallow oak stairs sounded the well-known pit-a-pat of high-heeled shoes, till the steps, staying a second at the smaller drawing-room, went on to the larger room, the door of which opened and shut with a bang; but nothing disturbed the little girl. As her mother read on, someone behind those folding doors was turning the handles softly, pacing up and down the floor, moving chairs and small tables, till at last the reader became so nervous she thought she even should have screamed. Instead of that, however, she made some excuse of resting for a moment, gave the book to her daughter, and taking up a lamp went bravely to the threshold of the other room and looked in. The footsteps ceased suddenly, but peer as she might into every corner, nothing could she see. Just as she was turning back to "The Snow Queen" and the fire, the child ran towards her. "Why, mamma," she said, pointing to a window seat on which the stream of lamplight fell brightest, "who is that pretty lady?" Since then Mrs. S., who is a Catholic, has had that restless ghost laid (this is the nineteenth century, five miles from Charing Cross), and with bell and book the priest and the acolyte have done their best to restore peace to No. —, Church row, the consequence being that after that afternoon, spent in sprinklings and prayer, the pretty lady has altogether ceased her visits.

Later accounts, most probably concerning the same ghost, explain that the footsteps were those of a child being pursued. These would stop suddenly and then would come a long, shuddering, sigh. September was the favourite month for the haunting to occur. Dawn would occasionally show the sinister figure of a red-haired serving-maid creeping from the house carrying a carpet-bag. Long ago, it was believed, she had murdered a child who was in her care, dismembered its body, and furtively left the house at first light with the remains in the bag.

The notebooks of John Emslie supply another ghost of this locality:

Mr Ashley, a student at Heatherley's Art Academy, and who lived for two years at the Priory at Hampstead, told me that the latter building was erected by a public-house auctioneer of the name of Thompson who, being supposed from his business to know every corner of a street, was called Corner Thompson: having, in his business capacity, acquired a great many oddities, he erected the odd-looking building (Priory) and furnished it equally oddly: his two daughters married, and one of them is said to have been immured in the walls of the house, and her ghost has been sometimes seen.

Emslie was told this tale in about 1880.

Dick Turpin figures prominently in Hampstead ghost stories. Mounted on his famous black horse, he has often been seen in the vicinity of the Vale of Health. The notorious highwayman gallops up at a furious pace, and just as you feel certain that you will be run down, he vanishes. Before the Second World War the clatter of Black Bess's hoofs was sometimes heard at the famous Spaniards Inn, on the Hampstead Heath, where he used to lodge.

Another ghost from about the same era was as recently as late 1980 experienced by the singer Lynsey de Paul, dining, appropriately, at Turpin's on Heath Road with James Coburn. John Blake, writing in the *New Standard*, quoted her as saying:

All of a sudden I said to James: 'There's a ghost here.' I felt she was a young woman who was strangled in the building in the 1700s. I told a waiter, and he said a girl was stabbed there long ago. Then he came back a few minutes later to tell me he had the story wrong. The girl had been strangled, as I originally thought.

Mr Michael Best, who co-runs the restaurant, told me: 'Lynsey is right – and she couldn't have known about the story beforehand. We took over the restaurant a year ago and heard the tale from an American tourist who lived in the building during the war and witnessed numerous sightings.

'Lynsey was sitting at Table Number Three, near the old fireplace. People have asked to be moved from there in the past because it made them feel uncomfortable.'

Turpin at work.

The William IV pub, in Heath Street, has a ghost which haunts the road outside. A girl in a white shroud and with long plaited hair is seen at the windows, sorrowfully staring in. She is said to be the shade of a young girl who committed suicide in the dentist's surgery that once stood opposite the pub. On the heath itself is a Whistling Stone that marks the spot where a highwayman was killed.

The Northern Suburbs

Bruce Castle, at Tottenham, is now a museum: once it was the home of Rowland Hill, the founder of the penny post and of the British Post Office. Thus it is appropriate that it now displays interesting items connected with the development of the postal system. The building itself dates from Elizabethan times when it was a manor-house. An earlier house was built by the father of Robert Bruce whose family owned the manor of Tottenham in early medieval times.

The mansion's ghost is that of Constantia, the beautiful wife of Lord Coleraine, who was so possessive that he kept her locked up in the small chamber high above the entrance porch. On 3 November 1680, she jumped to her death from the balustrade with her baby in her arms. Her terrible scream was heard on the anniversary of the sad event until early in this century, when a local vicar held a prayer meeting in the room in an attempt to quieten the ghost.

Recent reports of ghosts at Bruce Castle include a lively cavalcade of figures in eighteenth-century costume seen in the grounds in 1971. These ephemeral party-goers appeared twice within a week or so. On the second occasion the couple who saw the gathering approached it, whereupon the figures 'melted into the wall'.

J. P. Emslie was an enthusiastic collector of the folk-tales and traditions of London: his notebooks covered the period between 1860 and 1893 and show a particular interest in ghost stories. The notebooks were edited by F. Celoria for the first issue of *London Studies* in 1974, and are the source for the following stories.

Honeypot Lane, Stanmore, was the scene of a great battle when Caesar's armies first came to Britain. This is said to be the cause of its haunting – for a great rushing sound is sometimes heard on dark nights, and many have spoken of something horrible brushing past them at the same time. Old Church Farm, also at Stanmore, was once a rectory:

People have often seen a ghost rise out of a grave in the field opposite to the farm, go over to the farm, enter it, and come back and re-enter its grave. People have heard knocking, and all kinds of noises: last year a man was in the house, watching a dying woman; no other people were in the house. He saw the parson's ghost come into the room, lean over the woman and look at her, and then retire.

The district around Kingsbury Green and The Hyde at Colindale was haunted by the ghost of a haymaker who had quarrelled with a fellow worker and been fatally stabbed with a pitchfork. The ghost was supposed to be dangerous, and if you encountered it you ran the risk of being run through – with the pitchfork. Hyde Lane was also the haunt of a ghostly donkey, remarkable for being polychromatic, dazzling the beholder with its rainbow colours as it passed.

Another well-haunted thoroughfare, according to Emslie, is Colindeep Lane. The wife of Jack Griffiths drowned herself in a pond by the lane, and it is her ghost that is seen. She was ill-used by her husband, and was 'maddened by drink' when she threw herself in the pond. Another ghost was seen by a policeman in the lane one night, going towards Hendon:

He saw a man a little in front of him, and walked faster to catch up to him, for the sake of having his company. Not catching the man, he went on increasing his speed until he was running hard, and yet could never catch the man, who suddenly disappeared. The policeman was so frightened, that his hair stood up on end to that extent, that it lifted his hat off his head, and a few days after he died of fright.

In the days when Edmonton was a village, it had a haunted house called 'Wire Hall'. A cook once employed there had murdered a fellow servant. The room where the murder took place was so badly haunted that it had to be bricked up and remained so for fifty years until the house was pulled down. A spectral white dog also haunted this locality (close to Edmonton Church) which never harmed anyone who met with it as long as they ignored it. Another ghost is that of a labourer killed by a bullock at Wire Hall.

Nether Street, West Finchley, was haunted by the ghost of a white lady who frightened many of the local constabulary. One policeman became so preoccupied with the ghost after he had seen it that he spent much time '. . . reading all about the ghosts in the *History of Finchley* until he lost his reason. He is now in an asylum.'

Emslie was a wonderful collector of story and anecdote. A final extract from his work is this opinion, from another policeman:

A policeman at Bedfont told me something to the following effect: it is written that the time will come when we shall not know night from day, summer from winter, and that when those things shall

It is hard to believe that the northern suburbs could provide scenes like this only a hundred years ago!

A white dog is said to haunt the district around Edmonton church. (GUILDHALL LIBRARY)

come we may look for the end of the world; it does seem as if that time were coming, as the winters have lately been so mild, that workmen used to look to begin working again in the fields as soon as possible after Christmas, but now they look to be keeping at work in the fields up till Christmas time; extologers [*sic*] tell us that as the former world was destroyed by water, the present one will be destroyed by fire, about the year AD 2000, and it does seem as if the world were getting wicked enough for it, for you find that little children damn and bugger, and know as much as grown-up people.

Avenue House, East End Road, Finchley, now houses local government offices. It was once the home of 'Inky' Stephens, manufacturer of pens and ink, who gave the property to Finchley Council. During the war one of the upstairs rooms was converted into a dormitory for women working the switchboard. This was unsuccessful because of a ghost who constantly disturbed the girls sleeping there, always approaching one particular bed, having entered the room without opening the door. After a little it would leave the room in the same way.

Lawrence Street, Mill Hill, was troubled by the activities of a ghost in 1963 after men working in the grounds of St Joseph's Nursing College accidentally unearthed a coffin which turned out to contain the remains of a nun buried in the nineteenth century.

Several housewives living in the vicinity had strange experiences shortly afterwards. Two spoke of seeing a cloaked figure in the street which disappeared as it was approached. They, with several other people living near by, also said that they heard hymn-singing in their houses. At first they thought that this came from their radios, but in all cases their sets turned out to be switched off. A cloaked figure had previously haunted Lawrence Street in the 1920s but the reason for its presence was never discovered.

Leaving the far northern suburbs, and turning east, we come to the fire station at Ilford. Originally this was situated in the Broadway, where in Victorian times Geoffrey Netherwood was one of the firemen. In his spare time he enjoyed reading of the supernatural, which appeared to be his only interest apart from his duties at the fire station. He was well regarded by his colleagues, and when he died his coffin was borne by them to the grave; his gleaming brass helmet was buried with him. Shortly afterwards these same colleagues encountered his ghost in the building, and even in modern times, with the brigade depot having been moved to Romford Road, Geoffrey Netherwood continues to haunt it, still resplendent in his old-fashioned uniform.

In the early years of the present century Perryman's Farm, Ilford, was troubled by a poltergeist which caused damage by breaking crockery and dislodging pictures from the wall. The old lady who lived there resorted to traditional means in order to placate the troubled spirit: each night she left it a bottle of beer and a plate of food on the table. The account fails to tell us whether this generous treatment was successful.

A very traditional English haunting occurs in Bell Lane, Enfield. This is the appearance of the phantom stage-coach known as the 'Enfield Flyer' which strikes terror into the hearts of those it encounters when it dashes towards them out of the darkness. Just as they feel certain that it will run them over it vanishes. Since it seems to travel about five or six feet above the surface of the road, 'run over' is a literal expression. The coach is black and carries two lady passengers wearing large hats. Only a theoretical explanation for this haunting has ever been given: which is, that in olden days the level of the road was higher as the surrounding land had not been drained and was often flooded; the coach and its occupants may have come to disaster when it crashed off the road into the flood waters of the River Lea (the phantom coach has also been seen to vanish into this river).

Wanstead churchyard provides the frightening spectacle of a ghostly skeleton wheeling the coffin cart. As it approaches an ornate tomb, a spectre in white emerges and passionately embraces the bony frame. Do not be alarmed, though, as it is a family reunion – the ghosts are man and wife!

RE CRDS

Singular Execution of the Countess of Salisbury in 1541.

Cruikshanks. del.

The City

The Spectres of the Tower

This, the capital's foremost historical attraction, has a legacy of horror and suffering extending to comparatively recent times. The Romans placed a fortification here when they founded the city, principally to protect the approach to the city upriver from the sea. Parts of the walls they built to enclose their settlement are incorporated into the defences of the Tower and may still be seen today, but the main work dates from1078, William the Conqueror also appreciating the strategic value of the site. Many of his successors put up further defence-works to make it even more secure, necessary as weapons became more sophisticated. Living quarters were also made more elaborate until the Tower eventually became a town within a town – its life revolving round that of its most important citizen, at many times throughout history the monarch himself.

At the hub of the fortress is the Conqueror's White Tower: the defences surrounding it were designed for two functions – not only should they keep the enemy at bay, but they should also serve to make escape impossible for the prisoners held within. Many of the most illustrious figures of our history have been confined in the Tower's lodgings and dungeons: once incarcerated in the Tower most of them knew that their fate was already determined; even though execution might be delayed for many years, in most cases political expediency made the monarch sign the fatal decree in the end.

Execution by the axeman's hand at the block on Tower Green would have been a welcome end to the suffering of many held captive here. Terrible instruments of torture were used to extract confessions from prisoners, and many suffered the greatest agonies without repudiating their allegiance or faith. Thus it can hardly come as a surprise that the sufferings of these poor souls live on at the Tower in the psychic plane. For the variety of its manifestations it is unrivalled in Britain and, most probably, anywhere in the world. They are dealt with more comprehensively in G. Abbott's excellent

Ghosts of the Tower of London, published in 1980, and only a select few can be mentioned here.

Even as recently as the time of the Second World War the Tower was used as a prison. Spies and traitors were kept safe behind its massive walls, and a few of them met their ends facing a firing-squad close to the Traitors' Gate. Quite recently a yeoman warder, looking from the window of his house one evening, was startled to see a strange figure suddenly appear only yards from the old shooting-range where executions took place. The man, his head bowed, was dressed in a drab grey utility suit of the 1940s. As the warder strained his eyes to try to take in more details the figure vanished.

One evening in 1954, at fifteen minutes before midnight, a sentry saw a puff of white smoke come from the barrel of one of the ancient cannon that abound at the Tower. This lingered for a moment, then made the shape of a square and began to drift towards the guardsman, changing shape again as it did so. At this the sentry left the scene to fetch a colleague, and when he returned both saw the smoke 'dangling on the wrong side of the steps leading to the top of the wall'. The strange mass quivered in constant movement, but by the time the guard was turned out all trace of it had vanished. (*Proceedings of the Society for Psychical Research*, **53**, 150.)

The Traitors' Gate was the watergate entrance for prisoners condemned after trial at Westminster. It dates from 1240 when Henry III enlarged the fortress by building outer defence-works. There is a story that when work on the gate was almost complete a great storm undermined the foundations on St George's Day 1240, with the result that the gate collapsed. When the circumstances were repeated identically the following year an inquiry revealed that a priest claimed to have witnessed the ghost of St Thomas Becket striking the stonework with a crucifix, lamenting that the new defence-works were not for the common good but 'for the injury and prejudice of the Londoners, my brethren'. Since it was the King's grandfather who had caused the death of the Saint he felt it politic to include a small oratory in the tower of the new building dedicated to St Thomas Becket. Even so its rooms have always had the reputation of being haunted. Doors open and close without reason, the figure of a monk in a brown robe has been seen, and ghostly footsteps – the distinctive 'slap' of monastic sandals – are sometimes heard. As in many different parts of the Tower, these rooms also occasionally echo with the agonised groans and shrieks of long-dead prisoners suffering duress,

'The Night before the Execution' by George Cruikshank. (BRITISH LIBRARY)

but perhaps the saddest sounds of all are the heart-rending sobs of a baby that died centuries ago.

Only a few of the ghosts can be readily identified. Henry VI was stabbed to death, most probably by Richard, Duke of York (later King Richard III), during the hour before midnight on 21 May 1471. The chamber where this awful deed took place is reputed to be haunted by the figure of the victim which always appears at this time.

Anne Boleyn, the most celebrated of the wives of Henry VIII, was beheaded on Tower Green in 1536. Her ghost has frequently been seen both on the Green and, more spectacularly, in the Chapel Royal situated in the White Tower. Here a Captain of the Guard saw a light burning in the locked chapel late at night. Finding a ladder, he was able to use it to look down on the strange scene being enacted within. A nineteenth-century account described it thus:

> Slowly down the aisle moved a stately procession of knights and ladies, attired in ancient costumes; and in front walked an elegant female whose face was averted from him, but whose figure greatly resembled the one he had seen in reputed portraits of Anne Boleyn. After having repeatedly paced the chapel, the entire procession, together with the light, disappeared.
>
> (*Ghostly Visitors* by 'Spectre Stricken', London 1882.)

Another account of this story tells how the procession always occurs on the anniversary of the terrible execution of the Countess of

Salisbury in 1541. This brave old lady (she was over seventy at the time of her death) suffered because of her son's (Cardinal Pole) vilification of Henry VIII's religious doctrines, a campaign the Cardinal conducted from the safety of France. Thus his mother was brought to the block by Henry as an act of vengeance, but instead of submitting meekly to the axeman she refused to lay down her head and was pursued round the scaffold by him. Swinging wildly he inflicted the most hideous wounds on his victim till she at last succumbed. This event may also be the cause of the sinister shadow of an axe which passes over Tower Green before becoming clearly defined on the wall of the White Tower, where it stands 'menacingly erect'.

A further sighting of the ghost of Anne Boleyn is contained in the proceedings of a court martial that took place in 1864. A sentry standing guard at the Queen's House saw and challenged a white shape that appeared suddenly veiled in mist. When his challenge went unanswered he put his bayonet into the figure but was overcome by severe shock when it passed right through without meeting any resistance. The sentry's story was corroborated by two onlookers who saw the incident from a window in the Bloody Tower: he was acquitted of dereliction of duty by the court. In later years the same apparition was seen by other guards. It is not known what details convinced the sentry or his officers that the ghost was that of Anne Boleyn – we can only accept that a hundred years of tradition makes it so.

The ghost of Thomas Wentworth, Earl of Strafford, is another that has been identified. His bitter comment 'Put not your trust in Princes for in them is no salvation' sums up his relationship with Charles I, the King who found it expedient to condemn a friend to death to hide his own shortcomings. Strafford died bravely on the scaffold, yet his spirit proved restless, appearing to his old political rival Archbishop Laud, himself a prisoner at the time and with whom he had requested a final meeting. Perhaps because this was denied him, Strafford's ghost visited Laud in his cell, reproved him for his misdemeanours, and told him to have no fear. Later the same night, before Laud had recovered from the shock of Wentworth's visitation, the old man was further disturbed by the sudden appearance of the ghost of Cardinal Wolsey. Perhaps this was a premonition, as Laud was himself executed four years later.

Much of the Tower's reputation as a grim, evil fortress stems from the famous story of the little Princes of the Bloody Tower, murdered by order of their wicked uncle who was later to become Richard III. This happened soon after they had been imprisoned here in 1483: King Edward V was twelve years old and his brother Richard, Duke of York only nine. No one knew their fate for certain until 1674 when two small skeletons were found beneath a stairway outside the White Tower. It was generally assumed that this was where the Princes had been hidden after their murders, and their ghosts are said to have ceased to haunt the Bloody Tower after the bones had been reburied in Westminster Abbey. Certainly there have been no recent reports of a pathetic pair of little-boy ghosts clad in long white nightgowns.

On 24 October 1618 Sir Walter Raleigh was executed at Westminster after enduring thirteen years of imprisonment in the Bloody Tower. His ghost frequents 'Raleigh's Walk' where the old adventurer used to exercise during his long captivity.

Although their ghosts have never been identified, James, Earl of Derwentwater, and Charles Radcliff, his younger brother, have good cause to haunt this place. Their family had a curse of extinction laid that was fulfilled with the death of the two brothers:

When a green oakleaf is turned to red
The last earl shall die in his gory bed.
The fox and the owl shall inhabit his halls,
The bat and the spider shall cling to his walls,
His lands from his house the strong arm shall sever
And the name of his race be extinguished forever.

As they were a Catholic family it was only too easy for this curse to be effective in the seventeenth and eighteenth centuries. James, the last Earl, was persuaded to take up arms against George I in the first Jacobite Rebellion. It is a tradition that he came to his decision riding by the banks of a stream – the Devil's Water – on his estate. Glancing up through the foliage of an oak tree he saw one red leaf prematurely sere amongst a thousand green ones.

Both brothers fought at Preston for the Jacobites and both were captured – James being sent to the Tower of London and imprisoned in the Devereux Tower. He was sentenced to death for insurrection and he lost his title and estates by attainment. Much pressure was brought to bear upon the King to secure the reprieve of this young and popular nobleman. However, when it was learnt that Robert Walpole, one of the chief Ministers, had been offered a bribe of

£60,000 to save him from execution, the sentence was ordered to be carried out and he was beheaded on Tower Hill on 24 February 1716. He was twenty-seven years old.

Meanwhile his younger brother had been imprisoned at Newgate and might have been pardoned but instead of waiting for this he took the chance to escape with thirteen other prisoners. Settling on the Continent and marrying a wealthy widow, he was for a time Secretary to Prince Charles Edward ('Bonnie Prince Charlie'), and made many clandestine trips to England to rally support for the Stuart cause. However in 1745 he was captured off the Dogger Bank, a passenger in a French ship laden with arms for the Jacobite armies. Like his brother he was incarcerated in the Tower and condemned to death under the former sentence. He was allowed one concession: although he was not a member of the peerage (his brother had forfeited the title as part of his punishment) he was allowed death by decapitation rather than by hanging, which would have been his fate otherwise. The sentence was carried out on 8 December 1746.

Thus the curse was fulfilled, as was a gipsy prophecy made to Charles Radcliff in his youth. He was told that all his palm showed was the shape of a bloody axe, its blade turned towards him.

The Martin Tower, at the north-eastern corner of the inner defence-works, has the unenviable reputation of being the haunt of some of the most persistent of the ghosts of the Tower. In the upper rooms there is the phantom of George Boleyn, brother of Anne, who was imprisoned in these chambers before suffering the most hideous form of execution devised by the English system: being hung, drawn and quartered. This was usually reserved for traitors, though others in particular disfavour might also suffer its agonies. The victim was first half-strangled, then cut down and, while still alive, disembowelled, finally the body was cut up into quarters. There were instances of people surviving until the final part of the sentence.

Thomas Percy received a more merciful sentence – he was imprisoned in this tower for sixteen years for his part in the Gunpowder Plot. However his spectre is supposed to be the one that caused the sentries such apprehension during the last century that they would only mount guard in pairs. In the last few years visitors have felt unseen hands attempt to push them down the steep stone steps by the tower.

The Martin Tower was the location of the most famous, and to many the most convincing, of all the supernatural occurrences in the

Tower. This happened during the early years of the last century: it was witnessed by a very credible and distinguished man – Edward Lenthal Swifte, then the Keeper of the Crown Jewels. His position made it impossible for him to tell of his experience at the time, but when he left office he was able to recount it at length in *Notes & Queries* (1860). He wrote:

I have often purposed to leave behind me a faithful record of all that I personally know of this strange story. Forty-three years have passed, and its impression is as vividly before me as on the moment of its occurrence but there are yet survivors who can testify that I have not at any time either amplified or abridged my ghostly experiences.

In 1814 I was appointed Keeper of the Crown Jewels in the Tower, where I resided with my family till my retirement in 1852. One Saturday night in October, 1817, about the 'witching hour', I was at supper with my wife, her sisters, and our little boy, in the sitting-room of the Jewel House, which – then comparatively modernised – is said to have been the 'doleful prison' of Anne Boleyn, and of the ten bishops whom Oliver Cromwell piously accommodated therein.

For an accurate picture of the *locus in quo* my scene is laid, I refer to George Cruikshank's woodcut in p. 384 of Ainsworth's *Tower of London*. The room was – as it still is – irregularly shaped, having three doors and two windows, which last are cut nearly nine feet deep into the outer wall; between these is a chimney-piece, projecting far into the room, and (then) surmounted with a large oil-painting. On the night in question the doors were all closed, heavy and dark cloth curtains were let down over the windows, and the only light in the room was that of two candles on the table; I sat at the foot of the table, my son on my right hand, his mother fronting the chimney-piece, and her sister on the opposite side. I had offered a glass of wine and water to my wife, when, on putting it to her lips, she paused, and exclaimed, 'Good God! what is that?' I looked up, and saw a cylindrical figure, like a glass-tube, seemingly about the thickness of my arm, and hovering between the ceiling and the table; its contents appeared to be a dense fluid, white and pale azure, like to the gathering of a summer-cloud, and incessantly mingling within the cylinder. This lasted about two minutes, when it began slowly to move *before* my sister-in-law;

The illustration from Ainsworth's Tower of London *referred to in the text.* (BRITISH LIBRARY)

then, following the oblong-shape of the table, *before* my son and myself; passing *behind* my wife, it paused for a moment over her right shoulder (observe, there was no mirror opposite to her in which she could there behold it). Instantly she crouched down, and with both hands covering her shoulder, she shrieked out, 'O Christ! It has seized me!' Even now, while writing, I feel the fresh horror of that moment. I caught up my chair, struck at the wainscot behind her, rushed up-stairs to the other children's room, and told the terrified nurse what I had seen. Meanwhile the other domestics had hurried into the parlour, where their mistress recounted to them the scene, even as I was detailing it above stairs.

The marvel of all this is enhanced by the fact that *neither my sister-in-law nor my son beheld this 'appearance'.* When I the next morning related the night's horror to our chaplain, after the service in the Tower church, he asked me, might not *one* person have his natural senses deceived? And if *one*, why might not *two*? My answer was, if *two*, why not two thousand? an argument which would reduce history, secular or sacred, to a fable.

Mr Swifte's story stimulated a bevy of correspondence to *Notes & Queries*. Readers suggested logical explanations for the phenomena, most of which Mr Swifte was able to demolish effectively. Thus when it was alleged that some prankster might have projected images into the room he pointed out that not only did the thick curtains make this impracticable, but if it had been accomplished then all the people present would have seen the illusion. In one of his replies Mr Swifte mentioned a more sinister episode that occurred at the Tower only a few days after his own experience:

One of the night sentries at the Jewel Office, a man who was in perfect health and spirits, and was singing and whistling up to the moment of the occurrence, was alarmed by a figure like a huge bear issuing from under the Jewel Room door. He thrust at it with his bayonet, which stuck in the door, even as my chair had dinted the wainscot; he dropped in a fit, and was carried senseless to the guard-room.

When on the morrow I saw the unfortunate soldier in the main guard-room, his fellow sentinel was also there, and testified to having seen him at his post just before the alarm, awake and alert, and had even spoken to him. I saw the unfortunate man again on the following day, but changed beyond all recognition; in another day or two, the brave and steady soldier, who would have mounted a breach, or led a forlorn hope with unshaken nerves, *died* – at the presence of a shadow.

Confirmation of this story came from another officer stationed at the Tower at this time. This is his account:

Before the burning of the armouries there was a paved yard in front of the Jewel House, from which a gloomy and ghost-like doorway led down a flight of steps to the Mint. Some strange noises were heard in this gloomy corner; and on a dark night at twelve the sentry saw a figure like a bear cross the pavement and disappear down the steps. This so terrified him that he fell, and in a few hours after, having recovered sufficiently to tell the tale, he died. It was fully believed to have arisen from phantasmagoria. . . . The soldier bore a high character for bravery and good conduct. I was then in my thirtieth year, and was present when his body was buried with military honours in the Flemish burial ground, St Catherine's.

George Offor.

Bear-baiting.

Two footnotes may give this story added interest. In his book *Haunted Houses* Charles Harper wrote:

Whether or not the soldier died from the effects of seeing a genuine apparition, or was merely the victim of a practical joke, was never known; but the guards were doubled immediately after this affair and no more apparitions appeared. It is remarkable, however, to read in the memoirs of Sir John Reresby, a hundred years earlier, how a somewhat similar apparition was observed at York Castle where a piece of paper, fluttering along the ground, was seen to change into a monkey, and then into a bear,* and then to accomplish the amazing feat of squeezing between the door and the doorstep, through a space that would hardly have done more than admit the passage of a coin.

Perhaps it is hardly surprising that the ghost of a bear should haunt the Tower, for these creatures were put to incredible suffering here over the centuries when bear-baiting was a sport. Moreover the Royal Menagerie was housed here from early medieval times until the reign of William IV. Leopards, tigers, lions and elephants were among the animals kept, and it is on record that bears, brown and white, were in captivity. The polar bears were taken on leash to the river to catch their own fish! Another ghostly bear haunts Cheyne Walk, Chelsea.

In 1964 G. W. Lambert put forward the 'vortex' theory to explain the 'glass-tube' seen by Mr Swifte and his family. In Volume 42 of *The Journal for Psychical Research* he wrote:

*Another, earlier account says that it finally turned into a turkey-cock.

In certain conditions, which are not well understood, vortices are set up in the atmosphere. They are only rendered visible (a) if they pick up light objects like dust or sand into a sort of column, or (b) occur in very humid conditions, with the result that the air in the centre of the vortex, cooler than that surrounding it, precipitates moisture into a visible cloud of roughly columnar shape. Vortices, which have often been observed picking up hay in hayfields in the summer, are seen to move horizontally at about 4 m.p.h., i.e. at about the rate at which a man walks. Thus a misty 'figure', some 5 or 6 feet high, moving at 'walking' speed, may easily be mistaken for a 'ghost'. If it is taller than a man, it is even more terrifying. Vortices are usually encountered out of doors, but there is no obvious reason why small ones should not occasionally form indoors.

Lambert developed his theory to show that there have been stories of unaccountable clouds of mist forming in old castles since the seventeenth century. Further, the primitive methods of sanitation in such a place could bring about sufficient generation of methane gas to give a cold flame effect ('corpse candles', or will o' the wisps). This was particularly likely to occur in a building close to the Thames, which in 1817 was virtually an open sewer.

Tower Hill, the open space in front of the entrance to the Tower, also has its ghosts. During the Second World War a sentry guarding the main gate (the Tower was then used as a prison for spies and turncoats) watched aghast as a stately procession passed his post. Priests and soldiers clad in the dress of a bygone age came first, then a stretcher borne by solemn attendants. On it lay the body of a man, his head rested in the crook of his arm, in the classic manner of ghosts. Not surprisingly the sentry called the guard out, but by the time they arrived the cortège had vanished. The next day the sentry wrote down his account of the incident. His description of the costume enabled experts to identify the uniforms as those worn by the Sheriff of London's men in medieval times. Then, prisoners were taken from the Tower and handed over to the Sheriff for execution on Tower Hill. Afterwards the body was brought back for burial in the churchyard within the precincts of the Tower, while the head was often taken for display on one of the series of spikes erected for the purpose on London Bridge.

The City Churches

All Hallows-by-the-Tower, in Byward Street, suffered badly from bomb damage but was restored by the efforts of the founder of the Toc H movement, 'Tubby' Clayton, who was its vicar. Before the war there were reports of it being haunted by the ghost of a white Persian cat which in its lifetime had been owned by the organist, Miss Liscette Rist. She was a great animal-lover and made it her personal task to sand the road that led from the docks up to Tower Hill so that the horses working there should not slip. Her Persian cat would accompany her to church for services, and when it died she asked that she should be allowed to bury it in consecrated ground. This request was refused, which may account for the cat returning to haunt All Hallows. There are no reports of its having been seen in the restored church.

The Church of St Magnus the Martyr is on Fish Street Hill, close to the Monument and to London Bridge. The previous church on the site was the first to be burnt down in the Great Fire; the present one is by Wren. Its ghost is a monastic figure who wears an old-fashioned cowled robe. He had been seen by many people inside the church and seems to be a gentle sort of spirit, though he did once frighten one good lady of the church by appearing without a head. The ghost is often seen close to the tomb of Miles Coverdale, Bishop of Exeter, who first translated the Bible into English – this gives rise to speculation that it is Coverdale's spirit that haunts the church. A peculiar aura of sadness emanates from the figure, and many people alone in the church have the feeling that they are being secretly watched, a sense generated by lots of old buildings which is very disquieting to some people.

Before the Great Fire the King's Wardrobe – which contained the ceremonial clothing used on State occasions – was situated close to St Andrew's Church, Queen Victoria Street, which thus carried the suffix '-by-the-Wardrobe'. It is a church built by Wren that suffered badly in the Blitz but has been rebuilt and is now the headquarters of the Redundant Churches Fund. In 1937 a bell named Gabriel was hung in its tower. This was cast in Worcester in the mid fifteenth century and had previously been at Avenbury in Herefordshire until the belfry there became unsafe. Gabriel is said always to have rung of his own accord on the death of a Vicar of Avenbury, and one

St Andrew's-by-the-Wardrobe.

authority (Jack Hallam) maintains that he heralded the demise of an Avenbury vicar from the tower of St Andrew's during his brief sojourn there.

Wren's masterpiece – St Paul's Cathedral – has a ghost: he is an elderly clergyman who haunts All Souls' Chapel at the west end of the cathedral, just by the visitors' entrance. The chapel was rededicated after the First World War and is now the Kitchener Memorial Chapel, commemorating not just the Field-Marshal but all who served in the Army and died in that conflict. It is said that when the chapel was redesigned a secret stairway was revealed at the very spot where the ancient cleric would disappear, melting into the stonework. Two accounts say that the stairway led directly to the dome – this is clearly ridiculous since the length of the nave separates the chapel from the crossing. However all the vergers who have seen the ghost mentioned one unusual characteristic – its high-pitched, tuneless, whistle.

From St Paul's let us walk up the steps and pass through the

Paternoster Square development to emerge on Newgate Street. Opposite is a quiet oasis amid the bustle of the City – Greyfriars churchyard, which also has the sparse remains of Christ Church. This was founded by the Franciscans in 1209, and soon became a powerful monastery. Queen Isabella was buried here, with the heart of her husband, whom she had brutally murdered, on her breast. Little wonder that she is supposed to haunt the churchyard. Another murderess to walk here is Lady Alice Hungerford. She was acclaimed as the great beauty of her generation, but poisoned her second husband and was hanged at Tyburn in 1523. On one infamous occasion her ghost met that of Queen Isabella and such was their rivalry that an unholy row broke out among the tombstones. The onlookers fled in terror. The third lady to haunt Greyfriars is Elizabeth Barton, 'the Holy Maid of Kent', a humble serving-girl prone to spectacular fits who was manipulated so that in delirium she seemed to speak against Henry VIII's plan to divorce his first wife in order to marry Anne Boleyn. She was supposed to have prophesied that he would lose his throne should he remarry. In the event Henry survived but the Holy Maid perished, being executed, again at Tyburn, in 1534. She was buried in Greyfriars but never takes sides in the dispute between the other two lady ghosts.

'Stop stranger, stop as you pass by. As you are now, so once was I. As I am now, you soon will be, so pray prepare to follow me.' So read the inscription on the case containing old Jimmy Garlickhythe, the mummified remains of an unknown medieval gentleman which used to be on display in the Church of St James, Garlickhythe, in Upper Thames Street. His ghost became particularly active after a bomb crashed through the roof of this beautiful Wren church in 1942. Miraculously it failed to explode, and ended up harmlessly in the crypt. Old Jimmy did not take kindly to the disturbance, and was seen on several occasions in different parts of the church. No one knows who 'Old Jimmy' was, though it seems certain that he was of considerable importance as he was buried in a coffin made of glass, a great status symbol in the Middle Ages (keeping down with the Jones's, in fact). Perhaps he was one of the six Lord Mayors of London to be buried in this church.

A ghostly cat is also said to have been seen in St James's: it would be more appropriate if this were seen in the neighbouring Church of St Michael Paternoster Royal, in College Hill. This is another Wren church, again restored after bomb damage, where a mummified cat,

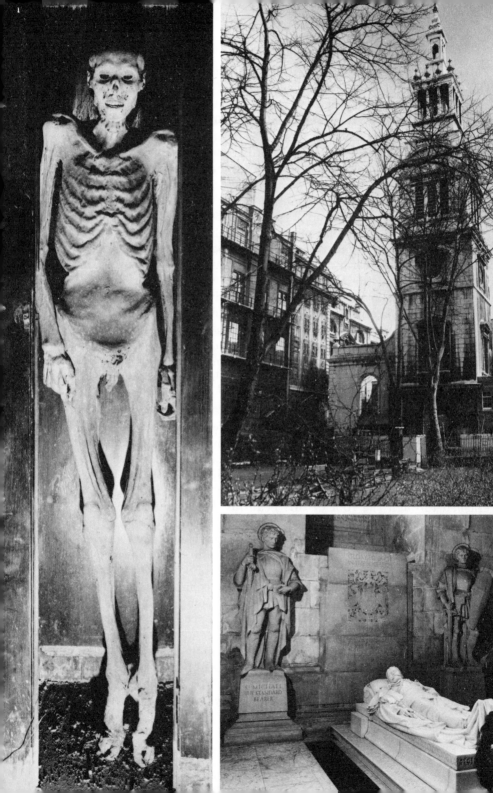

found when the church was rebuilt, is kept in a glass case. This is a highly appropriate trophy for the church, as the original building contained the tomb of Dick Whittington, who died in 1423.

Legend tells how as a young man Richard Whittington came to London from the country to seek his fortune. At first he was unsuccessful and he decided to return home, accompanied by a cat who had, in the ways of those animals, adopted him. When he reached Highgate Hill he paused and heard Bow Bells say: 'Turn again Whittington, thrice Mayor of London.' He obeyed them and with his cat returned to the city where he soon became wealthy and was, in fact, Lord Mayor three times. An inscribed stone surmounted by a cat marks the place on Highgate Hill where he heard the bells.

The massive Norman pillars of the nave give the Church of St Bartholomew-the-Great a completely different atmosphere to that of the Wren churches. Perhaps that is why it is the most haunted of the City churches, or is it because of the awful scenes which took place in front of its beautiful gatehouse, which faces Smithfield?

At a spot known as 'The Elms' many hundreds of people met their deaths, in a variety of hideous ways. A poisoner was boiled alive, and a Prior of Greenwich roasted to death in an iron cage, on the orders of Henry VIII whose authority over the Church he had denied. Most, however, were burned at the stake. If they were fortunate, and the executioner could reach them before the flames grew too fierce, they were strangled first – but many were burnt alive. In the reign of Mary 270 were put to death in this way in England for heresy. Many of them died here in Smithfield, facing east, and the old gateway to the Church of St Bartholomew-the-Great. Small wonder that their ghostly cries still echo through the ether, and these, with the sound of crackling faggots, have been heard by people passing by here alone, on dark nights. Some have even spoken of also smelling the hideous stench of charred flesh.

The ghostly monk said to haunt the church itself is usually taken to be its founder, Rahere, who built the original priory here in 1123, and thus founded the famous hospital as well. He was apparently a minstrel or jester at the Court of Henry I who became a convert to the religious way of life when he was sickened by the frivolity of the Court. While on pilgrimage to Rome he caught malaria and came very close to death. He promised in his prayers to build a hospital for the poor if his life should be spared, and after recovering dreamed that St Bartholomew visited him and directed him to Smithfield,

Left: 'Old Jimmy' Garlickhythe. Right, top: Greyfriars; below: All Souls' Chapel, St Paul's Cathedral (note the shadowy figure in the doorway, the negative has not been tampered with).

69

Wale del.

Grignion sculp.

Manner of BURNING the MARTYRS in Smithfield.

where he was to build the hospice and church.

The Reverend W. F. G. Sandwith was Rector of St Bartholomew's during the early years of this century. He was a man sensitive to ghosts, and saw here not only the monkish figure of Rahere, but another, even more intriguing spectre:

I was taking two ladies round the church, and quite suddenly, looking at the pulpit, I saw in it a man in the black gown of Geneva, evidently a Divine of the Reformation period, preaching away most earnestly to an invisible congregation. No sound was to be heard, but he appeared to be exhorting the unseen audience with the greatest fervour, gesticulating vehemently, bending first to the right, then to the left over the pulpit, thumping the cushions in front of him, and all the while his lips moving as though speech was pouring from them. I looked at him in some dismay because I was afraid that the ladies who were with me might be upset, but as the moments passed and they made no remark about the apparition, I determined to ascertain whether they did, or did not, see it. With this object I pointed straight at the pulpit where the man was preaching and remarked——

'I don't think that pulpit is quite worthy of the church, do you?'

'No, perhaps not,' she replied without further comment, and after a while I turned to her companion and pointed to a monument near the pulpit.

'That is a very interesting old Jacobean effigy there,' I remarked, thus making her, also, look in the direction of the pulpit. She agreed with me, indifferently, in a manner which showed me conclusively that she saw nothing unusual in the direction to which I thus caused her to look. Yet for fully a quarter of an hour I remained in the church seeing that man in the pulpit as clearly as I see you beside me.

(From *Ghosts Vivisected* by A. M. W. Stirling.)

Mrs Stirling also describes a meeting Mr Sandwith's wife had with Rahere:

It seems that on the previous Christmas Eve, Mrs. Sandwith was arranging flowers at the altar in the church when she heard a faint sound behind her, and, looking round, she saw the figure of a monk standing at a little distance. His cowl was drawn over his head and his face was invisible. She spoke to him, but he did not answer, and as she watched him, he glided away noiselessly into the vestry. She at once followed, but to her astonishment found no one there; whereupon she went home and told her husband of her uncanny experience.

'The next day, Christmas Day,' said Mr. Sandwith, continuing his wife's story, 'I was celebrating Holy Communion when I looked up, and, to my astonishment, on the capital of one of the pillars adjacent, apparently looking down at me, was a monk's face encircled by a cowl. I was so amazed that I paused in the middle of the service, and only when I became aware that the congregation were looking at me in surprise, did I continue, while the face above me faded away; but the curious thing was that my wife saw the body of the apparition without the face and I saw the face without the body.'

Rahere has been seen many times since then. He is a tranquil ghost, and his aura sheds a feeling of peace over those he appears to. The Lady Chapel is a location particularly favoured by him, though one elderly lady connected with the church believed that he was always certain to appear in the nave on the first day of July, at seven in the morning.

All hospitals have ghosts, though most of the staff feel that it would be unsettling for the peace of mind of their patients to have them publicised, for so often they appear before death. This does not, however, apply to the Grey Lady of Grace Ward, who is supposed to be the ghost of a nurse killed by a mentally disturbed patient.

A ghostly monk also haunts Charterhouse, once a Carthusian monastery and the original home of the famous school. This was founded by Thomas Sutton in 1611 as a hospital for forty poor boys and men. The boys moved out to Godalming in 1872, but the charity still provides accommodation for a few elderly men here, who have the chance of seeing the headless ghost of Thomas Howard, fourth Duke of Norfolk, descend the staircase of the Great Hall. He was executed for treason in the reign of Elizabeth I.

When the school occupied the building, the square was used as an area for recreation. Some 500 years previously it had been a burial-ground for some of the 500,000 inhabitants of London who died of the Black Death, and boys of the school would dare one another to listen, with ear to the ground at dead of night, for the moans of those mistakenly buried alive long ago.

Newgate

Newgate was the most infamous of London's gaols: its history extends back to Norman times, and it lasted until 1901, when it was demolished to make room for the Central Criminal Court (Old Bailey). The judges there are reminded of the old prison by a curious custom that still survives – at the beginning of each case held in the summer the judge is presented with a nosegay originally intended to mask the aroma emanating from Newgate. Amen Court, where many of the churchmen from St Paul's live, backs on to the site of the old prison and its graveyard, and a particularly horrific ghost crawls along the old wall that originally separated the Court from the prison.

The Black Dog of Newgate is the most venerable of all the ill-famed ghosts here. It must have been known in folklore long before anything was written down: the earliest record of its existence dates from about 1596 and was written by an inmate named Luke Hutton. This version of the story is a diatribe against the evil of his fellow prisoners, and tells of the terrible tricks which have brought them

Amen Court – the shapeless monster would crawl along the ivy-covered wall at the end.

The Blacke Dogge of Newgate:
both pithie and profitable
for all Readers.

Vide, Lege, Caue.

Time shall trie the trueth.
by Luke Hutton

Imprinted at London by G. Simson and W. White.

there. Hutton dedicated his work to the Lord Chief Justice, Sir John Popham, and it may have helped him get his release. Nevertheless he failed to take to the straight and narrow subsequently and in 1598 was hanged in York 'for his robberies and trespasses committed thereabout'. The following is taken from the version of 1638, *The discovery of a London Monster, called, the Blacke Dogg of Newgate.*

This tells of the narrator entering a pub (appropriately 'The Black Dog') where he orders his pint of wine and gets into conversation about the dog with a stranger ('a poore Thin-gut fellow'):

I maintained that I had read an old Chronicle that it was a walking spirit in the likenesse of a blacke Dog, gliding up and down the streets a little before the time of Execution, and in the night whilst the Sessions continued, and his beginning thus.

In the raigne of King *Henry* the third there happened such a famine through England, but especially in London, that many starved for want of food, by which meanes the Prisoners in Newgate eat up one another altue, but commonly those that came newly in, and such as could make but small resistance. Amongst many others cast into this Denne of misery, there was a certaine Scholler brought thither, upon suspition of Conjuring, and that he by Charmes and devilish Whitchcrafts, had done much hurt to the kings subjects, which Scholler, mauger his Devils Furies, Spirits and Goblins, was by the famished prisoners eaten up, and deemed passing good meate. This being done, such an idle conceit possessed the mindes of the poore Prisoners, that they supposed, nightly to see the Scholler in the shape of a black Dog walking up and downe the Prison, ready with his ravening Jawes to teare out their bowels: for his late human flesh they had so hungerly eaten, and withall they hourely heard (as they thought) strange groanes and cries, as if it had been some creature in great paine and torments, whereupon such a nightly feare grew amongst them, that it turned to a Frenzie, and from a Frenzie to Desperation, in which desperation they killed the Keeper, and so many of them escaped forth, but yet whither soever they came or went they imagined a Blacke Dog to follow, and by this means, as I doe thinke, the name of him began.

"Not so" quoth Signior Thin-gut, "I thinke it rather an idle fiction than a probable truth; but this I must tell you Sir, I know it for a truth, that there is no other blacke Dog, that I ever saw or

heard of, but a great blacke stone standing in the dungeon called *Limbo*, the place where the condemned Prisoners be put after their Judgement, upon which they set a burning candle in the night, against which I have heard that a desperate condemned Prisoner dashed out his braines."

Is this 'the black shape' that creeps along the high wall at the end of Amen Court? The shape is never seen definitely enough to say whether it is man or beast, or a nameless, amorphous horror, but over the long centuries of its history Newgate has seen enough evil to have generated not just one ghost, but legions.

Which brings an interesting coincidence to mind – for this particular wall was a part of the original, Roman, boundary wall of London. On the Newgate side of it there was a narrow passage which ran from the prison to the pits where the bodies of those executed were buried in quicklime. This was known as 'Dead Man's Walk', and for much of its length its paving was a cast-iron grating which gave footsteps a distinctive, ringing sound. The last man to be buried in the lime-pit was lame, and the hesitant sound of his feet on the iron sometimes disturbs the night-time peace of the City. However as interest in anatomy increased, fewer bodies reached the pits at the end of Dead Man's Walk. There was eager demand from the hospitals for the corpses of executed felons. *The Diary of a Resurrectionist* tells of the procedure:

The executions generally took place at eight o'clock on Mondays, and the 'cut down,' as it is called, at nine, although there was no cutting at all, as the rope, with a large knot at the end, was simply passed through a thick and strong ring, with a screw, which firmly held the rope in its place, and when all was over, Calcraft, *alias* 'Jack Ketch,' would make his appearance on the scaffold, and by simply turning the screw, the body would fall down. At once it would be placed in one of those large carts with collapsible sides, only to be seen in the neighbourhood of the Docks, and then preceded by the City Marshal in his cocked hat, and, in fact, all his war paint, with Calcraft and his assistant in the cart, the procession would make its way to 33 Hosier Lane, West Smithfield, in the front drawing room of which were assembled Sir William Blizard, President of the Royal College of Surgeons, and members of the Court desirous of being present, with Messrs. Clift (senior and junior), Belfour, and myself. On extraordinary occasions

The gallows and drop at Newgate. (GUILDHALL LIBRARY)

visitors were admitted by special favour. The bodies would then be stripped, and the clothes removed by Calcraft as his valuable perquisites, which, with the fatal rope, were afterwards exhibited to the morbidly curious, at so much per head, at some favoured public-house. It was the duty of the City Marshal to be present to see the body 'anatomised,' as the Act of Parliament had it. A crucial incision in the chest was enough to satisfy the important City functionary above referred to, and he would soon beat a hasty retreat, on his gaily-decked charger, to report the due execution of his duty. These experiments concluded, the body would be stitched up, and Pearson, an old museum attendant, would remove it in a light cart to the hospital, to which it was intended to present it for dissection.

In 1783 the New Prison had been completed at Newgate, and executions took place there rather than at Tyburn. These events were eagerly awaited, and great crowds gathered to see the poor wretches suffer. On 23 February 1807, John Holloway and Owen Haggerty were brought to the scaffold for the murder of a Mr Steele, a lavender-merchant. Both men denied committing the crime to the last: the *Newgate Calendar* tells how they met their fate, and of the dreadful events that followed:

Owen Haggerty first ascended the scaffold. His arms were pinioned, and the halter had been already placed round his neck: he wore a white cap, and a light olive shag great-coat: he looked downwards, and was silent. He was attended by a Roman Catholic clergyman, who read to him, and to whom the unfortunate culprit seemed to pay great attention; he made no public acknowledgement of guilt. After the executioner had tied the fatal noose, he brought up Holloway, who wore a smock frock and jacket, as it had been stated by the approver that he did at the time of the murder: he had also a white cap on, was pinioned, and had a halter round his neck: he had his hat in his hand; and mounting the scaffold, he jumped and made an awkward bow, and said, "I am innocent, innocent, by God!" He then turned round, and, bowing, made use of the same expressions, "Innocent, innocent, innocent! Gentlemen!—No verdict! No verdict! No verdict! Gentlemen. Innocent! Innocent!" At this moment, and while in the act of saying something more, the executioner proceeded to do his office, by placing the cap over his face; to which he, with apparent reluctance, complied; at the same time uttering some words which were not heard. As soon as the rope was fixed round his neck, he continued quiet. He was attended in his devotions by an assistant at Rowland Hill's Chapel.

The last that mounted the scaffold was Elizabeth Godfrey. She had been a woman of the town, aged 34, and had been capitally convicted of the wilful murder of Richard Prince, in Mary-le-bone parish, on the 25th of December 1806, by giving him a mortal wound with a pocket-knife in the left eye, of which wound he languished and died. Immediately on receiving sentence, this woman's firmness and recollection seemed to fail her, and she appeared bordering upon a state of frenzy. At the place of execution she was dressed in white, with a close cap, and long sleeves, and was attended by the Rev. Mr Ford, the Ordinary of Newgate; but her feelings appeared to be much overpowered, that notwithstanding she bore the appearance of resignation in her countenance, her whole frame was so shaken by the terror of her situation, that she was incapable of any actual devotion.

They were all launched off together, at about a quarter after eight. It was a long time before the body of the poor female seemed to have gone through its last suffering.

The crowd which assembled to witness this execution was unparalleled, being, according to the best calculation, near 40,000; and the fatal catastrophe, which happened in consequence, will cause the day long to be remembered. By eight o'clock, not an inch of ground was unoccupied in view of the platform, and the pressure of the crowd was so great, that before the malefactors appeared, numbers of persons were crying out in vain to escape from it. The attempt only tended to increase the confusion, and several females of low stature, who had been so imprudent as to venture among the mob, were in a dismal situation: their cries were dreadful. Some, who could be no longer supported by the men, were suffered to fall, and were trampled to death, and this was also the case with several boys. In all parts there were continual cries of "Murder! murder!"

particularly from the female part of the spectators and children, some of whom were seen expiring without the possibility of obtaining the least assistance, every one being employed in endeavours to preserve his own life. The most affecting scene of distress was seen at Green Arbour lane, nearly opposite the Debtor's-door. The terrible occurrence which took place near this spot was attributed to the circumstance of two pie-men attending there to dispose of their pies, and it appears that one of them having his basket overthrown, which stood upon a sort of stool upon four legs, some of the mob, not being aware of what had happened, and at the same time being severely pressed, fell over the basket and the man, at the moment he was picking it up, together with its contents. Those who fell were never more suffered to rise, and were soon numbered with the dead.

At this fatal place a man of the name of Herrington was thrown down, who had in his hand his youngest son, a fine boy, about twelve years of age. The youth was soon trampled to death; but the father recovered, though much bruised, and was amongst the wounded in St. Bartholomew's Hospital. A woman, who was so imprudent as to bring with her a child at the breast, was one of the number killed: whilst in the act of falling, she forced the child into the arms of the man nearest to her, requesting him, for God's sake, to save its life; but the man, finding it required all his exertions to preserve himself, threw the infant from him. It was fortunately caught at a distance by another man, who, finding it difficult to ensure its safety or his own, got rid of it in a similar way. The child was then again caught by a person, who contrived to struggle with it to a cart, under which he deposited it until the danger was over, and the mob was dispersed.

In other parts, the pressure was so great that a horrible sense of confusion ensued, and seven persons lost their lives by suffocation alone. A cart which was overloaded with spectators broke down, and some of the persons falling from the vehicle, were trampled under foot and never recovered.

During the hour for which the malefactors hung, little assistance could be afforded to the unhappy sufferers; but after the bodies were cut down, and the gallows removed to the Old Bailey yard, the marshals and constables cleared the street, and then, shocking to relate, there lay near one hundred persons dead, or in a state of insensibility, strewed round the street. Twenty-seven dead bodies were taken to St. Bartholomew's Hospital; four to St. Sepulchre's church; one to the Swan on Snow-hill, one to a public-house opposite St. Andrew's church, Holborn; one, an apprentice to his master's, Mr. Broadwood, pianoforte maker, Golden-square; a mother was seen carrying away the body of her dead boy; and the body of Mr. Harrison, a respectable gentleman, was taken to his house at Holloway. There was a sailor-boy killed opposite Newgate by suffocation: he carried a small bag, in which he had some bread and cheese, from which it was concluded that he had come some distance to witness the execution.

The fate of Mary Green, who came to the scaffold at Newgate in 1819, had a happier outcome:

MARY GREEN, WHO AFTER BEING HUNG CAME TO LIFE AGAIN.

This young woman, being left an orphan at three years of age, was brought up in a respectable family till her fifteenth year, when she was placed in service, where she continued till her marriage in 1810. Her husband treated her badly, but for eight years she bore it uncomplainingly, when he suddenly left her altogether and totally destitute. She followed him to Battle Bridge, where he was at work, but he refused her any aid. At this time, and thus situated, she fell into the company of a set of forgers of bank notes, but though earnestly entreated to become one in passing them, she steadily refused. At length stern necessity left her no other resource; she yielded, was arrested, tried, convicted, and sentenced to expiate such a crime (which was more justly her husband's than her own) on the scaffold. Exertions were made to save her, but they all failed, and this unhappy woman was doomed to undergo her sentence. She was executed at Newgate on March 22nd, 1819, and after hanging the usual time, was cut down and her body delivered to her friends. When preparing for her burial, they were startled by finding signs of returning life. Dr Beddell was sent for, and in twenty minutes she perfectly recovered. God had more mercy on her than her judges, and thus showed His mercy in restoring her to life. What her wretched husband's feelings must have been on hearing of her execution, is known only to his Maker. Thus singularly released from her husband, she lived under a feigned name, in the neighbourhood of Old St. Pancras, as a reputable and thrifty woman, and on her decease, many years afterwards, was buried in the old graveyard. (*History of St Pancras.*)

Thurston Hopkins, a writer about the supernatural working about fifty years ago, told a chilling story of Newgate in his book *Ghosts over England*. He became friendly with the Chief Warder of Newgate, Mr Scott, who attended the execution of Mrs Amelia Dyer, the Reading baby-farmer, on 10 June 1896. Paid handsomely to look after unwanted babies, she saved herself the expense by drowning them in the Thames and other rivers. Mrs Dyer was a well-behaved prisoner, yet she had a way of looking at Mr Scott which made him acutely uncomfortable. Her small, evil eyes, which belied the greasy smile on her face, brought a chill to his soul. As she passed him on the way to the scaffold, she paused, and said to him quietly, 'I'll meet you again, some day, sir.' Hopkins described the sequel to this:

> One night just before Newgate was closed down for good several of the warders were having a bottle of whisky together to celebrate the final week of duty in the prison. They were sitting in the Keeper's room next to the Women Felons Yard. There was a door with a glass observation wicket looking out to the yard. Suddenly Scott felt aware that someone's eyes were fixed on him, and he heard a voice ringing in his head: 'Meet you again . . . meet you again some day, sir.' . . . Then he looked towards the door and Mrs. Dyer's face was framed in the grille. There was no mistaking her oily benevolent smile, the little dark, snake-like eyes and the thin lips trying to look kind and harmless. She gave Scott one sad enigmatical look and passed on. Scott jumped up and opened the door and saw nothing except a woman's handkerchief which fluttered at his feet on the wet flagstones.
>
> There was no woman convict in the prison at that time – indeed the reception of women prisoners had been discontinued for some years.

Later in the same book Thurston Hopkins describes how when Chief Warder Scott was photographed outside the execution shed, Mrs Dyer's face appeared behind his shoulder on the print.

Elliott O'Donnell, in his book on London ghosts, tells how the night before demolition was due to commence the watchman and his wife were in the kitchen having supper when the bell in the condemned cell began to ring. The watchman hurried to investigate, only to find no one there but the bell still gently swinging. . . .

82   *Chief Warder Scott and the Medical Officer of Newgate pose beneath the grating which gave Birdcage Walk its name. The bodies of executed prisoners were buried in quicklime beneath the flagstones.*
(GUILDHALL LIBRARY)

The Cock Lane Uproar

Sold by A Dicey & Co in Aldermary Church Yard.

At Miss Fanny's New Theatre in Cock Lane
By particular Desire of Several Persons of Distinction
This Evening will be preformed
The old Watch by Miss F——s

At the end of the last Act will be introduced the Procession to the Vault
any Lady or Gentleman may have a private Scratching or Knocking in
another Room for one guinea each with or without Candles.

The Cock Lane Ghost

Cock Lane is a narrow thoroughfare that leads off Giltspur Street opposite St Bartholomew's Hospital. In 1762, the year it became famous for its ghost, Cock Lane was a seedy street of tenements with tradespeople occupying the ground floor of many of the properties.

One such house was the home of William Parsons, a Verger at St Sepulchre's, Holborn. He had met a well-to-do Norfolk gentleman, William Kent, at the church, and when their conversation gave him to understand that Kent was looking for rooms in the City, he was able to offer him accommodation in his own house. Kent was a widower and was living with his late wife's sister, whom he was forbidden to marry by the laws of the Church, much to their mutual regret. At first the arrangement worked well, but Parsons borrowed money from his lodger which he proved reluctant to repay: naturally this led to ill-feeling which was at its height when Kent was called away to a family gathering in Norfolk, leaving his common-law wife, 'Miss Fanny', in the care of the Parsons family. She was a nervous lady, and because of this persuaded the Parsons' eleven-year-old daughter, Elizabeth, to sleep with her. This was the start of the disturbances – both Miss Fanny and the child were kept awake by extraordinary noises, which at first they attributed to a neighbouring cobbler. However this proved not to be the case as they continued unabated, even on the Lord's Day, causing Miss Fanny considerable disquiet, as she had begun to believe that they foretold her death. On his return Kent took his 'wife' away from the house to new lodgings in Clerkenwell. In the meantime the noises went on in the Parsons' house, disturbing the elder daughter and her sister in their bedroom, but not the rest of the household. Mr Kent began the process of suing Parsons for the money that was owed him.

By January of the following year Miss Fanny was dead. Officially the cause of death was given as smallpox, but events in the Parsons' house in Cock Lane soon threw suspicion on this. Firstly the scratching and knocking was resumed with renewed vigour, and the elder of the daughters actually saw the ghost, and identified it as Miss Fanny. She had appeared in her shroud, without hands, 'all luminous and shining'.

By now the ghost had achieved considerable local notoriety, and many visitors came to the house to hear the strange noises that it produced. A 'one tap yes, two taps no' means of communicating with the spirit was devised, and by means of this it was found that the spirit was indeed that of Miss Fanny, who believed that she had been poisoned by a glass of purl (a mixture of hot beer and gin) which contained red arsenic.

When news of this got abroad everyone flocked to Cock Lane. Horace Walpole visited the house with the Duke of York:

Even Horace Walpole was magnetically drawn to the clerk's house in Cock Lane. The clever fribble writes to Sir Horace Mann, January 29, 1762: 'I am ashamed to tell you that we are again dipped into an egregious scene of folly. The reigning fashion is a ghost – a ghost, that would not pass muster in the paltriest convent in the Apennines. It only knocks and scratches; does not pretend to appear or to speak. The clergy give it their benediction; and all the world, whether believers or infidels, go to hear it. I, in which number you may guess, go to-morrow; for it is as much the mode to visit the ghost as the Prince of Mecklenburg, who is just arrived. I have not seen him yet, though I have left my name for him.'

Again Walpole writes: – 'I went to hear it, for it is not an apparition, but an audition. We set out from the opera, changed our clothes at Northumberland House, the Duke of York, Lady Northumberland, Lady Mary Coke, Lord Hertford, and I, all in one hackney-coach, and drove to the spot. It rained torrents; yet the lane was full of mob, and the house so full we could not get in. At last they discovered it was the Duke of York, and the company squeezed themselves into one another's pockets to make room for us. The house, which is borrowed, and to which the ghost has adjourned, is wretchedly small and miserable. When we opened the chamber, in which were fifty people, with no light, but one tallow candle at the end, we tumbled over the bed of the child to whom the ghost comes, and whom they are murdering by inches in such insufferable heat and stench. At the top of the room are ropes to dry clothes. I asked if we were to have rope-dancing between the acts. We heard nothing. They told us (as they would at a puppet-show) that it would not come that night till seven in the morning, that is, when there are only 'prentices and old women. We stayed, however, till half an hour after one. The Methodists have promised them contributions. Provisions are sent in like forage, and all the taverns and ale-houses in the neighbourhood make fortunes.'

(Walpole to George Montagu, Feb. 2nd, 1762.)

Already there were many who were suspicious about the authenticity of the ghost, and to allay them Elizabeth was moved to another house (with better accommodation for visitors). The scratching and knocking continued, attracting all the celebrities of the day to the house. A sceptical pamphleteer wrote:

To have a proper idea of this scene, as it is now carried on, the reader is to conceive a very small room, with a bed in the middle; the girl at the usual hour of going to bed, is undressed, and put in with proper solemnity. The spectators are next introduced, who sit looking at each other, suppressing laughter, and wait in silent expectation for the opening of the scene. As the ghost is a good deal offended at incredulity, the persons present are to conceal theirs, if they have any, as by this concealment they can only hope to gratify their curiosity; for, if they show, either before or when the knocking is begun, a too prying, inquisitive, or ludicrous turn of thinking, the ghost continues usually silent, or, to use the expression of the house, 'Miss Fanny is angry.' The spectators, therefore, have nothing for it but to sit quiet and credulous, otherwise they must hear no ghost, which is no small disappointment to persons who have come for no other purpose.

The girl, who knows, by some secret, when the ghost is to appear, sometimes apprizes the assistants of its intended visitation. It first begins to scratch, and then to answer questions, giving two knocks for a negative, but one for an affirmative. By this means it tells whether a watch, when held up, be white, blue, yellow, or black; how many clergymen are in the room, though in this sometimes mistaken. . . . It is sometimes mistaken in questions of a private nature, when it deigns to answer them. For instance, the ghost was ignorant where she had dined upon Mr. K—'s marriage; how many of her relations were at church upon the same occasion; but, particularly, she called her father John, instead of Thomas – a mistake, indeed, a little extraordinary in a ghost. But perhaps she was willing to verify the old proverb, that 'It is a wise child that knows its own father.' However, though sometimes right, and sometimes wrong, she pretty invariably persists in one story, namely, that she was poisoned, in a cup of purl, by red arsenic, a poison unheard of before, by Mr. K—, in her last illness, and that she heartily wished him hanged.

87

THE "GHOST'S" HOUSE IN COCK LANE. (*See page* 436.)

It is no easy matter to remark upon an evidence of this nature; but it may not be unnecessary to observe, that the ghost, though fond of company, is particularly modest upon these occasions, an enemy to the light of a candle, and always most silent before those from whose rank and understanding she could most reasonably expect redress.

However in the end the ghost became too ambitious and brought about its own downfall. It promised that if certain learned gentlemen would enter the vaults of St John's, Clerkenwell, she would prove her ghostly presence there by knocking three times on the lid of her coffin. A distinguished company accordingly gathered at St John's at the appointed hour, one o'clock in the morning. Dr Johnson was one of them. But when the ghost was called upon to prove itself there was no response. Its fall from grace was complete when subsequent tests were undertaken. With the girl's hands and feet bound no noises were heard. She was threatened with imprisonment in Newgate and not surprisingly she broke down and confessed. A small sounding-board was found concealed in her stays.

Many of the perpetrators of the hoax were prosecuted, and Kent was compensated for the damage done to his character. Yet public sympathy remained with Parsons, and little harm befell him when he was pilloried for three days (perhaps because of the prosperity that the haunting had brought to the area). He was also sentenced to two years in prison. Elizabeth was thought an unwilling accomplice, and did not have to face trial. She was subsequently twice married and died in Chiswick in 1806. An interesting postscript is printed in Walford's *Old and New London*:

"While drawing the crypt of St John's, Clerkenwell," says Mr. J. W. Archer, "in a narrow cloister on the north side, there being at the time coffins, fragments of shrouds, and human remains lying about in disorder, the sexton's boy pointed to one of the coffins, and said that it was 'Scratching Fanny.' This reminding me of the Cock Lane Ghost, I removed the lid of the coffin, which was loose, and saw the body of a woman, which had become adipocere.* The face was perfect, handsome, oval, with an aquiline nose. Will not arsenic produce adipocere? She is said to have been poisoned, although the charge is understood to have been disproved. I inquired of one of the churchwardens of the time, Mr. Bird, who said the coffin had always been understood to contain the body of the woman whose spirit was said to have haunted the house in Cock Lane."

In 1893, 325 coffins were removed from the vaults at St John's; one, unidentifiable, was unmistakably stained with arsenic. . . .

Adipocere: fatty, waxy substance generated in dead bodies buried in moist places.

"Hackney Coachman."

From Fleet Street to Aldgate

Considering how many strange stories have been concocted there in the past, it would seem strange to leave Fleet Street out of this book for want of a ghost, yet only an incident dating from 1684 saves 'the Street of Shame' from neglect. This is the story of the misfortune of Thomas Cox, who on the night of 31 October (is this a significant date?) drove his Hackney carriage up Water Lane, off Fleet Street, and dropped his passenger there. He continued to the bottom of the lane in order to turn the carriage round, and then called in at a pub 'for a pot or two' before gently driving up the lane again. When he was within three or four doors of Fleet Street at the top, he was stopped by the dark figure of a gentleman who appeared to hold a roll of paper or parchment in his hand. Cox was told to drive to Lower Church Yard, by St Bride's Church, and he immediately climbed up on his box and lashed his horses to get them to start. But for some reason they became so difficult to control that he was eventually forced to get down, thoroughly frightened by their unnatural behaviour. Even with the coachman at their heads the horses remained excited and dangerous, lashing out with their hooves. Cox shouted to his passenger to get down, as he could go no further, and the man alighted, and held out his hand towards Cox:

> ... which the Coach man saw, but no money in it; but when he went to take it could feel no hand, though he saw the same shape of the Gentlemans person in the Coach as before, who presently stept out, at which the Horses started and flying out drew the Coach man back, who having stopped his Horses and looking back to his fare, he saw a great black thing in the form of a Bear with great flaming Eyes which lay by the Wall side and made up to him, at which the Horses press'd forward, and the Coach man with much ado stop'd them, and taking the Reins from his Whip into his Hand, as it approached him whip't at it, and as he thought lash'd it; when on a sudden it vanished away in a terrible flash of Fire with great sparks, as if a Flambeaux had been dashed against the Wall and all flashed in his face, that he was so stoun'd that he did not know where he was, and lost all Sense in the Horrour and Consternation he was in.

(The True Relation of the Devils Appearing to Thomas Cox, a Hackney-Coach-Man.)

Cox was fortunate that the Devil offered him no money, for had he taken any his soul would have been claimed and he would have suffered eternal damnation. As it was, he managed somehow to return to his stables, where he was found speechless, and remained so until the following day, when he was able to tell his story to several divines who seemed to have accepted it as authentic. However his limbs remained benumbed, without sense or feeling, and 'not sensible of any heat though fire is applied to them which you may burn his flesh withall, without making him sensible of any pain or anguish; and it is very much fear'd by his friends that he will never recover the use of them again, but remain in that sad condition as long as he lives.'

As a reproach to those who might say he was drunk, the writer of the above pamphlet was at pains to stress that Cox was 'as free from being fudled as ever he was in his life', yet there is such a tongue-in-cheek quality about the telling of the story that it would convince only the most gullible, even if Cox's encounter had taken place on another night, and not at Hallowe'en.

No. 186 Fleet Street was the address of Sweeney Todd, 'The Demon Barber of Fleet Street'. The famous story tells how the barber's shop

'Easy shaving' – an illustration by Phiz for Martin Chuzzlewit.

Sweeney Todd's premises in Fleet Street in 1832. (GUILDHALL LIBRARY)

had a special chair with a tilting mechanism so that the occupant (usually a customer chosen as probably being 'up from the country', and therefore with no one likely to miss him for a week or so) could be shot neatly straight into the cellar below. If he were unfortunate enough to survive the fall, then Todd would be there almost immediately to finish the job off with his razor. The story spoke of an old underground passage that led from his cellar, below St Dunstan's Church, to another cellar in Bell Yard, part of the premises of Mrs Lovett, a pastrycook. She was Todd's accomplice, and her pies were acclaimed as the best in London by her customers, many of whom worked in the Courts of Justice on the other side of Bell Yard. Of course Todd's victims ended up in Mrs Lovett's pies.

The story made a wonderful melodrama but there is no supporting evidence to show that Sweeney Todd ever existed. Such a villain would have made a great stir when brought to book, and there are no newspaper accounts of his capture or trial. His origins may have derived from a terrible Scottish outlaw named Sawney Bean, who, with an ever-increasing family, terrorised Galloway in the fifteenth century. They set upon travellers, robbed and murdered them, and then cut up the bodies and pickled them in barrels. This is said to have been their only sustenance, and over the years the family interbred with such success that they became a fierce clan menacing the order of the whole district. Innkeepers were arbitrarily executed because vanished travellers had last been seen using their hostelries, and many innocent wayfarers were lynched in the belief that they were members of the gang. In the end, after twenty-five years of butchery, Sawney and his family found the fate they had deserved for so long. Their downfall is described in John Nicholson's *Historical and Traditional Tales connected with the South of Scotland* (1843):

A man and his wife behind him on the same horse, coming one evening home from a fair, and falling into the ambuscade of these merciless wretches, they fell upon them in a furious manner. The man to save himself as well as he could, fought very bravely against them with sword and pistol, riding some of them down by main force of his horse.

In the conflict the poor woman fell from behind him, and was instantly butchered before her husband's face, for the female cannibals cut her throat, and fell to sucking her blood with as great a gusto as if it had been wine: this done, they ript up her belly, and pulled out her entrails. Such a dreadful spectacle made the man make the more obstinate resistance, as he expected the same fate, if he fell into their hands.

It pleased Providence while he was engaged that twenty or thirty who had been at the same fair, came together in a body; upon which Sawney Bean and his bloodthirsty clan withdrew and made the best of their way through a thick wood to their den.

This man, who was the first who had ever fallen in their way, and came off alive, told the whole company what had happened, and showed them the horrid spectacle of his wife, whom the murderers had dragged to some distance, but had not time to carry her entirely off. They were all struck with stupefaction and amazement at what he related: they took him with them to Glasgow, and told the affair to the magistrates of that city, who immediately sent to the King concerning it.

The result of this was that a force of about 400 men were sent to the area who hunted Sawney and his people down ruthlessly. When the men of the gang were captured their legs and hands were cut off and they were left to bleed to death, their womenfolk being compelled to watch the spectacle. When the last of the men expired it became the turn of the women and children, who were all burnt alive in three separate fires. None, it is said, showed any sign of penitence, but cursed their captors to the last.

From this edifying detour to the south of Scotland, we return to the City of London, and an equally ghoulish account from Houndsditch:

The Divils cruelty to Mankind.
BEING

A true Relation of the Life and Death of *George Gibbs*, a *Sawyer* by his Trade, who being many times tempted by the *Devill* to destroy himselfe, did on *Friday* being the 7 of *March* 1663. Most cruelly Ripp up his own Belly, and pull'd out his Bowells and Guts, and cut them in pieces: to the Amazement of all the Beholders, the sorrow of his Friends, and the great grief of his Wife, being not long married: and both young People.

If the synopsis of the ballad (by Charles Hammond) is amusing, the verses themselves prove to be horrifically hilarious:

94

At twelve a clock at night he rose,
  his Wife being then a bed,
And down to ease himself he goes,
  thus to his Wife he said,
His Wife perswaded him to stay,
  but he was fully bent,
The Divill prompting him on's way,
  and out he present went.

When he came there he shut the door,
  and out his Penknife slip't,
His Belly with it Cut and tore,
  and out his Bowells rip't,
His careful Wife did present rise,
  but when she did come there,
And did behold it with her eyes,
  she trembled with such fear.

Few words she spoke to him but went
  and in some Neighbors brought,
Thinking the worst for to prevent,
  and save his life they thought.
Whilst she was gone he made the Door
  fast to himself within,
But they did break and down it tore,
  and suddenly got in.

His Belly he had rip't up quite,
  and out his Bowels tore,
That such a Devillish bloody sight,
  scarce shown by man before,
The Divill did do it to be sure,
  elce he could nere proceed,
His strength and heart could nere endure,
  to do that cruell deed.

Some of his Gutts were cut in two,
  and mangled in such sort,
That he himself could never doe,
  but had some helper for't.
Eight hours or more this man did live,
  in grievous woe and pain,
What Sustinance they did him give,
  came straight way forth again.

The Divil he said did tempt him long,
  and many times before,
For all he did resist him strong,
  he nere would give him ore,
Thus have you heard the doleful end,
  of *Gibbs*, which is too true,
And take this councill from a Friend,
  for fear you after rue.

Pamphlets and ballads of the seventeenth and eighteenth centuries are a much more profitable source of ghosts for this area than more modern newspapers, etc., probably because so many more people actually lived in the City in those days. An account of poltergeist activity in a house at Puddle-dock is in the Guildhall Library and is dated 1674:

News from

PUDDLE-DOCK

IN

LONDON

OR,

A Perfect particuler of the strange Apparitions and Transactions that have happened in the House of Mr. EDWARD PITTS next Door to the STILL at PUDDLE-DOCK

The House of Mr. *Edward Pitts* at *Puddledock* hath in a very strange and stupendious manner been disturbed these 15 or 16 Nights last past: The House is two Rooms of a Floor; and the two Rooms up one pair of stairs have been for these 15 or 16 Nights between 12 and 1 of the Clock continually haunted. When *Mr. Pitts'* Family are gone, or going to Bed, he looks to see those two doors fast; but in the morning he hath always found them open, except once, which was the last week, and then after he had fastened both those doors, he takes a rope and fastens it to the handle of the door, and from thence to a nail on the stairs; that Night he found that door as he left it, but the other wide open; not one night in all this time but his Goods in these Rooms (the one his Kitchin, the other his Parler) have been removed from one place to another in a most strange manner; In the Kitchin the Pewter hath been taken off the shelves and laid any where about the Room. A Box of Candles of 5 or 6 pound have been taken out of the Box and planted about the Room, some put in Candlesticks, and others laid by two and two, the ends laid contrary ways; but that which is the most remarkable is this, on the last Lords-day at Night, *March* 15. 1674. when this Mr. *Pitts* and his Family were going to Supper, a

Fold-up Table (which stood on one side of the Kitchin) was brought to the fire side; upon which the Meat was set, *Mr. Pitts* takes the Loaf off the Dresser to cut bread to lay on the Table, as he was cutting the Bread he spied upon the Dresser a great thing like a Catt, at which being a little affrighted, he started back Presently calling to his Wife, saying, here's a Catt, I never saw a Catt in this house before, upon which, this Cat-like thing seemed to slide off the Dresser, giving a thump on the Boards, and so vanished away. All *Mr. Pitt*'s Family then in the Room, but none could perceive this strange Catt but only his Daughter of about 15 years of Age, and himself; and they say it was as bigg as any Mastiff Dog; but they could not perceive that it had any Leggs.

The pamphlet goes on to describe other strange incidents that befell the household. In the middle of the night the Watchman reprimanded Mr Pitts for keeping a light burning in the house, though the latter was certain that he had been careful to put out all the lamps and candles before retiring (of course in 1674 fire precautions were very strict). Although he knew that he had to get up to investigate the strange light he found himself utterly unable to do so; at the same time he was conscious of the great light in the bedchamber diminishing little by little until the whole room was dark

... then of a sudden he had as much Light as if it had been clear day. In the morning when it was day he got up and went (as every morning he had been used to do) to see what alterations he could find in his 2 haunted Rooms, when he came down he found his Kitchin-door wide open, as it use to be, but his Parler door was off the Latch a little ajar, barricadoed with a great 2 handed Chair, he thrust the Chair aside and opened the door; when he came into the Room, upon the Table there he found a great Wooden Sand-box, upon which was 2 snuffs of Candles burnt to Ashes, a 3d. Candle had been upon that Box, but that had burnt all one side of the Box, and made such a stink in the house (which I should have mentioned before) that the Woman of the house admired what was Burning that should cause such a stink. This Sand-box Candlestick Mr. Pitts had never seen before, nor had ever been master of such a one in his Life; but that which is yet more Wonderful is this, by this Sand-box was placed upon the Table two Splinters of Wood cross ways, exactly like the form here following.

Three Ends or Corners of this Cross was cleft, and in each cleft there was stuck a Paper printed on both sides as you have here *verbatim.*

Right against this Cross and Papers by the Table was placed a Chair, as if some one had sat there viewing them over.

This night, *March* 16 Mr. *Pitts* intends to have some people to sit up, that may speak to any thing that shall appear, and to demand in the name of the Father, *what are you?*

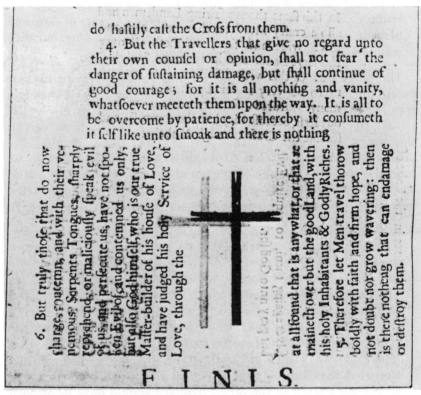

The cleft cross from the pamphlet. (GUILDHALL LIBRARY)

Although there must be some suspicion about the authenticity of the account, there are many features of the haunting that ring true, being typical of poltergeist activity; but one cannot help feeling that the printer had most enjoyment out of this, choosing relevant blocks of type from his old chases with his tongue in cheek.

In 1647 there was a great stir in Lombard Street when the yard of a Mr Youngs was haunted by a very curious ghost. Not only were its pranks troublesome, but it sent divines and other learned men who came to investigate into 'distracted extasy' so that they were able to neither speak or stand. Certainly it was a formidable ghost, able to slam shut a casement window injudiciously opened by a spectator on the third floor of the house that overlooked the yard. The ghost usually disappeared in a spectacular manner, too:

> . . . this hideous MONSTER . . . usually vanishes away, (to the thinking of the beholders) into the ground, then immediately ensueth a noise like to claps of thunder and flashes of fire like lightning seemes to ascend out of the Earthe, and after that a stinking mist, and a noysome sulferous smoake.

An even more harmful ghost was described in *Mercurius Democritus*, a Commonwealth news-book, in February 1654. It walked 'every night among the Butchers at *Smithfield Barrs*, the *Shambles*, *White-chappell* and *Eastcheap*, in the habit of Mallet'.

This probably referred to Sir Thomas Mallet, a Royalist Judge hated by the supporters of Parliament. He had been imprisoned in the Tower but was released in 1644 in an exchange of prisoners. For the remainder of the Commonwealth he was disabled 'as if dead' from being a judge, on the ground of being 'the fomenter and protector of the malignant factor'. At the Restoration he returned to the Bench, but by this time he was seventy-eight years of age, and it was soon discovered that he was too old to serve efficiently. Mallet was given a handsome pension and spent his last years at his country estate.

Since he was still alive at the time of the haunting, it could not be claimed that his ghost was responsible for the chaos it caused: it was sufficient propaganda to say that the ghost looked like him. It passed through the butchers' stalls like a whirlwind, scattering their tables and dislodging carcasses from their hooks. In fury the butchers would slash at the spectral form with cleavers and knives, but the blades always passed through it without doing any harm. However the ghost could be malevolent as well as mischievous: on one occasion he pursued a fair maid, and when he caught her, ate her alive!

Several books on the supernatural were written in the nineteenth century by H. Welby. This extract is from *Signs before Death* (1875):

A shoemaker's wife in the parish of Cripplegate, being thought

Sir Thomas Mallet by an unknown artist. (NATIONAL PORTRAIT GALLERY)

dead, was, agreeable to his desire, buried in her wedding cloaths;
her ring being on her finger, induced the sexton to open the grave in
the night, in order to steal it: when finding it not easy to come off, he
took his knife to cut the finger from the hand; which operation
recalled the woman to her senses, and she rose from her coffin. The
affrighted villain took to his heels: and she, taking his lanthorn,
walked home, knocked up her husband, and lived several years
after. Her monument is yet standing in Cripplegate-church.

Remarkably, 250 years before, another H. Welby was living in Cripplegate in a curious style. He was a wealthy gentleman, happily married, with a daughter engaged to be married to a baronet. For some reason he fell out with his younger brother, who fired at him with a pistol. Even though the shot missed, the incident changed Henry Welby's life completely. He shut himself up in three rooms of a house in Grub Street, off Cripplegate, and became a recluse, being attended only by an old maid. He lived the life of a hermit for forty-four years, his only solace being his books, and died in 1640 at the age of eighty-four. He had lived on a diet of gruel, with an occasional salad of herbs, and, even more rarely, the yolk of an egg on feast days. His housekeeper died six days before him.

Returning to the proper subject of this book from these curious detours, the building at the very hub of the City is haunted. This is the Bank of England, whose site covers four acres. The Bank moved to its present position from the old Grocers' Hall in 1734. At the heart of the building is a small enclosed garden haunted by the ghost of Sarah Whitehead since the 1840s.

The Dividend Pay Office at the Bank of England. (GUILDHALL LIBRARY)

Miss Whitehead. insane. she daily attended the Bank of England.

(GUILDHALL LIBRARY)

102

She was the sister of Philip Whitehead, a young bank employee who was arrested in 1811 for forgery. Sarah was devoted to him, and when he was hanged for his crime her mind refused to accept his fate. Instead she used to visit the Bank each day to inquire if her brother had been seen there. Politely they would reply that he had not been in yet that day, and so she would wait for him outside – a sad figure dressed in black, her face garishly rouged.* This was the routine she followed for more than twenty-five years until her death. She is supposed to have been buried in the churchyard of St Christopher-le-Stocks, which was within the environs of the Bank, and later became the garden where she was frequently seen as a sad ghost, still looking for her missing brother.

The ghost of a giant also haunts the Bank. In the days of the 'resurrectionists' one of the cashiers was a man of enormous stature, being nearly eight feet tall. He had an awful dread of his body being disinterred after death by grave-robbers and so persuaded the Governors of the Bank to allow his body to be buried within its precincts. His ghost often terrified members of the Bank picquet, frequently shaking their rifles. Sadly, there are no reports of the electronic surveillance equipment, which took over the Guardsmen's duties in 1973, having ever picked up the echo of his (or Sarah's) ghost, but during excavation work an eighteenth-century lead coffin was discovered. It was seven feet eight inches long, and had an iron chain bound round it.

The Bank Station is believed by London Transport staff to be haunted. Most of the maintenance personnel dislike working there at night because of the strange feeling of despondency and dread which can overcome them. This is accompanied by a smell described as being like that of a newly opened grave.

More 'tangible' is the ghost of Aldgate Station: an old woman who was once seen stroking the hair of an electrician working on the track. Within minutes he had made a mistake which should have been fatal, sending 22,000 volts through his body. Yet though he was knocked out he suffered no other ill-effects, neither did he see or feel the ghost.

*Eric Maple tells of a different motive for her vigil at the Bank. In *Supernatural England* he says that she believed that she was owed a vast fortune, including the whole of the Muswell Hill estate. 'On one occasion she approached Baron Rothschild on the steps of the Stock Exchange and accused him of defrauding her of her fortune. Tactfully Rothschild presented her with a half-crown on account and she cheerfully proceeded on her way.'

The Bethnal Green Ghost

The haunting of 132 Teesdale Street was, literally, a nine-day wonder in February 1938. Although at the end of the affair the ghost was discredited, many aspects of the case remain a mystery, and it may well be that a supernatural occurrence triggered off hysteria which eventually infected two households.

The house in Bethnal Green (which is now demolished) was a three-storey 'workers' dwelling' built in early Victorian times. In the winter of 1937–8 its tenants were the Davis family, headed by sixty-one-year-old Mr George Davis whose wife had died the previous September. She had been born in the house, as had her father, and had brought up a large family there. This consisted of four sons (Albert, Walter, Charles and Sydney, only the latter living at home) and three daughters (Minnie, Nellie and Gracie). The youngest of the daughters, Gracie, was twenty and looked after her father and the young Sydney. Both Minnie and Nellie had married and moved away, though the latter was a frequent visitor to the house with her husband, Alfred Rose, a policeman. The upper floor was sub-let to the Harrisons, a family consisting of husband, wife, and eighteen-month-old baby. They had been tenants for five years and Mrs Harrison was paid a small amount each week to keep an eye on Mrs Davis, who was an invalid.

The late Mrs Davis had suffered from violent epileptic fits for the last twenty-nine years of her life, and from badly ulcerated legs which made movement about the house difficult for her. Although she had been friendly with Mrs Harrison when she first became a tenant, the relationship had soured over the years, generated by Mrs Davis's jealousy of her husband's liking the company of Mrs Harrison – though this friendship appears to have been perfectly innocent.

When Mrs Davis was at last taken to hospital Mrs Harrison visited her there and said that her visit pleased the old lady. Presumably this ended the six weeks of silence from Mrs Davis that she had endured before the latter was taken off to hospital. Mrs Davis did not survive long in hospital but died there on 12 September and was buried at Manor Park Cemetery. The subsequent happenings were described in the *Evening Standard* for 4 February 1938 – the first of many accounts of the disturbances at 132 Teesdale Street:

POLICE AT HOME OF "GHOST" by Garry Allighan

I spent last night in a haunted house in London, investigating the manifestations of a 'ghost' which the BBC are to try to broadcast and televise.

Ghostly manifestations actually occurred while I was there – and were heard by a large crowd gathered in the street.

The fame of the haunted house has spread far and wide, and so great are the crowds attracted that three policemen have been on duty to keep the road clear.

The house is in Bethnal Green. The lower part of it is tenanted by Mr George Davis, a 61-year-old compositor.

'My wife died on September 12th,' Mr Davis told me when I arrived.

Furniture Upset

'On Armistice Day I visited the cemetery with my daughter Grace and my son Sidney. When we returned we heard a strange tapping noise.'

'Like a Morse code signal,' said Sidney, who is 16.

'The noise was repeated at varying intervals during the day, and continued for about two weeks.

'Then, one day, we were having tea in the kitchen when we heard a long-drawn-out moan, followed by heavy footsteps overhead. We rushed up.

'The very heavy tallboy in my father's bedroom which usually stands against the wall, had been moved in the centre of the room. The bedclothes were thrown on the floor. A chair had been overturned.'

Since then the family have not had a minute's peace. Grace Davis, a girl of twenty, told me that the furniture is disturbed about three or four times a day and often during the night.

'It is useless making the beds until the evening,' she said.

'On one occasion the bedroom door was unlocked and a chair was thrown down the stairs.

Picture Turned Over

At another time Grace was standing in the hall talking to Mrs Harrison, who occupies the upper part of the house, and another person.

Suddenly they saw one of the pictures on the wall begin to twist and turn round.

'As I moved forward to steady the picture it was snatched from my hand and dashed to the floor with a crash,' Mrs Harrison told me.

Often when Grace comes down in the morning she finds all the crockery cleared from the kitchen dresser and standing on the table. So far no crockery has been smashed.

Mrs Harrison has had trinkets removed from her dressing-table and placed on the floor.

I had been talking to Mr Davis for about five minutes, when suddenly there was an eerie cry, like that of a woman in pain. I heard heavy footsteps overhead, followed by a loud crash.

We all ran up the stairs, and when we reached the bedroom the door, which Mr Davis swore he had bolted only 15 minutes previously, was standing wide open.

Furniture was overthrown, bedclothes were on the floor.

Mr Davis told me that he had covered a sheet of paper with treacle and placed it on the floor, but although footsteps were heard and furniture was overturned, *there were no marks on the treacle.*

'Last Saturday I tied a chair to the rail of my bed,' he said. 'Three times the string was untied and the chair was overturned. On the

The upturned bedroom chair. (SOCIETY FOR PSYCHICAL RESEARCH)

fourth occasion the chair was overturned and the string disappeared. We called in the police, and they searched every nook and cranny, but the piece of string has not been seen since.'

The family are overwrought and in despair.

It was this report that must have excited the interest of Dr Fodor, the eminent investigator of the International Institute for Psychical Investigation. All but the first of his reports survive in the files of the present-day Society for Psychical Research to whom they were passed when the Institute became defunct. I am most grateful to the Society for allowing me to use them for this account.

Dr Fodor first visited the house on 6 February, accompanied by two assistants, Mr Laurence Evans and the Marquis des Barres.

'We were received with a story of great wonders,' wrote Dr Fodor. Apart from one bang at four in the morning, which had awoken Mr Davis, the night had passed relatively quietly for the occupants of the house, but when Mrs Harrison came downstairs at eight o'clock she found chaos. In the sitting-room, crowded with ornaments, few items were left in their proper place. Pictures of Mrs Davis were upside-down in an armchair when they should have been on the piano; the heavy glass bowl which protected an ornamental pincushion had been removed and the pincushion itself was on the sofa. The cover was also off the birdcage and two chairs were overturned. Furniture was disturbed in other parts of the house too, notably in Grace's bedroom where all the chairs were upside-down and a heavy wardrobe had been moved away from the wall. The family had left everything for the investigators to see.

During the day, Dr Fodor was told, the cry had been heard six times. Mrs Rose, the married daughter, said that it was just like the cry given by her mother before she went into a fit. It was also heard by Mr Abrahams who lived across the street, the newsagent Mr Atkins, and the milkman who had called at eleven o'clock. Usually the cry was followed by a bang and many people smelt a strong and unpleasant odour subsequently which lasted for about five minutes after the bang. The family explained this by associating the bang or thud with Mrs Davis falling at the start of her fit. She would clutch at anything in her distress and often pull it over with her. She would be unconscious for about half an hour and would signal her gradual return to sensibility by a mumbling sound which, it was said, was also frequently heard.

Gradually the investigators were able to discover significant points and learn something of the characters of the people occupying the house. They found the strongest personality to be Mrs Harrison who was inclined to embroider a story given the least encouragement. She exerted considerable influence over the young and timid Gracie with the power of her will. Her husband had little patience with the investigation and when questioned in detail was hostile and evasive. By contrast Mr Davis appeared under-assertive, almost pathetic. After the Harrisons had given Dr Fodor an explicit account of meeting the misty, ethereal form of Mrs Davis on the stairs, Mr Davis was asked whether he had also seen the ghost of his wife. He replied, 'I think she should naturally come to me.'

One of the most significant factors discovered by the investigators was that for the most part the disturbances occurred when the Harrisons were on the top floor. In this report their suspicions about the source of the disturbances fall squarely on the Harrisons:

> As to the chair which Mr Davis tied with a string to his bedstead, the string was half a yard long and it was knotted. It was found undone and the chair overturned three times. The string was always lying straight and without knots on the floor. The fourth time Mrs Harrison tied it with a double knot. The chair was overthrown again but the string was gone.
>
> (It seems as if Mr and Mrs Harrison wanted to put an end to an unnecessary complication which required more time to be spent in the bedroom of Mr Davis and was, therefore, more risky. The simplest way out was to take the string.)

They are also sceptical about the picture-turning incident mentioned in the *Evening Standard*, perhaps implying that the picture could have been jerked from the wall by means of a piece of thread held by Mrs Harrison (the classic *modus operandi* of many fake ghosts, including the famous Stockwell Ghost).

> The picture was a group photograph on the wall in the passage. It was found turned to the wall. In the presence of Mrs Harrison, Grace turned it round. It seemed to be pulled out of her hand, the nail came out, the picture fell down, and the glass broke.

Finally, they decide that the cry is that of the Harrisons' baby, Maureen, who had made a similar sound earlier during their visit. Her parents maintained that she had only been making that

particular noise for a fortnight or so.

The behaviour of Mr Harrison at the end of their visit had a bizarre touch to it that makes the account border on the hilarious:

> We tried an experiment. We asked Mrs Harrison to lie on Grace's bed and put out the light. The bed did not move, but first three, and later four or five soft taps were heard. It was, however, not impossible for Mrs Harrison to cause them by tapping on the wall. As we went down Mr Evans stayed behind. He heard a noise. Something was thrown down the stairs. It was an onion. He called me back and we called up to Mr Harrison. After some delay he answered. Mr Evans asked him "Was he outside his room just now?" He hesitated and then muttered the baby had thrown down an onion. It was an unusual time for an eighteen-month-old baby to be out in a dark passage throwing onions.

The same investigators visited the house again on the following evening. Their report, remaining sceptical, nevertheless betrays a slight bewilderment with the case; as they get to know the participants better they find it harder to understand why anyone should want to contrive a haunting to frighten the occupants of the house especially since the Harrisons had already expressed their wish to leave it as soon as alternative accommodation could be found. They, like the Davis family, told Dr Fodor of their belief that the disturbances were being caused by the jealous spirit of Mrs Davis trying to force Mrs Harrison from the house.

By questioning the two women separately Fodor was able to show that when two policemen called earlier in the afternoon (Mr Rose was a policeman) and the cry was heard (followed by the throwing down of a chair upstairs) Mrs Harrison had run up to her flat to tend the baby, which was crying. Grace, questioned earlier, had been adamant that all the occupants of the house were present when the policemen called and the cry was heard. The policemen hearing the cry added substantially to the notoriety of the haunting.*

Concluding this report the investigator wrote:

> Mrs Harrison told me that in early November and December, when the cry was new, she used to stand with Grace outside in the rain and cold. They were afraid of the cry and of the opening doors.
>
> 'The first night we heard the cry,' Mrs Harrison stated, 'Mr

*Though this is again contradicted in a later, fifth, report when the policeman, interviewed for a second time, swears that everyone *was* downstairs when the cry was heard.

Harrison was reading and I was knitting. He said "Quick, Mrs Davis". I said, "Don't say that. It is funny, it is her cry". I thought it was Sydney playing a joke on us. I found Sydney below at the door biting his nails. He asked me "Did you hear my Mam?"'

I asked Grace whether anything has been found overthrown in any of the rooms without the door being opened. She said 'Yes'. We then decided to seal up Grace's bedroom on Tuesday afternoon (*the next day*) and leave it sealed up until Thursday afternoon.

Fodor's point about the lack of motive for a phoney haunting was echoed the next day in a statement made by Walter Davis (the unemployed son) to the *Hackney Gazette*. 'People have accused us of telling lies about these things, but it's all perfectly true. What point would there be in making our lives unbearable with crowds packing outside the house and children tormenting us and breaking windows?'

Strangely, no mention of the following strange occurrence is given in the notes of the psychic investigators. Again Walter told the story:

'We hear these cries at all times of the day and night, and they are just the cries my mother used to make when she was ill. Shortly before you arrived we had a visit from a gentleman interested in psychic research. He told us he could see a woman standing in the corner of the room. He described her to us, and the description was exactly that of my mother when she was alive.'

Typically, Mrs Harrison cannot refrain from chipping in:

There was no doubt at all about the description. It was Mrs Davis all right. He also said that she wanted to tell us that she was turning the house up to show us that it was hers, but that we would not have much more of it.

That night must have been a restless one for the Harrisons and the Davis family, but this was due not to the attentions of the ghost but to the crowds which had been drawn to the scene by the publicity. The headline in the *Daily Express* the next morning told of the popular excitement:

'HAUNTED' HOUSE BESIEGED BY 2,000 'GHOST' HUNTERS
DEAD WIFE'S 'I SHALL COME BACK'

Police had to be called last night to control 2,000 determined 'ghost hunters' who were besieging a Bethnal Green house reported to be haunted.

The house is in Teesdale Street, and police had to draw cordons across each end of the road to keep away curious, incredulous sightseers. . . .

Dr Nandor Fodor, research officer of the International Institute for Psychical Research, has been called in by the families, and last night, with two assistants, he took photographs in the house with a special camera. . . . While Dr Fodor was hunting with his camera last night feelings were running high in Teesdale Street.

One woman in the crowd shouted: 'We can't even get into our own street now without having to ask a copper'.

When Laurence Evans came to the house at three in the afternoon he found the occupants still seething with indignation at this report. 'Mrs Harrison was in a high state of hysterics over the *Daily Express* story of the morning,' he wrote. 'She decleared she would not be able to go out of the house owing to the hostility of the women outside.'

Although the night had been peaceful, more disturbances had occurred in the house during the day. After showing the house to Harry Price (a famous psychic investigator later to become notorious for his dubious research at Borley Rectory) Evans began his work of sealing off the front bedroom:

. . . I then went upstairs into the front room and securely fastened both the windows with 2-inch steel screws, so that neither the top or the bottom could be moved. The Marquis des Barres was helping me, and together we marked the position of every piece of furniture in the room by marking the floor in blue pencil exactly under the leg of each piece. I then sprinkled about two pounds of powdered starch on the floor in the vicinity of the door. We took particular care to make no mark on the floor with our own feet, by sprinkling the floor in front of us and backing out of the room. We then shut the door and I took the following precautions to prevent entry. I had obtained six one-inch steel screw-eyes which I placed in pairs, on the door, one on the lintel in three different places. I then fastened each pair together with 7–22 copper wire. After that I threaded tape through each pair of eyes, wound it round the wire, tied it, and sealed it with my own private seal. I am quite satisfied that it is impossible for normal entry to be made without it being quite apparent to us.

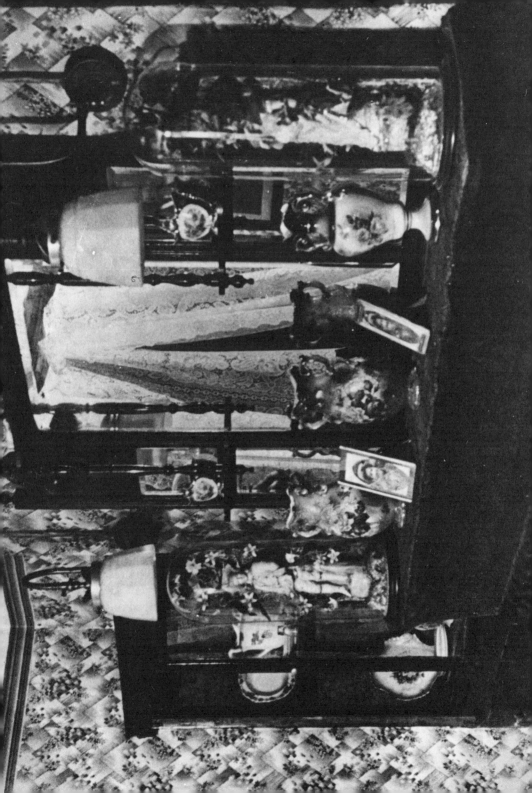

As I was coming down the stairs, preparatory to leaving the house, I heard the moan. It appeared to come from below where Grace, Mrs Harrison and the baby were sitting in the kitchen. I asked them if they had heard it also, and they said that they had and that it had come from the front-room. I went into the front-room and found the glass cover had been taken completely off the near pin-cushion and had been placed on the piano beside it, and the glass cover had been slightly moved from the second pin-cushion.

We left the house at 5 p.m.

On emerging from the house, Evans made the following comments to the reporter from the *Hackney Gazette*:

'So far our investigation has been hampered by a number of things, not the least of which is the presence of large and noisy crowds outside the house. During my stay here this afternoon I have heard the "cry", but I was unable to satisfy myself where it came from.

'I also found that a glass bowl in the sitting room had moved from one part of the room to another, but, as there were fingerprints, this was not very conclusive. However, I have now rubbed all the fingerprints off, and if the bowl moves again the test will be more reliable.

The families in the house have given us the fullest assistance in making our investigation, and in my experience of these matters there would so far appear to be good grounds for believing that something sub-normal is taking place, and that these events are genuine.'

The next visit to the house was made on the Thursday (10 February) to open the room sealed by Laurence Evans two days before. Firstly, however, Dr Fodor investigated articles that had been moved in the front room.

We were told that half-an-hour after Mr Evans left on Tuesday afternoon, the pin-cushion in the sitting room went from under the glass cover on the piano to the sofa. Mr Evans had wiped the glass cover clean before he left. Now, on the glass shade which was moved from the piano to the top of the table we found fingerprints. It would have been an impracticable suggestion to ask the members of the household for fingerprints. Any one of them might have touched the glass shade and forgotten all about it.

The mantelpiece in the front room.
(SOCIETY FOR PSYCHICAL RESEARCH)

It seems today that Fodor was hasty in finding it impracticable to take the fingerprints of everybody in the house. After all the results need not have been revealed, but a closer watch could have been kept on one person in particular.

Another curiosity, in view of the harassment that both families were suffering, is why they stayed in the house at all during this time. Apparently it was suggested that they should all move out and leave it to the investigators for a few days, but this course of action, which seems to be obvious in retrospect, was rejected by all concerned.*

Although the opening of the room proved to be an anti-climax (no furniture had been moved, the starch dust showed no footprints) the usual highly charged atmosphere of the house was quickly re-established with Grace once more in hysterics:

> While Mr Evans and myself were talking to the reporters in the sitting-room below, the *Daily Sketch* reporter saw through the glass door of the sitting room Grace showing signs of great agitation and uttering a scream. At that moment the door opened and we were told that they had heard the scream. It seemed to come from above. Mr Evans felt Grace's pulse. Her heart was beating wildly and she was almost crying. Mrs Harrison, at the time the scream was heard, was out in the backyard.
>
> Mr Walter Davis (*the elder son*) heard the scream quite plainly. He said he went cold just before, and expected to hear it.
>
> After the reporters left, Grace went upstairs to sweep up the starch powder. I was with her for some time, then a policeman (No. H 620) who had called, stayed with her while she was doing this work. Below I was questioning Mr Walter Davis whom I met for the first time. He told me about three weeks ago he saw one portrait of Mrs Davis, which was on the mantelpiece in the sitting room, slowly turning around and facing the other. This happened in full light. A number of people have seen it at the same time, including Mrs Harrison and Grace. I asked Mr Walter Davis about the hand which Grace saw coming around the door, and which she recognised as her mother's hand. He said: 'The kitchen door slowly moved. There appeared to be a white shadow behind it, trying to get a grip on the door. I saw no wrist or fingers. I do not know whose hand it might have been.'

Later that day Mrs Pierce, a neighbour, confirmed Walter's tale of the picture turning:

*Similarly, this stratagem was also resisted in two other famous instances of poltergeist activity, at Cock Lane, and much more recently, at Enfield.

I think it is very mysterious. I have known these people for 33 years. I was there when the picture turned on the mantel-piece to face the other way. Walter and his brother-in-law were there. Mr Harrison was in the kitchen. Ten or fifteen people saw it.

At this time the Vicar, the Reverend F. G. S. Nicholle, was also paying a visit to the house. He had been a witness to strange disturbances there the previous evening when he heard the cry and found a chair thrown across the doorway of the back bedroom. While Fodor was being interviewed by a reporter in the front sitting-room, Sydney, the youngest son, rushed into the room in great excitement and asked them whether they had heard anything. Neither of the men had heard any unusual sounds but both followed Sydney back to the kitchen. Fodor's account continues:

In the kitchen the Vicar told me that tapping noises were heard from above. I went upstairs and found both doors open; the chair in the back bedroom was overthrown. The bolt of that door was drawn. The bolt of the other door was not drawn but this bolt is really not held by the bolt-hole, which is broken through. A little pressure would be sufficient to open it. Such pressure, however, would make a definite noise. I rushed downstairs and asked the Vicar: 'Was everybody in the kitchen whilst this happened?' The Vicar was positive that Mrs Harrison, Mr Walter Davis, Sydney, and Grace were all in the kitchen and no-one had gone upstairs at all.

Mr Evans, while this happened, was outside in the street at the telephone. When he came back he fastened the front door of the sitting-room with copper wire drawn through staples, and placed a large plant-pot at the bottom of the door. He then turned the key in the lock leaving the key inside. Then we turned both pictures of Mrs Davis on the mantel-piece backwards, put one of the pincushions with its cover in the kitchen, and fastened the door between the kitchen and the sitting-room with copper wire drawn through two staples and sealed it. Then we proceeded to the room upstairs and placed the pincushion and its glass cover on the top of Grace's dresser. On the mantel-piece opposite there was a picture of Mrs Davis. This I had turned backwards previous to the door-opening phenomenon. It was still backwards, and so we left it. We fastened the door with copper wire drawn through the top staples and sealed it.

By this time the media had enthusiastically adoped the 'Bethnal Green Ghost' and each day there were reports of the latest developments in the newspaper and on the wireless, as radio was called then. Even that new prodigy television was involved, it being suggested that there should be a transmission from the house. In the Press pundits were being called upon to give their expert interpretations of events, and in the *Evening Standard* of 10 February the authoress Miss Rachael Ferguson commented:

On the evidence, it seems to me that, in view of the fact that the disturbances did not begin until after the burial of Mrs Davis, the trouble comes under the category of 'spirit of the dead', and is, in point of fact, her effort to re-establish communication with her family.

May I suggest, therefore, that Mr Davis and his family should pay serious attention to these 'rappings'?

The method is very simple and is that adopted in table-turning. If these rappings should be heard again, Mr Davis, and his family, should assemble in the room in which the sounds appear to be the clearest and ask, 'Is there anyone there?' If the answer is a rap, he should say, 'We want to help you, and will ask you questions. Rap once for "yes" and twice for "no".'

If this fails, after a thorough test, it has often been found a complete solution to call in a priest to exorcise the house. I say 'often' not 'always' because some spirits are too low in the superphysical scale to be susceptible to prayer.

In this class come poltergeists and elementals, about which there is nothing to be done except to give up the house altogether.

This upsetting of furniture rather points to the poltergeist, but it also possibly indicates the annoyance of the dead at the obtuseness of her family. She probably has something on her mind – remorse, advice, warning, or help – to convey, and should be given every possible help by the living.

The great fame of the haunting brought forward many suggestions of ways of ending the disturbances, both from ordinary members of the public and from the usual cranks. Many suggested exorcism but this remedy was never tried. Contact with a medium was tried at the end of the affair, though since the medium concerned already knew members of the family her pronouncements were too easy to discredit. She failed to disclose anything not already known to the

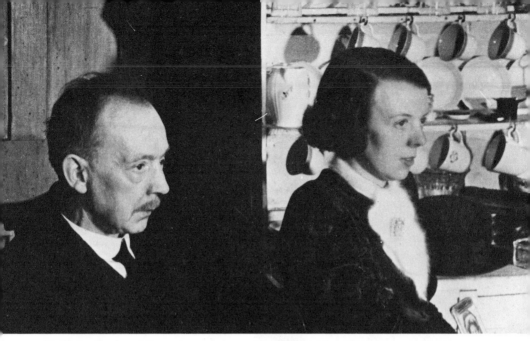

Mr Walter Davis and Grace. (SOC. FOR PSYCHICAL RESEARCH)

family, and Dr Fodor's correspondence with her shows him to have his tongue very much in his cheek.

The report in the *Daily Express* on Friday, 11 February, was also sceptical – pointing out that a ghost able to leave fingerprints was certainly worth investigating. That afternoon the three investigators again visited the house. They asked Grace whether she could see anything strange in the sitting-room through the glass panel of the locked door from the kitchen. She said that she had clearly seen the pictures of Mrs Davis, that Fodor had turned to face the wall, turned back to face the room: then they had turned themselves back to the original position. Mrs Harrison confirmed this, and, indeed, the pictures now faced the wall just as the investigators had left them. Young Sydney Davis was also asked whether he had seen this incident but replied that he was too scared to look for fear of what he might see. In his report Fodor commented:

This statement of the ladies is very odd and throws considerable light on the power of their imagination. I have no doubt whatsoever in my mind that they only imagined the pictures facing them. It would be extremely capricious behaviour on the part of the ghost if in the sealed room it suddenly performed this curious feat.

119

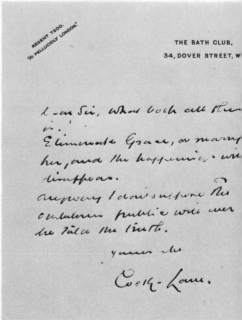

Left: *Another view of the front room.* Right: *The researchers received this amusing letter from the Bath Club.* (SOCIETY FOR PSYCHICAL RESEARCH)

Again, on the Saturday, Dr Fodor and his two assistants visited the house. Newspapermen were maintaining a vigil even though the ghost had scarcely been heard for twenty-four hours, though while they were talking to Grace in the sitting-room she claimed to hear faint moans coming from the kitchen. No one else present heard them. Nothing had been disturbed in either of the sealed rooms. Dr Fodor concluded:

> It is my impression that it has given a shock to the family that the Ghost could not, or would not, manifest in a sealed room. . . . It is as if this shock had set up a doubt in their minds regarding these phenomena, and by this very fact deprived the ghostly agency of one of the principal elements in the psychic atmosphere which made the disturbances possible.

The *Sunday Dispatch* of 13 February carried the story that the Harrisons were to leave the house on the following Tuesday. 'They say they are unable to bear the worry any longer.' The next day in the *Evening Standard* Dr Fodor was forecasting that the disturbances would end within the week. 'I do believe', he is quoted as saying, 'that

120

something very strange is abroad in the house. It is, in fact, one of the strangest cases I have ever met.' He concluded by stressing the difficulties a practical joker would have had playing his tricks in a house so crowded with family, newsmen, police and investigators. Many newspapers writing of the affair noted that poltergeist activity is a haunting of *people* and that in theory the events could continue away from the house. In most cases, they admitted, once a person is persuaded to go by a poltergeist the disturbances cease. As a columnist wrote in the *Daily Mail* on Monday, 14 February:

If we believe in the possibility of poltergeists we shall attribute to them all manner of low cunning and nasty intentions. We cannot be tolerant of them or of their mean, underhand ways. They are altogether different from the honest, upright ghosts of decaying castles and ancient halls. These are respectable ghosts; some are even amiable. Not so poltergeists: they are beyond the pale of this world and the other.

The *North London Recorder* contained a piece on poltergeists by a local occult expert, J. Bardell Smith, suggesting a means of ending the disturbances:

In all poltergeist cases it has been found that there lives in the house a woman in dawning womanhood say from 16 to 21 years of age; and through some mysterious make-up of her physical body 'power' or energy can be drawn by the 'ghost' to move articles, make noises and other very unpleasant demonstrations.

How can these happenings be stopped? The most drastic and certain remedy is the removal of the 'power station' – if the lady of 16 to 21 leaves the house these ghostly demonstrations will certainly come to an end.

In fact this course of action was about to be taken, for the Davis family, like the Harrisons, had also had enough and were looking for accommodation elsewhere. They were increasingly reluctant to speak with the Press or even Dr Fodor. The last mention of the haunting comes in the *City and East London Observer* whose 'Special Representative' accompanied the Doctor when he paid his final visit to the house on 18 February.

Upon our arrival, we were met by Mrs Harrison, the tenant who was moving out that day, and conducted into the kitchen where

Grace Davis, her two brothers and sister-in-law were sitting.

The first question the Doctor asked was 'Has anything happened since I was here last?' The reply came from Grace Davis: 'Owing to the publicity we have received I prefer not to say anything about it.'

After a while, however, Grace and Mrs Harrison told us the following story.

'Last Sunday afternoon we were sitting in this room when Mrs Harrison happened to glance through the communicating door of our front room and saw the outline of a man standing in front of the piano, gazing at an object.'

'She called me and I saw it too,' said Grace. 'Mrs Harrison asked my father to move from the position he was standing in. He did so and the vision still remained. We noticed that my father was in his shirt sleeves, whereas the apparition had a black coat on and a moustache, while my father is clean shaven. This occurred in broad daylight.'

Mrs Harrison here took up the conversation and described once again the sensations she experienced on Friday, when Dr Fodor's assistant and myself persuaded her to lie down on the bed of the late Mrs Davis. She then complained of feeling 'deathly cold', and said she felt as if the back of her head were being pressed in. She seemed to be in a state of coma and clutched her throat, declaring her mouth and throat were dry and sore.

By careful questioning I discovered that Mrs Harrison was the first to see or hear any untoward happening three months ago. She said, 'I saw the figure of Mrs Davis clearly and the word "Go" was uttered distinctly. Immediately after this I visited a London spiritualist who warned me that unless I moved something serious might happen on the middle floor.'

A fear has been on the household for some time due to the disappearance of a piece of string from the bedroom of the late Mrs Davis when a chair was tied to the bed and the 'ghost' decided, after several times untying it, to remove it completely. Every member of the household definitely states that this piece of string was not removed by themselves, and they have spent many hours looking for it, owing to fear of strangulation.

Mrs Harrison, continuing her conversation, stated that she had not told anybody of the fact that she had been to the spiritualist.

Dr Fodor and myself visited the rooms which, it was suggested, had been disturbed since our last visit and could find no traces of upheaval. A quick test by the Doctor showed no results.

He has decided that imagination is playing a part in the later happenings and discounts the theory that the 'ghost' is still present in the house.

As far as the new 'vision' is concerned, we discovered that when the house was being built, a man* was supposed to have fallen off the scaffolding and was killed. Dr Fodor suggested to me that the tenants knowing this, it reacted on their agitated minds, which readily associated the 'vision' with this past occurrence.

To demonstrate his theory, he showed me that a person passing or standing outside the house, their shadow would be thrown and reflected through the front window, and owing to the number of glass objects in the room, could possibly be seen in outline.

Mrs Harrison leaves the house today (Thursday) and Dr Fodor is convinced that the manifestations will not recur.

'I believe in the first place there was a genuine phenomenon behind it,' said Dr Fodor, summing up his conclusions. 'I refuse to believe all that has happened in the house could be due to imagination alone, neither could it have been a hoax. Many things could be explained but others were inexplicable.

'The later happenings are, in my opinion, an aftermath of the original manifestations, due to overwrought nerves. It is the well known last phase of all ghostly disturbances.'

Dr Fodor's notes show that this was not quite the end of the affair. When he contacted the spiritualist she told him that Mrs Harrison had first visited her twelve months previously – well before the death of Mrs Davis. She had been told then to move, 'before there is trouble'. Six weeks before Christmas (after the old lady had died) she again saw Mrs Harrison, this time accompanied by Grace Davis. She was asked to 'psychometrise' Mrs Davis's wedding-ring. Again the message was that Mrs Harrison should go. A few days later the medium came to the house and sat in the chair that Mrs Davis used. This time the warning was even stronger: Mrs Harrison was suspected of helping herself to money while Mrs Davis was in a fit (Mrs Harrison had said earlier that her landlady would often set fire to pound notes when in such a condition). Finally the spiritualist saw the ceiling falling on top of her, which charitably she put down to the condition of the house.

*This was, in fact, Mrs Davis's father, a master builder, who fell to his death while repairing the roof.

There is no escape from the hostility that Mrs Davis felt for Mrs Harrison. The Vicar, the Reverend Francis Nicholle, wrote of it in a letter to Dr Fodor:

> I could not discover that Mrs Davis had missed any money after her fits, but she did lose several pieces of jewellery about which I gather she had her suspicions. Mrs Harrison was in the habit of running into debt, and of borrowing money and household things, which was a source of annoyance to Mrs Davis. I understand that she is in Mr Davis' debt, and that is why they have not got rid of her before now.
>
> Mrs Davis evidently disliked her excessively, and kept saying that there would be no peace in the house while she was in it. . . . There can, I think, be no doubt that Mrs H. is the cause of these disturbances, and that their purpose has been either one of hostility, or perhaps of concern for the peace of the family.

Many of the local people thought that the disturbances were caused by the Harrisons, their motive being to escape repaying the money they owed to the Davis family. However there was evidence that the noises, etc. continued even when Mrs Harrison was with reliable witnesses, who claimed that the upper floors were completely empty (presumably Mr Harrison was known to be out at work on these occasions). A daughter of Mrs Davis has written to the author asserting that there was no ill-feeling between the two families, yet dislike and distrust are the emotions that are evoked by the old reports, letters and cuttings. Even Grace, who appears an inseparable companion of the upstairs tenant, expressed her dislike of Mrs Harrison to the Vicar.

Thus the strange story ends, full of contradictions to the last. Nevertheless it would seem that at the heart of the matter there was a genuine supernatural occurrence. Modern stories of poltergeists, such as the one at Enfield described by Guy Playfair, have many facets in common with the happenings at Teesdale Street. More remarkable are the similarities with the Cock Lane Ghost which so disturbed the gentry of London in the eighteenth century. Although part of Teesdale Street survives, the site of the Davis' home (where the family continued to live until the house was demolished in 1956) is now occupied by a great block of council housing, and few people remember the scenes in 1938 when upwards of 2000 people would congregate here in the hope of seeing the ghost.

Crowds outside 132 Teesdale Street. (SOCIETY FOR PSYCHICAL RESEARCH)

Dreams and Omens

The story of Dick Whittington 'turning again' to find fortune in the City of London and become its Lord Mayor three times over is probably the most famous tale of an omen concerning London. The dream of the Swaffham Tinker is hardly less remarkable and has also passed into the folklore of the City. This is how it is told in *Glimpses of the Supernatural* by the Reverend F. G. Lee (1875):

This Tinker, a hard-working, industrious man, one night dreamed that if he took a journey to London, and placed himself at a certain spot on London Bridge, he should meet one who would tell him something of great importance to his future prospects. The Tinker, on whom the dream made a deep impression, related it fully to his wife in the morning; who, however, half-laughed at him and half-scolded him for his folly in heeding such idle fancies. Next night he is said to have redreamed the dream; and again on the third night, when the impression was so powerful on his mind that he determined, in spite of the remonstrances of his wife and the ridicule of his neighbours, to go to London and see the upshot of it. Accordingly he set off for the metropolis on foot, reached it late on the third day (the distance was ninety miles), and, after the refreshment of a night's rest, took his station next day on a part of the Bridge answering to the description in his dream. There he stood all day, and all the next, and all the third, without any communication as to the purpose of his journey; so that towards night, on the third day, he began to lose patience and confidence in his dream, inwardly cursed his folly in disregarding his wife's counsel, and resolved next day to make the best of his way home. He still kept his station, however, till late in the evening, when, just as he was about to depart, a stranger who had noticed him standing steadfastly and with anxious look on the same spot for some days, accosted him, and asked him what he waited there for. After a little hesitation, the Tinker told his errand, though without acquainting him with the name of the place whence he came. The stranger enjoyed a smile at the rustic's simplicity, and advised him to go home and for the future to pay no attention to dreams. 'I myself,' said he, 'if I were disposed to put faith in such things, might now go a hundred miles into the country upon a similar errand. I

Left top: *Old London Bridge.* (GUILDHALL LIBRARY)
Left: *The Swaffham Tinker on a stall-end in the church at Swaffham*

dreamed three nights this week that if I went to a place called Swaffham in Norfolk, and dug under an apple-tree in a certain garden on the north side of the town I should find a box of money; but I have something else to do than run after such idle fancies! No, no, my friend; go home, and work well at your calling, and you will find there the riches you are seeking here.' The astonished Tinker did not doubt that this was the communication he had been sent to London to receive, but he merely thanked the stranger for his advice, and went away avowing his intention to follow it. Next day he set out for home, and on his arrival there said little to his wife touching his journey; but next morning he rose betimes and began to dig on the spot he supposed to be pointed out by the stranger. When he had got a few feet down, the spade struck upon something hard, which turned out to be an iron chest. This he quickly carried to his house, and when he had with difficulty wrenched open the lid, found it, to his great joy, to be full of money. After securing his treasure, he observed on the lid of the box an inscription, which, unlearned as he was, he could not decipher. But by a stratagem he got the description read without any suspicion on the part of his neighbours by some of the Grammar School lads, and found it to be

'Where this stood
Is another twice as good.'

And in truth on digging again the lucky Tinker disinterred, below the place where the first chest had lain, a second twice as large, also full of gold and silver coin. It is stated that, become thus a wealthy man, the Tinker showed his thankfulness to Providence by building a new chancel to the church, the old one being out of repair. And whatever fiction the marvellous taste of those ages may have mixed up with the tale, certain it is that there is shown to this day a monument in Swaffham Church, having an effigy in marble, said to be that of the Tinker with his Dog at his side and his tools and implements of trade lying about him.

A remarkable dream led to the arrest of a man for murder in 1695. On 23 December of that year a Grub Street grocer named Stockden was killed and no clue to the identity of the murderer was found. A few days later a Mrs Greenwood visited a local magistrate and told him that Stockden had appeared to her in a dream and begged her to tell the authorities that the man who had killed him lived in a house in Thames Street, which she was able to describe. The following night she had dreamed again, and this time Stockden showed her a portrait of the murderer, saying that his name was Maynard.

The magistrate accordingly sent for Maynard and questioned him about the killing, whereupon he confessed that he had been one of those who had killed the unfortunate grocer, but that he had three accomplices, whose identity he refused to divulge at first. However Mrs Greenwood dreamed yet again, and this time Stockden showed her a portrait of one of the accomplices, and through this identification the man was arrested. The third culprit was then betrayed by Maynard, and all three were hanged for the crime, which had been solved by a dream.

A further example of how a dream, and a ghost, led to justice being done comes from J. H. Ingram's *Haunted Homes and Family Traditions of Great Britain.* (1884). He found the story in *The History and Reality of Apparitions*, published in 1770 and edited by Defoe, who says that its source, the Reverend Dr Scott, was not only a man 'whose learning and piety were eminent, but one whose judgment was known to be good.' This is the story as told in *Haunted Homes*:

Dr. Scott was sitting alone by his fireside in the library of his house in Broad Street; he had shut himself in the room to study and, so it is alleged, had locked the door. In the midst of his reading happening to look up, he was much astounded to see, sitting in an elbow-chair on the other side of the fire-place, a grave, elderly gentleman, in a black velvet gown and a long wig, looking at him with a pleased countenance, and as if about to speak. Knowing that he had locked the door, Dr. Scott was quite confounded at seeing this uninvited visitor sitting in the elbow-chair, and from the first appears to have suspected its supernatural character. Indeed, so disturbed was he at the sight of the apparition, for such it was, that he was unable to speak, as he himself acknowledged in telling the story. The spectre, however, began the discourse by telling the doctor not to be frightened, for it would do him no harm, but came to see him upon a matter of great importance to an injured family, which was in danger of being ruined. Although the doctor was a stranger to this family, the apparition stated that knowing him to be a man of integrity it had selected him to perform an act of great charity as well as justice.

At first Dr. Scott was not sufficiently composed to pay proper attention to what the apparition propounded; but was rather more inclined to escape from the room if he could, and made one or two futile attempts to knock for some of his household to come up; at which his visitor appeared to be somewhat displeased. But, as the doctor afterwards stated, he had no power to go out of the room, even if he had been next the door, nor to knock for help, even if any had been close at hand.

Then the apparition, seeing the doctor still so confused, again desired him to compose himself, assuring him that he would not do him the slightest injury, nor do anything to cause him the least uneasiness, but desired that he would permit him to deliver the business he came about, which, when he had heard, he said, he would probably see less cause to be surprised or apprehensive than he did now.

By this time Dr. Scott had somewhat recovered himself, and encouraged by the calm manner in which the apparition addressed him, contrived to falter out:

'In the name of God, what art thou?'

'I desire you will not be frightened,' responded the apparition. 'I am a stranger to you, and if I tell you my name you will not know it. But you may do the business without inquiring further.' The doctor could not compose himself, but still remained very uneasy, and for some time said nothing. Again the apparition attempted to reassure him, but could only elicit from him a repetition of the ejaculation, 'In the name of God, what art thou?'

Upon this, says the narration, the spectre appeared to be displeased, and expostulated with Dr. Scott, telling him that it could have terrified him into compliance, but that it chose to come quietly and calmly to him; and, indeed, made use of such civil and natural discourse that the doctor began to grow a little more familiar, and at last ventured to ask what it wanted of him. Upon this the apparition appeared to be very gratified, and began its story. It related that it had once owned a very good estate, which at that time was enjoyed by its grandson; two nephews, however, the sons of its younger brother, were then suing for possession of the property and, owing to certain family reasons which the doctor could not or would not specify, were likely to oust the young man from his property. A deed of settlement, being the conveyance of the inheritance, could not be found and without it the owner of the estate had every reason to fear he would be ejected.

'Well,' said Dr. Scott, 'what can I do in the case?'

'Go to my grandson,' said the apparition, 'and direct him where to find the missing deed, which is concealed in a place where I put it myself.' And then it gave the doctor minute particulars of the chest wherein the needed document was hidden stowed away in an old lumber-room. When the apparition had impressed the matter thoroughly upon the doctor's mind, Dr. Scott not unnaturally asked his visitor why it could not direct the grandson himself to recover the missing deed. 'Ask me not about that,' said the apparition; 'there are divers reasons, which you may know hereafter. I can depend upon your honesty in it in the meantime.'

Still Dr. Scott did not like to take upon himself the strange mission, whereupon the apparition seemed to grow angry, and even begin to threaten him, so that he was at last compelled to promise compliance. The apparition then assumed a pleasant aspect, thanked him, and disappeared.

The strangest part of this strange story yet remains to be told. At the earliest opportunity Dr. Scott posted away to the address given him by the apparition, or dream as some persons deemed it. He asked for and was at once introduced to the gentleman the apparition had sent him to, and to his surprise was received most cordially by him. Dr. Scott's surprise was, indeed, quickened when the stranger entered most unreservedly into the particulars of his law-suit, telling him that he had had a dream the previous night, in which he had dreamed that a strange gentleman came to him, and assisted him to find the deed which was needed to confirm him in the possession of his estate.

This assured Dr. Scott that it was not a dream which he had had, and that he was really selected to discover the missing document. Making himself agreeable to his host, he eventually got him to take him all over his splendid old mansion. Finally, he beheld just such a lumber-room as the apparition had told him of, and on entering it, saw an exact *fac-simile* of the chest described to him by his supernatural visitant. There was an old rusty key in it that would neither turn round, nor come out of the lock, which was exactly what the apparition had forwarned him of! At the doctor's request a hammer and chisel were sent for, and the chest broken open, and, after some difficulty, a false drawer was found in it. This being split open, *there lay the missing parchment* spread out flat over the whole breadth of the bottom of the trunk!

The Crypt at Bow Church. (GUILDHALL LIBRARY)

The joy of the young heir, and of his family, may be imagined, whilst their surprise can have been no less. Whether Dr. Scott informed them of the means by which he was led to make the discovery is not stated; but it is alleged the production of the needed deed confirmed the owner in the possession of his estates. As this gentleman was still living, the narrator was not inclined to publish his name; and, now-a-days, the chances of discovering it are, doubtless, far less than they were in his time of finding the missing document. Regard it how we may, as a dream or a coincidence, certainly Dr. Scott's adventure was a very marvellous one.

A more macabre episode is described in a great source of material on dreams, the Reverend F. G. Lee's *Glimpses of the Supernatural*. It shows again how greatly the ghoulish activities of the 'resurrectionists' were feared at that time:

The Rev. Mr. Perring, Vicar of a parish which is now a component part of London, though, about forty-five years ago it had the appearance of a village at the outskirts, had to encounter the sad affliction of losing his eldest Son at an age when parents are encouraged to believe their children are to become their survivors; the youth dying in his seventeenth year. He was buried in the vaults of the church.

Two nights subsequently to that interment, the father dreamed that he saw his Son habited in a shroud spotted with blood, the expression of his countenance being that of a person enduring some paroxysm of acute pain: 'Father, father! come and defend me!' were the words he distinctly heard, as he gazed on this awe-inspiring apparition; 'they will not let me rest quietly in my coffin.'

The venerable man awoke with terror and trembling; but after a brief interval of painful reflection concluded himself to be labouring under the influence of his sad day-thoughts, and the depression of past sufferings; and with these rational assurances commended himself to the All-Merciful, and slumbered again and slept.

He saw his Son again beseeching him to protect his remains from outrage, 'For,' said the apparently surviving dead one, 'they are mangling my body at this moment.' The unhappy Father rose at once, being now unable to banish the fearful image from his mind, and determined when day should dawn to satisfy himself of the delusiveness or verity of the revelation conveyed through this seeming voice from the grave.

At an early hour, accordingly, he repaired to the Clerk's house, where the keys of the church and of the vaults were kept. The Clerk after considerable delay, came down-stairs, saying it was very unfortunate he should want them just on that very day, as his son over the way had taken them to the smith's for repair, – one of the largest of the bunch of keys having been broken off short in the main door of the vault, so as to render it impracticable for anybody to enter till the lock had been picked and taken off.

Impelled by the worst misgivings, the Vicar loudly insisted on the Clerk's accompanying him to the blacksmith's – not for a key but for a crowbar, it being his resolute determination to enter the vault and see his Son's coffin without a moment's delay.

The recollections of the dream were now becoming more and more vivid, and the scrutiny about to be made assumed a solemnity mingled with awe, which the agitation of the father rendered terrible to the agents in this forcible interruption into the resting-place of the dead. But the hinges were speedily wrenched asunder – the bar and bolts were beaten in and bent beneath the heavy hammer of the smith, – and at length with tottering and outstretched hands, the maddened parent stumbled and fell: his son's coffin had been lifted from the recess at the vault's side and deposited on the brick floor; the lid, released from every screw, lay loose at top, and the body, enveloped in its shroud, on which were several dark spots below the chin, lay exposed to view; the head had been raised, the broad riband had been removed from under the jaw, which now hung down with the most ghastly horror of expression, as if to tell with more terrific certainty the truth of the preceding night's vision. *Every tooth in the head had been drawn.*

The young man had when living a beautiful set of sound teeth. The Clerk's Son, who was a barber, cupper, and dentist, had possessed himself of the keys, and eventually of the teeth, for the purpose of profitable employment of so excellent a set in his line of business. The feelings of the Rev. Mr. Perring can be easily conceived. The event affected his mind through the remaining term of his existence; but what became of the delinquent whose sacrilegious hand had thus rifled the tomb was never afterwards correctly ascertained. He decamped the same day, and was supposed to have enlisted as a soldier. The Clerk was ignominiously displaced, and did not long survive the transaction. Some years afterwards, his house was pulled down to afford room for extensive improvements and new buildings in the village.

As regards the occurrence itself, few persons were apprised of it; as the Vicar – shunning public talk and excitement on the subject of any member of his family – exerted himself in concealing the circumstances as much as possible. The above facts, however, may be strictly relied on as accurate.

The most spectacular portents heralded the Plague which struck London in the early summer of 1665. Similar signs were seen a year later, before the Great Fire. This description of the first omens that were seen comes from *The Terrific Register* of 1825:

In the first place, a blazing star or comet appeared for several months before the plague, as there did the year after another, a little before the fire; the old women, and the phlegmatic hypochondriac part of the other sex, who I could almost call old women too, remarked (especially afterwards, though not till these judgments were over,) that those two comets passed directly over the city, and that so very near the houses, that it was plain they imported something peculiar to the city alone; that the comet before the pestilence, was of a faint, dull, languid colour, and its motion very heavy, solemn, and slow: but that the comet before the fire, was bright and sparkling, or as others said, flaming, and its motion swift and furious; and that accordingly, one foretold a heavy judgment, slow but severe, terrible and frightful, as was the plague; but the other foretold a stroke, sudden, swift, and fiery as the conflagration; nay, so particular some people were, that as they looked upon that comet preceding the fire, they fancied that they not only saw it pass swiftly and fiercely, and could perceive the motion with their eye, but even they heard it; that it made a rushing mighty noise, fierce and terrible, though at a distance, and but just perceivable.

Some heard voices warning them to be gone, for that there would be such a plague in London, so that the living would not be able to bury the dead: others saw apparitions in the air. Here they told us, they saw a flaming sword held in a hand, coming out of a cloud, with a point hanging directly over the city. There they saw hearses and coffins in the air, carrying to be buried. And there again, heaps of dead bodies lying unburied, and the like.

Another ran about naked, except a pair of drawers about his waist, crying day and night, like a man that Josephus mentions, who cried, 'Woe to Jerusalem!' a little before the destruction of that city: so this poor naked creature cried, 'Oh! the great and dreadful God!' and said no more, but repeated those words continually, with a voice and countenance full of horror, a swift pace, and nobody could ever find him to stop, or rest, or take any sustenance, at least, that ever I could hear of. I met this poor creature several times in

*Solomon Eagle became famous in London during the time of the Plague for his
denunciations of the weaknesses of Mankind. He was known as the Enthusiast.*
(GUILDHALL LIBRARY)

the streets, and would have spoken to him, but he would not enter into speech with me, or any one else; but held on his dismal cries continually.

In a narrow passage by Bishopsgate church-yard stood a man looking through between the palisadoes into the burying place; and as many people as the narrowness of the passage would admit to stop, without hindering the passage of others; and he was talking mighty eagerly to them, and pointing now to one place, then to another, and affirming, that he saw a ghost walking upon such a grave-stone there; he described the shape, the posture, and the movement of it so exactly, that it was the greatest matter of amazement to him in the world, that every body did not see it as well as he. On a sudden he would cry, 'There it is: now it comes this way:' then ''tis turned back;' till at length he persuaded the people into so firm a belief of it, that one fancied he saw it, and another fancied he saw it; and thus he came every day making a strange hubbub, considering it was in so narrow a passage, till Bishopsgate clock struck eleven; and then the ghost would seem to start; and as if he were called away, disappeared on a sudden.

The most curious portent of the Plague was given not in London but many miles to the west, in Cornwall. The Botathen Ghost is one of the greatest of our native ghost stories, and it needs little excuse to tell it again here.

The ghost first appeared to a schoolboy named Bligh, who encountered it each day as he crossed a field on his way to and from school. It was dressed 'in female attire' and would glide past him three or four times as he walked through the field. He became so upset by the apparition that he began to make a long detour to avoid going through Botathen (the name of the district where the ghost appeared – it is about three miles from Padstow). His family soon noticed a change in his demeanour and eventually got him to tell them what it was that was troubling him. When he told of the ghost they showed a little disbelief, but all the same approached his schoolmaster, the Reverend John Ruddle, a Prebendary of Exeter and Vicar of Alternan, and told him their son's story. When he heard it he was impressed by their sincerity and agreed to accompany the boy on a walk through the haunted meadow. In his diary the clergyman wrote of his first meeting with the ghost:

I arose the next morning, and went with him. The field to which he led me I guessed to be about twenty acres, in an open country, and about three furlongs from any house. We went into the field, and had not gone a third part before the *spectrum*, in the shape of a woman, with all the circumstances that he had described the day before, so far as the suddenness of its appearance and transition would permit me to discover, passed by.

I was a little impressed at it, and, though I had taken up a firm resolution to speak to it, I had not the power, nor durst I look back; yet I took care not to show any fear to my pupil and guide; and therefore, telling him that I was satisfied in the truth of his statement, we walked to the end of the field, and returned: nor did the ghost meet us that time but once.

There follows an account of several subsequent meetings with it. Mr Ruddle was an observant and fearless investigator: he noted that his spaniel was aware of the ghost's presence as it barked at it and then ran away. His description of the way it moved formed the pattern for many later 'ghost-writers':

> . . . secondly the motion of the *spectrum* was not *gradatim* or by steps, or moving of the feet, but by a kind of gliding, as children upon ice, or as a boat down a river, which practically answers the description the ancients give of the motion of these lemures.

By getting local people to accompany him to the field, Ruddle was able to identify the ghost as being Dorothy Durant (Dinglet in another account), a woman of the district who had often visited the Blighs and who had died a short time previously. His attempts to get the ghost to tell him what troubled it were unsuccessful. It answered in a voice that was hardly audible, and even the words he heard were unintelligible. Thus he decided that the only solution was to exorcise it: by these means the ghost could properly divulge the reason for its presence and thus be put to rest. Accordingly Ruddle set off secretly to Exeter to obtain permission from the Bishop. It proved difficult to persuade the latter that such action should be taken as he was reluctant to sanction anything that smacked of Popery.

'Our Church,' he told Ruddle, 'as is well known, hath abjured certain branches of her ancient power, on grounds of perversion and abuse.' But the country schoolmaster had done his homework, and by quoting from the seventy-second Canon of 1604 was able to convince his Bishop that permission should be granted.

Thus Ruddle was able to return to Botathen with the licence for exorcism signed and sealed, though as he knelt before the Bishop to receive his blessing, the old man had whispered: 'Let it be secret, Mr Ruddle, – weak brethren, weak brethren!'

The exorcism itself, as described in Ruddle's diary, seems to come straight from the pages of Denis Wheatley:

January 12th, 1665. Rode into the gateway of Botathen, armed at all points, but not with Saul's armour, and ready. There is danger from the demons, but so there is in the surrounding air every day. At early morning then and alone, for so the usage ordains, I betook me towards the field. It was void, and I had thereby due time to prepare. First I paced and measured out my circle on the grass. Then did I mark my pentacle in the very midst, and at the intersection of the five angles I did set up and fix my crutch of raun [rowan]. Lastly I took my station south, at the true line of the meridian, and stood facing due north. I waited and watched for a long time. At last there was a kind of trouble in the air, a soft and rippling sound, and all at once the shape appeared, and came on towards me gradually. I opened my parchment scroll, and read aloud the command. She paused and seemed to waver and doubt; stood still: and then I rehearsed the sentence again, sounding out every syllable like a chant. She drew near my ring, but halted at first outside, on the brink. I sounded again, and now at the third time I gave the signal in Syriac – the speech which is used, they say, where such ones dwell and converse in thoughts that glide.

She was at last obedient and swam into the midst of the circle: and there stood still suddenly. I saw, moreover, that she drew back her pointing hand. All this while I do confess that my knees shook under me, and the drops of sweat ran down my flesh like rain. But now, although face to face with the spirit, my heart grew calm and my mind composed, to know that the pentacle would govern her, and the ring must bind until I gave the word. Then I called to mind the rule laid down of old that no angel or fiend, no spirit, good or evil, will ever speak until they be spoken to. N.B. – This is the great law of prayer. God Himself will not yield reply until man hath made vocal entreaty once and again. So I went on to demand, as the books advise; and the phantom made answer willingly. Questioned, wherefore not at rest? Unquiet because of a certain sin. Asked what and by whom? Revealed it; but it is *sub sigillo*, and therefore *nefas*

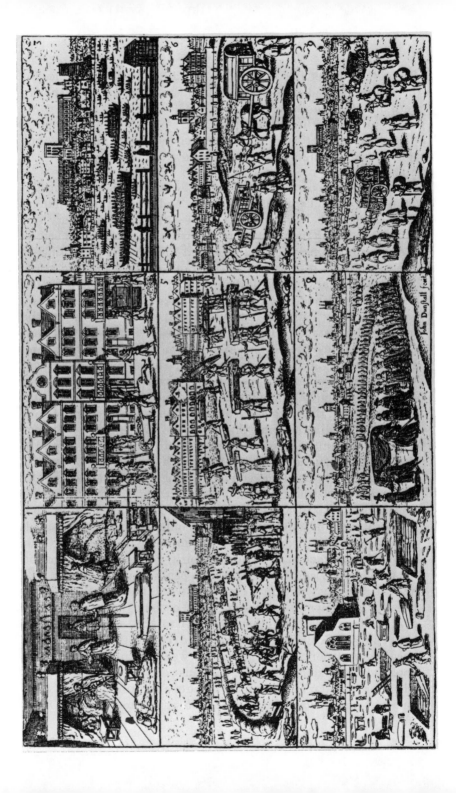

John Dunstall sculp.

dictu; more anon. Inquired, what sign she could give me that she was a true spirit and not a false friend? Stated [that] before next Yule-tide a fearful pestilence would lay waste the land; and myriads of souls would be loosened from their flesh, until, as she piteously said, 'Our valleys will be full.' Asked again, why she so terrified the lad? Replied, 'It is the law; we must seek a youth or a maiden of clean life, and under age, to receive messages and admonitions.' We conversed with many more words; but it is not lawful for me to set them down. Pen and ink would degrade and defile the thoughts she uttered, and which my mind received that day. I broke the ring and she passed, but to return once more next day. At evensong a long discourse with that ancient transgressor, Mr. B—. Great horror and remorse; entire atonement and penance; whatsoever I enjoin; full acknowledgment before pardon.

January 13, 1665. At sunrise I was again in the field. She came in at once, and, as it seemed, with freedom. Inquired if she knew my thoughts, and what I was going to relate? Answered, 'Nay, we only know what we perceive and hear: we cannot see the heart.' Then I rehearsed the penitent words of the man she had come up to denounce, and the satisfaction he would perform. Then said she, 'Peace in our midst.' I went through the proper forms of dismissal, and fulfilled all, as it was set down and written in my memoranda; and then with certain fixed rites, I did dismiss that troubled ghost, until she peacefully withdrew, gliding towards the west. Neither did she ever afterwards appear; but was allayed, until she shall come in her second flesh, to the Valley of Armageddon on the Last Day.

Thus ends a wonderful story; only Ruddle's triumph at the advent of the Plague strikes an unhappy note to modern ears. This is the entry in his diary for 10 July 1665:

How sorely must the infidels and hereticks of this generation be dismayed when they know that this Black Death, which is now swallowing its thousands in the streets of the great city was foretold six months agone, under the exorcisms of a country minister, by a visible and suppliant ghost! And what pleasures and improvements do such deny themselves who scorn and avoid all opportunity of intercourse with souls separate, and the spirits, glad and sorrowful, which inhabit the unseen world.

A pictorial broadsheet of 1665 showing the grim scenes during the Plague. (GUILDHALL LIBRARY)

The West End

Parks and Palaces

Of all the world's capital cities, London must wear the crown for the wealth of beautiful open spaces at its very heart. Although it is a common belief that only houses and other buildings are haunted, a remarkable regiment of ghosts may be found in these richly timbered sanctuaries of peace.

Unfortunately Dutch Elm Disease has been responsible for the demise of the haunted elm in Hyde Park known as 'Black Sally's Tree'. Black Sally was a woman tramp with Romany blood in her who disregarded the advice of other down-and-outs and slept beneath the gnarled branches of the ancient tree. She was found dead in the morning, confirming the belief of her fellow vagrants that something evil dwelt there. Her death occurred fifty or so years ago, and afterwards many spoke of hearing a sad moaning in the vicinity. There have been no reports of this since the tree has been felled.

Green Park also has an ill-famed tree, which invariably seems to be chosen by suicides looking for a branch suitable for holding a rope. It is said that it is even avoided by the birds of the park, who may be scared off by the half-heard evil chuckle that seems to come from it. Wardens know it as 'the tree of death' and say that a dark figure has been seen standing by it which disappears mysteriously when one draws near for a closer examination.

Buckingham Palace was built by John Sheffield, first Duke of Buckingham, in 1703. Subsequently it was bought by George III, and it was substantially rebuilt in the nineteenth century when the east wing (the side of the palace seen by the public) was added. The Royal Family normally occupy the north wing. The palace is supposed to be haunted by the ghost of a monk who dwelt in the priory that occupied the site before the Dissolution. He died in the punishment cell and

Above: Buckingham Palace (Guildhall Library).
Left: An old drawing of an elm in Hyde Park. Was this 'Black Sally's Tree'? (Guildhall Library).

Buckingham Palace today.

appears each year on Christmas Day, bound in irons, when he clanks along the great terrace which overlooks the forty acres of gardens.

St James's Palace is a more ancient building, dating from the time of Henry VII. After Whitehall Palace had been destroyed by fire, it was the monarch's official London residence until Buckingham Palace was so favoured by Queen Victoria. Two obscure royal mistresses were given apartments here – the Duchess of Mazarine, a favourite of Charles II, and Madame de Beauclair who was mistress of his brother and successor, James II. As the two ladies grew older they became close friends; they felt neglected by a world which could barely remember their moments of glory, and they came to depend greatly on the company of each other. One topic which came to interest them greatly was the likelihood of life after death, and they made a solemn compact that whichever one died first should return to report on conditions 'on the other side'.

The Duchess died first. During her final illness Madame de Beauclair reminded her of her solemn promise, and the Duchess confirmed her serious intention of keeping it. An hour later she was dead.

Madame de Beauclair lived on for many years, but since her great friend had failed to pay her a visit to confirm that another existence did, in fact, lie beyond the grave, she became bitter in her disbelief of life after death. She told a close friend the reason for her doubts – the broken promise made by the Duchess.

One evening this same male friend was at a card-party given by an acquaintance of Madame de Beauclair. They had just settled to play when a servant came to the room and begged the hostess to go at once to Madame de Beauclair: if she delayed the visit she would never again see her in this world. The lady had a severe cold, and on being assured that Madame was in excellent health, refused the request. Shortly afterwards another message arrived, expressed in even more urgent terms, and accompanied by the bequest of all the old lady's jewellery, which was of considerable value. Thus the hostess, accompanied by the male friend, was persuaded to go to Madame de Beauclair's apartment at the palace.

When they arrived at her bedside she told them that she would very soon leave this world for the eternity which she once questioned. She had seen the Duchess of Mazarine:

I perceived not how she entered but, turning my eyes towards

146   *The Duchess of Mazarine (Guildhall Library).*

yonder corner of the room, I saw her stand in the same form and habit she was accustomed to appear in when living: fain would I have spoken, but had not the power of utterance. She took a little circuit round the chamber, seeming rather to swim than walk, then stopped by the side of that Indian chest, and, looking on me with her usual sweetness, said, 'Beauclair, between the hours of twelve and one this night you will be with me.' The surprise I was in at first being a little abated, I began to ask some questions concerning that future world I was so soon to visit; but, on the opening of my lips for that purpose, she vanished from my sight.

(T. M. Jarvis, Accredited Ghost Stories, 1823.)

By the time Madame de Beauclair had told her story it was almost midnight, and thus far she had shown no signs of any ailment, but suddenly she cried out 'Oh! I am sick at heart', and although 'restoratives' were applied, she died within half an hour, 'it being exactly the time the apparition had foretold'.

The most bloody event in the history of the palace was the Duke of Cumberland's murder of his valet, Sellis. Cumberland was the fifth son of George III, and because of his boorish behaviour was the most unpopular man in London. On 31 May 1810, Sellis was found in his bedchamber, lying on the bed, his throat cut savagely from ear to ear, leaving the head almost separated from the body.

The Duke's other valet, Yew, had been called to the bedroom shortly before the discovery of the body, and found him standing shaking in his room, shirt covered in blood, with his sword, that had obviously just been used, lying on the floor. Cumberland claimed to have been murderously attacked by Sellis: indeed he was able to show a deep cut on his sword-hand which he said had been inflicted in the affray. When he had foiled his valet's attempt on his life, Sellis committed suicide.

Few believed the Duke's story; there was a rumour that he had seduced his valet's daughter – thus both men had a motive for murder. Sellis's ghost haunted the chamber where he was found long afterwards, always seen in the horrible state in which he was found, 'a most horrid ghost', especially as the smell of freshly spilled blood accompanied the haunting.

In January 1804, *The Times* carried the following story concerning a ghost which crossed Birdcage Walk to haunt St James's Park:

A few nights ago a figure was observed at a late hour by one of the

Coldstream Regiment, whilst on duty near the Royal Cockpit. The poor fellow is ready to swear he saw a woman pass him by without a head. He was sure that it was not a person dressed up in a white sheet, because he could plainly discover the arms; and notwithstanding his great alarm, he observed that the shoulders of the Ghost were the highest part of it; he therefore concluded, whatever it might be, that it had got no head. He was taken ill immediately on his leaving guard, and the next day taken to the hospital, where he still remains. On Tuesday one of his comrades having heard of the affair, and having taken the same watch that night, resolved to look out for the Ghost, and to speak to it; accordingly, at the usual time, her Ghostship paid him a visit. She appeared again without a head, and entered the Park from the end of Queen-street, near to the Royal Cockpit. This veteran was now panic-struck. He described himself to have got a locked jaw, and when he wanted to cry 'Who comes there?' he could not utter a word. Although he was tongue-tied, it does not appear that he was leg-tied; for on the Ghost seeming inclined to be better acquainted with him, he quitted his post and ran with all possible speed to the Guard-room, where he had scarcely recited his dismal story to the Serjeant, before he fell into strong fits, and continued so ill afterwards, that he was taken to the hospital on Wednesday, where he is now confined to his bed. Another night this headless Ghost held its midnight revels in an empty house behind the Armoury-room. Having finished its pranks in the empty dwelling, the soldier, who was a witness to this novel scene, observed this dreadful spectre to pass by him at a distance of fifty yards, and walked over the Park paling as easily as he could step over a straw; it then proceeded towards the Canal, and vanished from his sight. There are several other stories current amongst the Coldstream Regiment respecting the nocturnal gambols of this Ghost, and it is said, that several soldiers, besides those already mentioned, have seen, whilst on duty, what they suppose a supernatural phantom, which has so affected them, that they were taken ill immediately and sent to the hospital; but, be that as it may, it is an undoubted fact, that two sentinels have been sent there from the effects of fright, whatever may have been the real cause of it.

This newspaper report is slightly at odds with the sworn statements that the sentries had to sign before the Adjutant:

I do solemnly declare that whilst on guard at the Recruit House [now the Wellington Barracks], on or about the 3rd instant, about half-past one in the morning, I perceived the figure of a woman without a head, rise from the earth at the distance of about two feet before me. I was so alarmed at the circumstance that I had not power to speak to it, which was my wish to have done. But I distinctly observed that the figure was dressed in a red striped gown, with red spots between each stripe, and that part of the dress and figure appeared to me to be enveloped in a cloud. In about the space of two minutes, whilst my eyes were fixed on the object, it vanished from my sight. I was perfectly sober and collected at the time, and being in great trepidation called to the next sentinel, who met me half way, and to whom I communicated the strange sight I had seen.

(Signed) George Jones,

Of Lieut.-Colonel Taylor's Company of Coldstream Guards.
Westminster, *January* 15, 1804.

I do hereby declare, that whilst on guard behind the Armoury House (to the best of my recollection about three weeks ago), I heard at 12 o'clock a tremendous noise, which proceeded from the windows of an uninhabited house, near to the spot where I was on duty. At the same time I heard a voice cry out 'Bring me a light! bring me a light!' The last word was uttered in so feeble and so changeable a tone of voice, that I concluded some person was ill, and consequently offered them my assistance. I could, however, obtain no answer to my proposal, altho' I repeated it several times, and as often heard the voice use the same terms. I endeavoured to see the person who called out, but in vain. On a sudden the violent noise was renewed, which appeared to me to resemble sashes of windows lifted hastily up and down, but then they were moved in quick succession, and in different parts of the house nearly at the same time, so that it seems impossible to me that one person could accomplish the whole business. I heard several of the regiment say they have heard similar noises and proceedings, but I have never heard the cause accounted for.

(Signed) Richard Donkin,

12th Company of Coldstream Guards.
Whitehall, *January* 17, 1804.

(Printed in J. Larwood, *Story of the London Parks*, 1872.)

The Canal, St James's Park (Guildhall Library).

The ghost was popularly supposed to be that of the wife of a sergeant in the Guards who had been murdered by her husband about twenty years before. He had killed her by cutting off her head, and then threw the body into the canal (at this time the lake was little more than a broad dike – known as 'The Canal' – that drained the marshy area: the beautiful lake was made by John Nash in 1828 when he landscaped the park).

The fashionable streets surrounding the Royal Parks also have their ghosts. A house in St James's Street was notorious during the latter years of the nineteenth century, standing empty for many years because of its evil reputation. It had one room that was particularly sinister. Two incidents concerning it were mentioned by J. H. Ingram in *The Haunted Houses and Family Traditions of Great Britain*, 1884:

On one occasion a youth who, having been abroad for a considerable time, had not any knowledge of the evil reputation this chamber had acquired, was put there to sleep on his arrival, as it was hoped his rest might not be disturbed. In the morning, however, he complained sadly of the terrible time he had had in the night, with people looking in at him between the curtains of his bed, and he avowed his determination to terminate his visit at once, as he could not possibly sleep there any more.

After this period the house was again vacant for a considerable time, but was at length taken and workmen were sent in to put it in habitable repair. One day, when the men were away at their dinner, says our informant, 'the master builder took the key with him and went to inspect progress, and having examined the lower rooms, he was ascending the stairs, when he heard a man's foot behind him. He looked round, but there was nobody there, and he moved on again; still there was somebody following, and he stopped and looked over the rails, but there was no one to be seen. So, though feeling rather queer, he advanced into the drawing-room, where a fire had been lighted, and wishing to combat the uncomfortable sensation that was creeping over him, he took hold of a chair, and drawing it resolutely along the floor, he slammed it down upon the hearth with some force, and seated himself in it; when, to his amazement, the action, in all its particulars of sound, was immediately repeated by his unseen companion, who seemed to seat himself beside him on a chair as invisible as himself. Horror-stricken, the worthy builder started up and rushed out of the house.'

Around the corner from the palace is St James's Place where, in 1864, a ghost appeared at No. 19. The account of this ghost has curious echoes of the story of the Duchess of Mazarine. Two sisters had happily occupied the house for many years. In 1858 the elder sister died, the other continuing to live there. In November 1864, Miss Harriet, the surviving sister, was taken ill at Brighton and was eventually brought back to No. 19 to be nursed there by two of her nieces and the wife of a nephew. On the night of 23 December the nieces had retired to bed, leaving the door of their bedroom open. Both saw the figure of an old lady go past the door, and both recognised it as being old Aunt Anne, Harriet's sister who had died six years before. The nephew's wife, who was on duty in the sick-room, also recognised the ghost, and all three took it as a token of the death of Aunt Harriet: so it was, for she died at six o'clock on the following morning, having said that she, too, had seen her sister, who had come to call her away.

Apsley House was the home of the Duke of Wellington and stands on Hyde Park Corner. Devoted now to the relics of the Iron Duke's

From a Drawing by C.W.Walton, made from a photo taken in 1891.

career, it is one of the most rewarding, if neglected, of the sights of London. In the 1830s the Duke became so unpopular for his opposition to Parliamentary Reform that mobs gathered in Piccadilly to throw stones at him, and he was also besieged in his mansion. The Duke was forced to have iron shutters permanently fastened over the windows, and it was at this time that he claimed to have encountered the ghost of Cromwell, who pointed a finger at the mob outside in warning. This Wellington heeded, and gave up his opposition to the Reform Bill.

A remarkable haunting occurred at a house in Eaton Place, Belgravia, on 22 June 1893. On the evening of that day Lady Tryon, wife of Admiral Sir George Tryon, Commander-in-Chief of the Mediterranean Squadron, was giving a reception at the house, her husband being at sea. Some of the guests there were startled when they saw the striking figure of the Admiral stride across the room in full uniform. Lady Tryon was asked whether she knew that her husband was present, but was puzzled by the question, not having seen the apparition, and could only reply that he was with the fleet. The next day news reached England of the disaster known as the 'Camperdown Incident'. At the time Lady Tryon was giving her reception the Mediterranean Fleet had been steaming in parallel columns off the coast of Syria. Admiral Tryon was on board his flagship *Victoria* which led one column of battleships. Abreast of him was the *Camperdown* with Admiral Markham aboard. For some inexplicable reason Sir George signalled the two columns to turn inwards towards each other, and did not rescind the order until collision between the *Victoria* and the *Camperdown* was inevitable. The *Victoria* sank, 400 men were drowned, Sir George Tryon going down with his ship. As the boat sank he turned to his Captain and said, 'It is entirely my fault.'

It is a difficult task to write the biography of a man whose career ended so ingloriously, yet Tryon's biographer, Rear-Admiral C. C. Penrose Fitzgerald concluded his work with this passage of purple prose:

> The bones of these sailors and their gallant chief rest peacefully in and around the wreck of the ship that they stood by till the last, beneath the blue waters of that classic Eastern sea, – at least as hallowed a sepulchre as any plot of mouldering clay, – and their spirits have returned to God who gave them.

Admiral Sir George Tryon (British Library).   155

THE
Tyburn-Ghoſt:

OR,

The Strange Downfall

OF THE

GALLOWS.

A moſt true RELATION
How the famous
TRIPLE-TREE
Neer *PADDINTON*

Was on Tueſday-night laſt (the third of this inſtant
September) wonderfully pluckt up by the Roots,
and demoliſht by certain EVIL-SPIRITS.

To which is added,

Squire *Ketch*'s LAMENTATION
for the loſs of his Shop, &c.

With Allowance.

LONDON: Printed for *L.C.* 1678.

Tyburn – 'Albion's Fatal Tree'

'The law is, that thou shalt return from hence, to the place whence thou camest, and from thence to the place of execution, where thou shalt hang by the neck, till the body be dead! dead! dead! and the Lord have mercy upon thy soul.'

This was the hanging sentence that committed so many to the simple gallows at Tyburn, which stood close to Marble Arch, where Connaught Place is today. The prisoner was taken from the court back to the condemned cell at Newgate and shortly had to make the dreadful three-mile journey to Tyburn to be '. . . a Dreadful and Awful Example to Others, a Sacrifice to his Country's Justice.'

Until the latter half of the eighteenth century to be hanged was to die of strangulation. The tumbril that had brought the victims from Newgate was drawn up beneath the triangular gallows, last prayers were said,* the nooses fixed, and then a sharp slap to the flanks of the horse would leave the poor felons dangling: they would usually be cut down twenty minutes or so later. This method of execution left considerable scope to the hangman and quite a few survived their sentence, being revived after the hanging. Bribes given to the hangman ensured that the knot was subtly altered, though in some cases, such as that of Dr Dodd in 1777, this did not save the criminal. The bodies of executed criminals were usually given for dissection by surgeons, who were occasionally startled by their first incision reviving the hanged man. In the seventeenth century the murderess Anne Green came round as the anatomist William Petty began to use his knife on her body. Revival was even more common in the sixteenth century when the Guild of Barber-Surgeons approved a minute passing on the expenses involved to the person who brought back the 'half-hanged man' to his home:

Yt ys agreed that yf any bodie which shall at anie tyme here after happen to be brought to o'r hall for the intent to be wrought upon by Thanatomistes of o'r Companie, shall revyve or come to lyfe agayne, as of late hathe been scene, the charge aboute the same bodie so revivinge, shall be borne, levied, and susteyned, by such person, or persons, who shall so happen to bringe home the bodie.

Dissection by the surgeons after execution was as dreaded by

---

* The prayers included the 51st Psalm, which spectators at the 'hanging matches' would join in reciting with the condemned man. It includes the verse: 'Make me to hear joy and gladness; that the bones which thou hast broken may rejoice.'

criminals hung at Tyburn as the execution itself. There were many riots between 'the mob' and the men employed by the surgeons to collect the body from the gallows. To most ordinary people in London it seemed unjust that a man could be twice punished, and many believed that dismemberment meant being deprived of the chance of an after-life. However the man about to be hanged did have one last opportunity to harm those who had prosecuted him (or persecuted him in other ways). This was to lay a much-feared dying curse on them, with a promise that his ghost would only be at rest when revenge was taken.

A seventeen-year-old youth, William Stevens, was hanged in 1748 for stealing eight ounces of tobacco and six gallons of brandy from a shop. He had taken the goods while the shopkeeper's back was turned, and thus, as he had not broken into the premises, he believed that he would escape the death penalty. However the prosecution maintained that since the value of the goods, according to the shopkeeper, was more than forty shillings, the offence was one which automatically carried a sentence of hanging. The condemned man wrote to the man he had robbed: 'We are sorry you valued your Goods at three pounds, which an eminent Distiller says, were not worth half the Money . . . so you will hear no more from us, till after our Decease.'

Such a threat, made public, could cause much disquiet to a man who had brought a petty criminal to the gallows for a minor offence. He also had to suffer public acrimony, and often his property would be badly damaged by riot on the day of execution. All this, and the promise of a ghost as well!

In 1678 there was a considerable sensation when the gallows at Tyburn was uprooted overnight. Many people attributed this to the action of a ghost; a pamphleteer put forward many witty reasons for its demise, but favoured a supernatural explanation:

The means how it received this fatal overthrow, is as dubious as strange; some think, that being arrived at its grand *Climactericke*, like mighty over-grown States, it sunk under its *own weight*; others say it broke like many an honest Citizen, because it had too many *Hangers on*; some will needs have it to be a design of a Company of Quack-Doctors, to steal it away, make it into Powder, and sell it amongst the rest of their *Universal Medecines*, since it has so often had a *Probatum est*, for the *Cure of all Diseases*. But the most probable Opinion is, That it was ruined by certain Evil Spirits;

The gibbet at the London Dungeon.

Perhaps the Ghosts of some that had formerly suffered there; for if persons Killed, retain so great an Antipathy against their Murderers, that scarce a Physitian dares come near his expired Patient, least the Corpse should fall a Bleeding, and discover that which the more Courteous Grave uses to hide. We may imagine amongst so many *Rank Riders* as have broken their Necks by *Falls* from this Skittish Three-leg'd Jade, some or other might resolve to be reveng'd on her.

Nay, it is reported, or may be for ought I know, That there was seen last Tuesday-evening a Spirit sitting on one of the Cross-beams with its *Neck awry*, making a strange noise like a Scrietch-Owl; which 'tis supposed did afterwards demolish all the *venerable Fabrick*: But of this there is yet no *Affidavit* made, though 'tis certain the sight was extremely surprizing to Travellers passing by the next morning, to behold its *scattered Members* lying on the ground, as if the Gallows it self had been *Hang'd, drawn, and quarter'd*.

The Tidings was quickly spread abroad, but when it arrived at Squire *Ketch's* Ear, 'twas thought at first he would have Truss'd up himself for grief, that he should thus lose his *Shop* just upon the *Nick* of Trading, and be disappointed of his next days Harvest, made him lose all Patience, and fill the Air with Exclamations against the villainous Authors of the Mischief.

But we would not yet have any that have occasion to make *use* of such a *Convenience*, to dispair, for we are informed, there is a care taken for erecting a *New Structure* more *Commodious* and Magnificent, of which all persons that intend to be *Concern'd*, are desired to take notice, and declare their Exceptions, if they shall think it not made *firm and substantial enough* for their service.

The pamphleteer mentions the magical properties which were supposed to belong to the body of a hanged man. Passing his hand over a cyst was a certain cure for this disfigurement, and the 'death sweat' of an executed criminal was a substitute for the touch of the King's hand in curing scrofula – 'the King's Evil' (or lymphatic tuberculosis). When the body hung on a gibbet many hands were cut down to be prepared as 'Hands of Glory'. They were much in demand from house-thieves who believed that people remained asleep as long as the candle placed in the dead fingers burned. Only by using milk to quench the flame of the candle could the spell be broken.

Mayfair

Lord Lyttelton died on 27 November 1779. The circumstances of his death were so curious that Boswell quoted Johnson as saying: 'It is the most extraordinary occurrence in my days. I heard it from Lord Westcote, his uncle. I am so glad to have evidence of the spiritual world, that I am willing to believe it.'

Lyttelton was a notorious figure in his day, with many of the attributes of the Wicked Lord of melodrama. Miles Peter Andrews, a friend and fellow rake, described him thus:

> . . . a man distinguished for abilities, but also for the profligacy of morals which few could equal. With all this he was remarkable for what may be called unnatural cowardice in one so determinedly wicked. He never repented, yet could never stifle his conscience. He never could allow, yet never could deny, a world to come, and he contemplated with unceasing terror what would probably be his own state in such a world if there was one. He was always melancholy with fear, or mad in defiance; and probably his principal misery here was, that with all his endeavours, he never could extinguish the dread of an hereafter. . . .

He was given forewarning of death by the appearance of a ghost – popularly supposed to have been that of Mrs Amphlett, who had committed suicide after her daughters had been seduced by the wicked Lord (yet he appears to have cared for them afterwards, as Lord Westcote's account shows):

REMARKABLE DREAM OF THOMAS, LORD
LYTTELTON

On Thursday, the 25th of November, 1779,

Thomas, Lord Lyttelton, when he came to breakfast declared to Mrs. Flood, wife of Frederick Flood, Esq., of the kingdom of Ireland, and to the three Miss Amphletts, who were lodged in his house in Hill Street, London (where he then also was), that he had an extraordinary dream the night before. He said he thought he was in a room which a bird flew into, which appearance was suddenly changed into that of a woman dressed in white, who bade him prepare to die. To which he answered, 'I hope not soon, not in two months.' She replied, 'Yes, in three days.' He said he did not much regard it, because he could in some measure account for it;

The ghost visits Lord Lyttelton (Mary Evans Picture Library).

for that a few days before he had been with Mrs. Dawson when a robin-redbreast flew into her room.

When he had dressed himself that day to go to the House of Lords, he said he thought he did not look as if he was likely to die. In the evening of the following day, being Friday, he told the eldest Miss Amphlett that she looked melancholy; but, said he, 'You are foolish and fearful. I have lived two days, and, God willing, I will live out the third.'

On the morning of Saturday he told the same ladies that he was very well, and believed he should bilk the ghost. Some hours afterwards he went with them, Mr. Fortescue, and Captain

Wolseley, to Pitt Place, at Epsom; withdrew to his bed-chamber soon after eleven o'clock at night, talked cheerfully to his servant, and particularly inquired of him what care had been taken to provide good rolls for his breakfast the next morning, stepped into his bed with his waistcoat on, and as his servant was pulling it off, put his hand to his side, sunk back and immediately expired without a groan. He ate a good dinner after his arrival at Pitt Place, took an egg for his supper, and did not seem to be at all out of order, except that while he was eating his soup at dinner he had a rising in his throat, a thing which had often happened to him before, and which obliged him to spit some of it out. His physician, Dr. Fothergill, told me Lord Lyttelton had in the summer preceding a bad pain in his side, and he judged that some gut vessel in the part where he felt the pain gave way, and to that he conjectured his death was owing. His declaration of his dream and his expressions above mentioned, consequential thereon, were upon a close inquiry asserted to me to have been so, by Mrs. Flood, the eldest Miss Amphlett, Captain Wolseley, and his valet-de-chambre Faulkner, who dressed him on the Thursday; and the manner of his death was related to me by William Stuckey, in the presence of Mr. Fortescue and Captain Wolseley, Stuckey being the servant who attended him in his bed-chamber, and in whose arms he died.

Westcote

February the 13th, 1780

This story would be remarkable enough in itself, but there was a simultaneous happening that was equally curious. Lord Lyttelton's friend, Miles Peter Andrews, was expecting Lord Lyttelton to stay with him at his home at Dartford on the day of his death. Because of the dream, Lyttelton chose to forget this engagement. That fatal night, Andrews felt unwell and retired early to bed. Between eleven and midnight he awoke from feverish sleep to find his bed-curtains being pulled apart. A face appeared and in a dark voice spoke to him saying that he had come to tell him all was over, the world informed him that there was another state, and bade him repent, but that was not so.

Andrews recognised the face as being that of Lord Lyttelton, and immediately thought that his friend must have arrived at Dartford and was now playing one of his famous practical jokes on him. So he threw the first objects that came to hand at the noble Lord's head.

They were his slippers and they served to drive the figure into a dressing-room whose only door opened into Andrews's bedroom. Thoroughly angry, Andrews leapt out of bed in pursuit, but was amazed to find the dressing-room empty. He searched his bedroom, the door of which had been locked from the inside, but could not find anyone there either. Next he roused the entire household, telling the servants to search every inch for an intruder. They discovered nothing and so Andrews was forced to accept that Lord Lyttelton's visit was a dream.

The next day one of his house guests left for London early. She had been woken up during the night by the search for Lord Lyttelton and so was amazed to be told that he had died that night at Pitt Place. She immediately sent an express message to Andrews at Dartford, who fainted when he read the news. It had a great effect on his way of life which he changed for the better, and he admitted that he 'was not his own man again for three years'.

A similar story of a dream telling of death concerns a house in Brook Street. It was first printed in *Strange Things Amongst Us* by H. Spicer:

One morning, some years since, the wife of a distinguished London physician was in bed, at her house in Brook Street. It was daylight, and she was broad awake. The door opened; but Lady Clark, concluding that it was her maid entering, did not raise her head, until a remarkable-looking figure, passing between her bed and the window, walked up to the fire-place, when, reflected in the mirror which hung above, Lady Clark recognized the features of her step-son, Dr. John Forbes Clark, then attached to a foreign embassy. He wore a long night-dress, and carried something on his arm.

'Good Heavens! Is that *you*, John, and in that dress?' cried Lady Clark, in the first surprise.

The figure turned slowly round, and she then became aware that the object he carried was a dead child, the body being swathed round and round in a large Indian scarf of remarkable workmanship, which Lady Clark had presented to Mrs. John Clark on the eve of her departure.

As she gazed, the outlines of the figure became indistinct, invisible, vanishing in the grey light, or blending with the familiar objects in the room.

Lady Clark neither fainted nor shrieked, nor even rang the bell.

She lay back and thought the matter over, resolving to mention it to no one until the return of her husband, then absent in attendance on an illustrious household. His experience would decide whether her physical health offered any solution of the phenomenon. As for its being a dream, it may be taken as an accepted fact that, though nobody is conscious of the act of going to sleep, everybody knows by the sudden change of scenery, by the snapping of the chain of thought, and so forth, when he has been sleeping.

Very shortly after, Sir James returned home. On hearing the story, he immediately looked at the tongue that related such wonders, and likewise felt the lady's pulse. Both organs perfect. Of her nerves he had seen proof. Touching veracity, she was truth itself. All his skill could devise nothing better than a recommendation to patience, and to see what came of it. In the meantime, the day and hour were noted down, and the next advices from T—— awaited with more than usual interest.

At length they came. Dr. John Forbes Clark informed his father that their child, an only one, had died on such a day (that of the apparition), and that his wife, anxious that it should be laid to rest in the land of its birth, had begged that it might be forwarded by the next homeward ship. In due course it arrived, embalmed, but enclosed in a coffin so much larger than was required for the tiny occupant, that the intervening spaces had to be filled up with clothes, &c., while the Indian scarf had been wound, in many folds, around the child's body.

The late Nancy Spain once encountered a ghost in Piccadilly, right outside Fortnum & Mason. She was cab-hunting, and was pleased when a cab drew up by her to drop its fare. A woman with red hair got out, and began fumbling in her handbag for change to pay the driver. As she was in a hurry, and the elderly lady seemed unlikely to find the money, Miss Spain paid the driver herself. Without a word, the red-haired woman made off for Fortnum & Mason, and as Miss Spain got into the cab the driver commented, 'You got caught there, Miss. That old gal could buy up both of us. That was Lady C.'

The following day Miss Spain told her mother of the incident. When she had finished the story her mother left the room without comment, but returned a moment later with a newspaper dated three days before. It carried the headline 'Lady C. Dies in Fire.'

Elliott O'Donnell wrote of an apartment in Piccadilly where strangers, sleeping there, would be awoken by stealthy footsteps approaching the bed. Suddenly a great clammy hand would grip them about the throat, and the victim would suffer all the pain of strangulation, finally lapsing into unconsciousness. Fortunately they always awoke unharmed, but with the resolve never to stay in the flat again.

Vine Street Police Station is one of the best known in London. It is haunted by the ghost of a Sergeant who committed suicide in one of the cells in the early years of this century. The sound of his hob-nailed boots clumping down an empty corridor has terrified many a brave copper.

One of the most popular places of entertainment in Regency London was the Argyle Rooms in Regent Street, frequented by such men of fashion as Brummell and Alvanley. The diary of Thomas Raikes is the source of a macabre story that is set there. The entry is dated 26 December 1832:

It is now about fifteen months ago that Miss M———, a connection of my family, went with a party of friends to a concert at the Argyle Rooms. She appeared there to be suddenly seized with indisposition, and, though she persisted for some time to struggle against what seemed a violent nervous affection, it became at last so oppressive that they were obliged to send for their carriage and conduct her home. She was for a long time unwilling to say what was the cause of her indisposition; but, on being more earnestly questioned, she at length confessed that she had, immediately on arriving in the concert-room, been terrified by a horrible vision, which unceasingly presented itself to her sight. It seemed to her as though a naked corpse was lying on the floor at her feet; the features of the face were partly covered by a cloth mantle, but enough was apparent to convince her that the body was that of Sir J——— Y———. Every effort was made by her friends at the time to tranquillize her mind by representing the folly of allowing such delusions to prey upon her spirits, and she thus retired to bed; but on the following day the family received the tidings of Sir J——— Y——— having been drowned in Southampton river that very night by the oversetting of his boat; and the body was afterwards found entangled in a *boat-cloak*. Here is an authenticated case of second sight, and of very recent date.

From Baker Street to Soho

The Volunteer pub is at the northern end of Baker Street. It is built on what was farmland in the seventeenth century, owned by the ill-fated Nevill family. All had perished in a fire that destroyed their manor-house in 1654, and it is the ghost of Rupert Nevill that is supposed to be seen at the pub: most often he lurks in one of the dark alcoves of the cellar, dressed in surcoat, breeches and fancy stockings.

At 228 Baker Street there is a London Transport electrical sub-station supposed to be haunted by the ghost of Sarah Siddons, the great actress whose London home once occupied the site.

The formidable Mrs Stirling tells a strange tale of a house in Hallam Street, close to Portland Place. She explains how in 1934 she went to visit a famous metallurgist, Sherard Cowper-Coles, who had a new flat there. He had taken it as it was more convenient for his work than his permanent home at Sunbury. In order to show his wife what the flat was like, he erected a tripod, fixed a camera on it, and took a time exposure of the living-room. When the photograph was developed he saw that an armchair was occupied by a man, yet he had been alone at the time. Extremely puzzled by this, he took further photographs in the room, ensuring that no one could enter while the film was being exposed by carefully locking the door. He accumulated a large album full of pictures of people *dressed in the styles of bygone days.* These he showed to Mrs Stirling, and she described the portraits:

> He had an armchair upholstered in pink and white chintz, and in this appeared a partially developed phantom with ectoplasm, like cotton-wool, forming about its head and mouth, while the striped chintz of the chair showed clearly through the transparent figure. But the majority of the photographs were precisely like photographs of living people, though belonging to diverse periods of history. One was that of a warrior in ancient armour with a winged helmet, another that of a man in a military cloak like those worn in the time of Wellington. Some were of women with lovely faces; all were distinct and full of individuality—they appeared to be photographs of living people, not those of unsubstantial wraiths.

She asked him whether he ever photographed repulsive or evil things; he replied that he had, on occasion, done so, but when this occurred he destroyed the results. Then she asked him whether he had ever been able to identify any of the subjects.

'Only one', he answered and handed it to me. It was the photograph of an old lady wearing a cap with lappets, reminiscent in date and style of the portrait of Whistler's mother. 'When my brother saw this,' Mr. Cowper-Coles said, 'he exclaimed, "What an excellent photograph of our old nurse". He was older than me and could remember her, which I could not, as I was a baby when she died; but he recognized the likeness instantly and wondered how I got her photograph.'

Mrs Stirling, and other experts, were unable to explain this enigma without throwing doubts on the integrity of Mr Cowper-Coles. She remained convinced, however, that the photographs came about through some form of supernatural agency.

This delightful story of Soho appeared in the short-lived Victorian penny magazine, *Mother Shipton's Miscellany*:

THE SHROUDED SPECTRE

In the year 1704, a gentleman, to all appearance of large fortune, took furnished lodgings in a house in Soho-square. After he had resided there some weeks with his establishment, he lost his brother, who lived at Hampstead, and who on his death-bed particularly desired to be interred in the family vault in Westminster Abbey. The gentleman requested his landlord to permit him to bring the corpse of his brother to his lodgings, and to make arrangements there for the funeral. The landlord, without hesitation, signified his compliance.

The body, dressed in a white shroud, was accordingly brought in a very handsome coffin, and placed in the great dining-room. The funeral was to take place the next day, and the lodger and his servants went out to make the necessary preparations for the solemnity. He stayed out late, but this was no uncommon thing. The landlord and his family conceiving that they had no occasion to wait for him retired to bed as usual about 12 o'clock. One maid-servant was left up to let him in, and to boil some water, which he had desired might be ready for making tea on his return. The girl was accordingly sitting alone in the kitchen, when a tall spectre-looking figure entered, and clapped itself down in the chair opposite to her.

The maid was by no means one of the most timid of her sex; but she was terrified beyond expression, at this unexpected apparition. Uttering a loud scream, she flew out like an arrow at a side-door, and hurried to the chamber of her master and mistress. Scarcely had she awakened them, and communicated to the whole family some portion of the fright with which she was herself overwhelmed, when the spectre, enveloped in a shroud, and with a death-like paleness, made its appearance, and sat down in a chair in the bed-room, without their having observed how it entered. The worst of all was, that this chair stood by the door of the bed-chamber, so that not a creature could get away without passing close to the apparition, which rolled its glaring eyes so frightfully, and so hideously distorted its features, that they could not bear to look at it. The master and mistress crept under the bed-clothes, covered with profuse perspiration, while the maid-servant sunk nearly insensible by the side of the bed.

At the same time the whole house seemed to be in an uproar; for though they had covered themselves over head and ears, they could still hear the incessant noise and clatter, which served to increase their terror.

At length all became perfectly still in the house. The landlord ventured to raise his head, and to steal a glance at the chair by the door; but behold the ghost was gone! Sober reason began to resume its power. The poor girl was brought to herself after a good deal of shaking. In a short time they plucked up sufficient courage to quit the bed-room, and to commence an examination of the house, which they expected to find in great disorder. Nor were their anticipations unfounded. The whole house had been stripped by artful thieves, and the gentleman had decamped without paying for his lodging. It turned out that he was no other than an accomplice of the notorious Arthur Chambers, who was executed at Tyburn in 1706, and that the supposed corpse was this arch rogue himself, who had whitened his hands and face with chalk, and merely counterfeited death. About midnight he quitted the coffin and appeared to the maid in the kitchen. When she flew up stairs, he softly followed her, and seated at the door of the chamber, he acted as a sentinel, so that his industrious accomplices were enabled to plunder the house without the least molestation.

Covent Garden

Covent Garden's best-known ghost owes more to the fame of the man who investigated it than the excitement it generated. Until the latter part of the last century there were two hotels in the south-east corner of Covent Garden – the Old and New Hummums. The former had been one of the first Turkish baths to be introduced into this country – hence the name – but it had become so disreputable that it was eventually converted into an hotel. This was the scene of the haunting that interested Dr Johnson. Boswell wrote of a visit they made to Mr Thrales's house at Streatham:

Amongst the numerous prints pasted on the walls of the dining-room of Streatham was Hogarth's 'Modern Midnight Conversation.' I asked him what he knew of Parson Ford, who makes a conspicuous figure in the riotous group. Johnson said: 'Sir, he was my acquaintance and relation; my mother's nephew. He had purchased a living in the country, but not simoniacally. I never saw him but in the country. I have been told he was a man of great parts; very profligate, but I never heard he was impious.' Boswell asked, 'Was there not a story of his ghost having appeared?' Johnson said, 'Sir, it was believed. A waiter at the Hummums, in which house Ford died, had been absent for some time, and returned, not knowing that Ford was dead. Going down to the cellar, according to the story, he met him; going down again, he met him a second time. When he came up, he asked some of the people of the house what Ford could be doing there. They told him Ford was dead. The waiter took a fever, in which he lay for some time. When he recovered he said he had a message to deliver to some women from Ford; but he was not to tell what, or to whom. He walked out; he was followed, but somewhere about St Paul's they lost him. He came back, and said he had delivered the message, and the women exclaimed, "Then we are all undone!" Dr. Pellet, who was not a credulous man, inquired into the truth of this story, and he said the evidence was irresistible. My wife went to the Hummums (it is a place where people get themselves cupped). I believe she went with the intention to hear about this story of Ford. At first they were unwilling to tell her; but after they had talked to her she came away

The duel between the Duke of Hamilton and Lord Mohun.

satisfied that it was true. To be sure the man had a fever, and this vision may have been the beginning of it. But if the message to the women, and their behaviour upon it, were true as related, there was something supernatural. That rests upon his word, and there it remains.'

The story of Covent Garden's other ghost also comes from a journal, John Aubrey's *Miscellanies*. Aubrey relates the sad story of the son of Lord Mohun, who installed a beautiful mistress he loved dearly in a house in James Street. Lord Mohun's heir was a dashing young man, famed for his skill with the sword and for his horseman-ship. For some reason he had a quarrel with 'Prince' Griffin, and a duel on horseback was arranged for Chelsea Fields the following morning.

Young Mr Mohun set off early for the appointment, but by Ebury Farm he was set upon by a gang who robbed him and then shot him dead. It was generally supposed that these rogues were instructed by the bogus Prince who knew that his adversary was much the better man in combat. The murder took place at ten in the morning

> ... and at the identical time of his death, his mistress, being in bed at her lodgings in James Street, saw her lover come to her bed-side, draw the curtains, look upon her, and then go away. She called after him, but received no answer. She then knocked for her maid, and inquired for Mr. Mohun, but the maid said she had not seen him, and he could not have been in the room, as she had the key of it in her pocket.
>
> This account the narrator had direct from the mouths of the lady and her maid.

The Mohun family were fated to participate in duels, and invariably disaster befell them. In 1711 a duel took place in Hyde Park between Charles, Lord Mohun, and the Duke of Hamilton. They 'pushed at each other but very little', and then both men fell. They each received fatal wounds from the other's sword, and died shortly afterwards in the arms of their seconds. One of these, Colonel John Hamilton, was afterwards charged with being an accessory to murder, but the jury brought in the lesser verdict of his being guilty of manslaughter, whereupon 'the prisoner prayed the benefit of the statute, which was allowed him'. Presumably he left the court a free man.

Holborn and Around

Ghosts of lawyers are particularly prevalent in this district, which is not surprising when it is considered how much of the legal business of the kingdom is done here. Quite a lot of this hinges on the records in Somerset House, in the Strand, though the building has not always served to house a major part of our archives. Originally a Tudor palace stood here, built by the Duke of Somerset in the mid sixteenth century when he was Lord Protector of the realm of King Edward VI, who was ten years old when he came to the throne. Unhappily for Somerset, his great house was unfinished when he was beheaded for treason on Tower Hill in 1551. After that it became a royal palace, a favourite with Anne of Denmark, wife of James I, and with Henrietta Maria who came here as the fifteen-year-old bride of Charles I. They had a fondness for dwarfs and on one occasion she was pleased to be presented with a pie which contained a nine-year-old midget, only eighteen inches tall. When two of the little people were married a lavish reception was arranged, and the King himself gave the bride away. One of the tiny members of the household fell to his death from a window of the palace – a tragedy that threw the whole Court into mourning. In 1776 the Tudor palace was demolished and the present magnificent building erected, to the designs of Sir William Chambers. These were drawn up specifically to house various Departments of State, and originally the Admiralty was housed here. It is thus appropriate that the unmistakable ghost of Nelson should be seen, a frail figure with an empty sleeve where an arm should be. He particularly favours the bright mornings of spring for his appearances, when he is seen to cross the uneven stones of the old quadrangle. Witnesses remark on the aura the spirit carries above its head – a wispy, vague cloud – and the unusual sharpness of the figure, which always disappears when approached.

The famous Wig and Pen Club at the eastern end of the Strand is an exclusive club reserved for lawyers and eminent journalists. In the small hours the footsteps of an unseen man are heard walking along a corridor on the second floor. They are supposed to be the last psychic relics of a solicitor who was found dead in his office during the reign of Queen Victoria.

Engraved by R. Page.

JEFFERY HUDSON,

Aged 30 Years. 18 Inches high.

Dwarf to King Charles the First.

Published by J. Robins & C. Albion Press, London March 31 1821.

Lincoln's Inn (Guildhall Library).

The Percevals were an ill-starred family, Spencer Perceval, the Prime Minister, being shot dead in the House of Commons (see the account of his murder on page 46. A cousin, Robert, came to an equally violent end when he was waylaid and murdered in the Strand.

Robert Perceval was reading for the law at Lincoln's Inn, but was too fond of 'riotous and unprofitable pursuits' to be successful at this. One night he was at his books, belatedly immersed in learning the complicated processes of law, when he heard the great clock strike midnight. As it did so a sinister figure appeared, standing as silent as death, as still as a statue. Perceval first challenged it, but when this went unanswered he rushed at the figure with his sword drawn: it passed right through the spectral form. All this time the figure had its arm raised so that its cloak masked the face. Perceval bravely snatched the cloak away to reveal a face bearing his own likeness, perfectly rendered. But terrible wounds were to be seen both on the face and at the breast. Then the unwelcome visitor disappeared.

At first Perceval took this as a warning and reformed his life by applying himself whole-heartedly to his studies. However he was soon tempted back to his former dissolute habits which made him many enemies. The meaning of the ghost was shown when he was set upon in the Strand by acquaintances he had cheated. His corpse bore the same wounds that the ghost had shown him earlier. After this the chambers he had occupied in Lincoln's Inn were haunted by his own ghost, and for many years few students enjoyed peace in them.

The Royal College of Surgeons occupies premises in Lincoln's Inn Fields. A macabre experiment took place here in 1803, with tragic results. A report of the experiment appeared in Volume IX of *The Medical and Physical Journal*:

> Professor Aldini, of the University of Bologna, availed himself of the opportunity afforded by the execution of Forster, on the 27th inst. for the murder of his wife and child, to repeat his experiments on the theory* of his uncle Galvani. A liberal offer had been made him of the use of that subject by Mr. Keate, surgeon to the king, who was himself present on this occasion. The result of this experiment promises the greatest advantages to the interests of humanity, especially in cases of apparent death by drowning, and other cases of asphyxia.
>
> We hope that Mr. Keate and the Professor will shortly gratify the public with a particular account of an experiment, the first of its kind in Great Britain. The corpse was made to exhibit very powerful muscular contractions before dissection, and that afterwards these contractions continued for seven hours and a half. On the first application of the process to the face, the jaw of the deceased criminal began to quiver, and the adjoining muscles were horribly contorted, and one eye was actually opened. In the subsequent part of the process, the right hand was raised and clenched, and the legs and thighs were set in motion. It appeared to the uninformed part of the bye-standers, as if the wretched man was on the eve of being restored to life.

Just how upsetting this exhibition was to the 'uninformed part of the bye-standers' is shown in *The New Newgate Calendar* which also printed an account of the affair. It concluded: 'Mr. Pass, the beadle of the Surgeons' Company, being officially present during the time of these extraordinary experiments, was so alarmed, that on going home he died of fright.'

* Namely the application of electricity to the muscles.

Red Lion Square is an oasis of quiet in Holborn, close to four busy roads. It is haunted by a famous trio – the ghosts of Cromwell, Ireton, and John Bradshaw, three leading Parliamentarians who were originally interred in Westminster Abbey. After the Restoration their remains were exhumed and brought to trial at Westminster Hall as though they were still alive. Being found guilty of regicide, they were sentenced to be hung, drawn, and quartered. Accordingly the decayed bodies were dragged on sledges to Tyburn, hung there till sunset, beheaded, and the remains flung into a pit dug beneath the gallows. The heads were fixed on poles on the roof of Westminster Hall.

How, then, does this accord with their ghosts haunting Red Lion Square? Records show that the bodies rested overnight at the Red Lion Inn, Holborn – but why were they dragged east, when Tyburn lay some distance north-west of Westminster? Michael Harrison's explanation, in his book *London Beneath the Pavement*, is convincing. He points out that Tyburn commonly stood for any place of execution, and that the Red Lion Inn was close to two well-used 'Tyburns' – one more or less on the site of Centre Point, the other at the northern end of Fetter Lane. The royal prerogative of having the bodies quartered after 'execution' was not demanded (this was carried out so that each quarter could be exhibited as a warning in different parts of the country) and consequently the remains were buried, not at the gallows, but in the convenient field behind the Red Lion – now Red Lion Square. In his 'History' Sir John Prestwick wrote that the remains were 'privately interred in a small paddock near Holborn on the spot where the obelisk in Red Lion Square lately stood'. This had the cryptic inscription: 'Obtusus obtusiorum ingenii monumentum. Quid me respicis, viator? Vade.'

The ghosts walk across the square diagonally, ignoring modern pathways. They appear to be deep in conversation, and their bodies are entire; this may seem strange as their heads were certainly not buried here. This advertisement was published in the *Morning Chronicle* of 18 March 1799:

THE real embalmed head of the powerful and renowned usurper, OLIVER CROMWELL, with the original dies for the medals struck in honour of his victory at Dunbar, are now exhibited at No. 5, in Mead Court, Old Bond Street (where the rattlesnake was shewn last year); a genuine narrative relating to the acquisition,

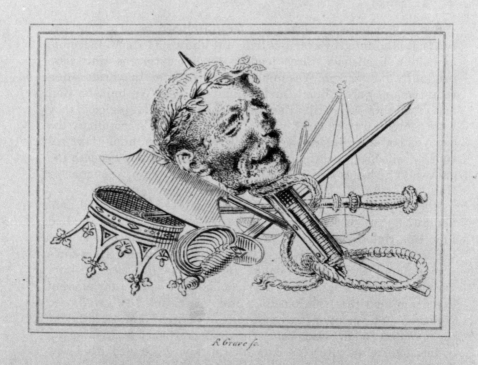

THE HEAD OF OLIVER CROMWELL.

as Expofed on the top of Weftminster Hall on the

RESTORATION OF KING CHARLES II.

(Guildhall Library)

concealment and preservation of these articles to be had at the place of exhibition.

The man who put the head on exhibition was named Cole, and he had obtained it from the Russell family, who at that time owned much of Holborn and most of Bloomsbury. Subsequently he sold the head three times, and on each occasion the purchaser suffered a sudden death soon after buying it. The family of the last of Cole's customers 'being nervous of keeping in the house a relic so fatal' quickly sold it to a medical man. It was last discovered in a vicarage in Norfolk.

The Embankment

Midway along the Victoria Embankment, between Waterloo and Hungerford bridges, is Cleopatra's Needle, a granite obelisk from Egypt about 3,500 years old. It is a strange fact, known to the police, that most suicide attempts along this stretch of river take place close to this column. Mocking laughter is occasionally heard here, with the sound of pain-racked moaning. There is also a tall, nude figure which dashes out of the shadows, jumps on the parapet, and dives into the river – yet there is never a splash.

The Temple is down-river, and these Inns of Court took their name from the English Knights Templar who were based here until their Order was dissolved in 1312. The Temple then passed to the Knights of St John who leased parts of it to lawyers. Its secluded courtyards and passages have seen many famous legal figures of the past, Judge Jeffreys of the Bloody Assize, for example, but it is not his ghost who haunts the Temple, but that of Sir Henry Hawkins (1817–1907), 'Hanging Hawkins', who rather unfairly gained this soubriquet not because he was unduly vindictive but because a great number of murder trials came his way. He is most often seen at midnight in wig and robes, carrying a bundle of papers. He silently glides through the arcades and crosses the courtyard, perhaps brought back by the curses of the evil men that he condemned.

Buckingham Street, close to Charing Cross Station, has several ghosts. William Etty the Victorian painter of sensuous nudes, lived at No. 14. Perhaps it is the ghost of one of his models who haunts the house: she is always remembered as a happy ghost. Samuel Pepys, the diarist and senior civil servant *par excellence*, lived next door at No. 12, and contrary to character is never seen pursuing the pretty, happy ghost of No. 14. He has been seen in the hall of his former home, facing the stairs – a grey figure with a kindly, smiling face: a ghost that never inspires fear.

Close by was the Adelphi, built by the Adam brothers. Because of the difficulties of building foundations so close to the unstable banks of the Thames (the Victoria Embankment had not then been built) great arches were put up to support the fashionable development above, pulled down in 1936.

Jenny was a Victorian whore who was strangled by one of her patrons and left on the squalid pile of sacks and rags here that she

179

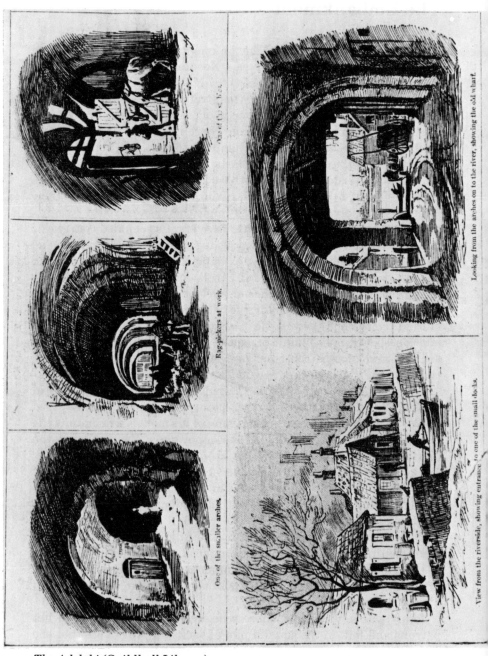

Out of the West.

Rag-pickers at work.

One of the smaller arches.

Looking from the arches on to the river, showing the old wharf.

View from the riverside, showing entrance to one of the small docks.

The Adelphi (Guildhall Library).

The discovery of the body at Scotland Yard, from the Illustrated Police News (British Library).

used as her place of work. The terrible sounds of her murder often used to echo through the vaults – a choking scream and then the death-tattoo of her heels drumming against the ground in final agony.

It is rare for politicians to get mixed up with ghosts, but this seems to have happened in 1969 when newspaper reports appeared concerning a ghost that haunted Mr Denis Healey's flat in Admiralty House, Whitehall (Mr Healey was Defence Secretary at the time). It is generally supposed that the ghost was that of Martha Ray (or Reay), mistress to the Earl of Sandwich who was Lord Commissioner of the Admiralty. She was shot dead on 7 April 1779, by a jealous lover, the Reverend James Hackman, as she was leaving Covent Garden.

The Black Museum is a part of New Scotland Yard, the great glass tower in Victoria Street. It used to be housed in the old building on the Embankment, distinctive with its red and white bricks laid in a chequered pattern, that served as Headquarters of the Metropolitan Police. When the foundations of this building were being dug in 1888 parts of the body of a young woman were found hidden in the excavations. The identity of this murder victim was never discovered, but it may have been her headless ghost which used to haunt the Black Museum before it was moved. The Curator of the museum frequently saw this ghost, but he was more worried by the whiskers that used to grow on the face of one of the death-masks of the executed criminals kept there. The hairs used to be trimmed regularly, but they continued to grow regardless. Apparently the man in question was a murderer whose beard was removed before execution as it was so bushy that it might have hindered the work of the rope.

Westminster

We have already met with the ghost of John Bradshaw who, with Cromwell and Ireton, walks in Red Lion Square (page 39). He also appears in the Deanery at Westminster where he signed the warrant for the execution of Charles I. However the most famous of the ghosts of Westminster is 'Father Benedictus' who haunts the Abbey, usually favouring the cloisters between five and six in the evening. The *Morning Post* of 30 August 1932, described a typical appearance:

> The story runs that an earthbound monk is supposed to materialise from time to time and walk along the cloisters, occasionally addressing persons, but always vanishing upon the least noise or other shock.
>
> The last recorded manifestation of this haunting took place in 1916.
>
> The latest phenomenon is described as a 'tall, lean cowled figure, which walked along the cloister gallery'. It paused to address two visitors and an American tourist, and described itself as a monk who had been killed in the Chapel of the Pyx by robbers during the reign of Henry VIII.
>
> There is no historical record of any such robbery, nor would robbers ordinarily have used a lance, the weapon to which the monk is stated to have referred. On the other hand, the same story has been told again and again throughout the centuries.
>
> One interesting feature of the haunting is said to be that the figure walks with the feet about an inch off the ground, indicating that the earthbound spirit still trod the same way as it had trodden in life before the years wore down the pavement.
>
> This characteristic is attributed to the spectre of Archbishop Laud in St John's College, Oxford, and to a thousand other lesser-known ghosts.

The tomb of the Unknown Warrior is perhaps the most poignant of all war memorials, and a ghost soldier in infantry uniform of the First World War has been seen by the tomb, his head bowed in sorrow. Some say that it is the ghost of the Warrior himself; others suggest that it is his brother.

A black-robed figure haunts Westminster's other cathedral, the Roman Catholic one which is actually situated in Victoria. He was

The profligate Duke of Buckingham (Mary Evans Picture Library).

last seen in 1966 standing by the High Altar, but 'faded into nothing' when approached by the Sacristan.

There is an intriguing legend concerning a phantom boat which is seen to approach and pass beneath Westminster Bridge but does not reappear on the other side. Lambeth Bridge cannot boast of a ghost but is connected with a celebrated incident in which the murder of the Duke of Buckingham (which took place on 23 August 1628, when he was stabbed at Portsmouth) was foretold in a dream to an officer of the King's Wardrobe.

This gentleman, whose name was Towse, had been well thought of by the Duke's father, Sir George Villiers, who appeared to him in a dream on three consecutive nights. He was urged to give the Duke this warning: 'That unless he did something to ingratiate himself with the people, he would be cut off in a short time.' When he protested that he was too humble to be given an audience with the Duke, the spectre told him of certain affairs which, if relayed to the Duke, would ensure that he would be seen. If he failed to do this, the ghost warned, then he could expect no peace of mind. Accordingly Towse made his way to the Court at Whitehall and told an official there of his dreams, including the secret details that the ghost had given him to ensure that he was given credence. The Duke quickly agreed to a meeting, arranging it for the day following when he was to hunt with the King. Towse was told to be at Lambeth Bridge at five in the morning.

Westminster Bridge, haunt of a phantom boat.

At the meeting the Duke and Towse drew apart from the retinue so that they could not be overheard. They spoke together for an hour or more, and at times the Duke's face showed great emotion. When he returned from hunting he went straight to his mother's apartment, and they were heard to exchange angry words. When news of his death was brought to her shortly afterwards she received it without showing the least surprise, as though it was something that she had foreseen for some time. The following comment appeared in the *Gentleman's Magazine* in 1756:

> Perhaps there may be some reason to suspect that the officer was employed by the Duke's mother, who finding her own remonstrances of no effect, and her son's danger increased with the popular discontent, pretends a message to him from his father's spirit, as the last effort to influence his conduct, and preserve his life.

The story of an equally ineffectual dream concerns the murder of a Prime Minister in the House of Commons. On the evening of 11 May 1812, Spencer Perceval, Prime Minister and Chancellor of the Exchequer, was shot dead by John Bellingham – a man who had become demented by a grudge that he held against the Government. On the same night a superintendent of mines in Cornwall, John Williams of Scorrier, dreamed of the episode three times. The dream was so vivid that he wrote it down before witnesses – he was able to describe the murder in amazing detail:

> Mr. Williams dreamed he was in the House of Commons, where he saw a small man in a blue coat and white waistcoat. Then, as he watched, a man in a brown coat with yellow buttons drew a pistol from his coat. He fired at the small man, who fell, blood pouring from a wound a little below the left breast. Mr. Williams heard clearly the report of the pistol, saw blood fly out and stain the waistcoat, saw the colour of the man's face change. He watched the murderer seized by men who were present, 'observed his countenance'; asked who had been shot, and was told 'the Chancellor'.

News of the assassination reached Williams in Truro two days later, much to the consternation of his family and friends who had ridiculed the importance that he had attached to his dream.

After the murder Bellingham clearly showed himself to be insane:

The murder of Spencer Perceval.

'He persisted in denying any personal enmity for Mr Perceval, for whose death he expressed the greatest sorrow, separating, by a confusion of ideas, the man from the minister; and seemed to think he had not injured the individual though he had taken away the life of the chancellor of the exchequer.'

Nevertheless he was found guilty and executed at the usual place – before the debtors' door at Newgate, a great crowd being present.

Bloomsbury

Sir Ernest Alfred Wallis Budge (1857–1934) was Keeper of Egyptian and Assyrian Antiquities at the British Museum from 1893 until 1924. He was responsible for sorting out the fantastic treasures of this department – identifying and dating them. His was a Victorian success story *par excellence*. His background had been humble, and his first job had been as an office boy with W. H. Smith, the newspaper distributors. However his talents were fostered by various school-masters and tutors (and even by Mr Gladstone the Prime Minister who was impressed by his learning and application) and eventually he won the scholarship which set him on course for a remarkable career. He claimed to have been aided by dreaming a vivid dream *three times* (a magic figure this) on the night before a vital examination. He remembered particulars of the dream the next day – details of the hall where the examination was held, the supervisors, and, most important, the questions – which concerned an obscure Assyrian language whose characters he knew little about. Early in the morning he began researching the subject, and so was prepared when the questions turned up later in the day. Perhaps it was this experience that made him take seriously the story of one of the exhibits in the Egyptian Rooms – the haunted mummy-case from the tomb of an unknown Theban princess of the XXIst Dynasty, *c.* 1050 BC.*

The exhibit in question is No. 22542, to be found in the First Egyptian Room. The hieroglyphics which richly decorate the body of the case below the extraordinarily beautiful portrait identify her as serving the priesthood of Amen-Re, 'King of the Gods'. This was founded at Thebes by Amenhetep I, the second King of the XVIIIth Dynasty.

The story began in the 1880s, when three English visitors to Thebes purchased a beautiful mummy-case from an Arab. The tourists packed it among their baggage and set out to return to Cairo, pausing for a day or two *en route* to take in some duck-shooting. This was when the first accident occurred: a gun exploded, badly injuring the arm of the sportsman – the owner of the mummy-case. Shortly afterwards another member of the party mysteriously disappeared and was never again seen – it was supposed that he had drowned. By the time the two Englishmen reached Cairo the injured arm had

* Today the caption in the case identifies the exhibit as a mummy-case for the mummy of an unnamed singer of Amen-Re.

turned gangrenous and so it had to be amputated. Feeling that the misfortunes of the expedition had somehow been caused by the mummy-case, the owner sold it to a dealer in Cairo. It is said that three of the subsequent owners of the case died mysteriously; in 1888 it reached London, being bought by a collector in Streatham. A famous mystic who was a friend of this collector immediately felt the evil emanating from the ancient treasure: 'Get rid of it or it will kill you,' she warned. This was heeded, and it was sold to another wealthy antiquarian who decided to have it photographed. He employed his usual man to undertake the job but never saw the results – the photographer died the day after taking the pictures. A well-known firm of West End photographers, Mansells, were next commissioned but once again misfortune followed the proceedings – both photographer and his assistant suffering minor injuries as they did the work. The result of the photograph was even more disturbing – the face on the coffin was shown as that of a hateful old hag, her dark eyes full of evil loathing. The new owner quickly decided to get rid of the object, and managed to sell it to a lady collector. On its first night in her house every piece of glass was smashed, and within a few days all her pet animals had died. Furthermore the lady herself, formerly in the best of health, fell into a mysterious sickness which appeared to be incurable, until she got rid of the coffin from Thebes.

The case was presented to the Trustees of the British Museum in 1889 by A. F. Wheeler, Esq. There is nothing to tell us what misfortunes befell this gentleman previously, but it is said that when porters brought the object to the museum one fell and broke his leg, and the other died a few days after.

By this time all sorts of stories were circulating about the coffin. No one, apparently, could make a satisfactory sketch of it, and its malice invariably caused injury to those unwise enough to make an attempt. Watchmen were terrified of patrolling the room where it was kept and complained of being followed by an unseen presence that left them quaking with fear. One security man actually saw the evil spirit emerge from the open coffin-cover. He described it as having a hideous face, yellow-green and wrinkled like a sheep's bladder: when it seemed about to pursue him he fled from the room. Another photographer, who had taken a picture of the case the day before, killed himself after seeing the results. Altogether the deaths of thirteen people were attributed to the priestess.

Her notoriety spread abroad. It was said that when the case

reached the museum it had, in fact, contained a mummy that Budge had privately sold to an American. This had been shipped in the *Empress of Ireland* which sank in the St Lawrence. A similarly absurd (?) story accounted for the mummy being responsible for the sinking of the *Titanic*, and its influence was also blamed for the loss of HMS *Hampshire* in 1916 which resulted in the death of Field-Marshal Earl Kitchener. Thus it acquired a nickname – 'the Ship Wrecker'. A strange, unexplained remark said to have been made by Sir Ernest Budge adds to the mystery: 'Never print what I say in my lifetime, but that mummy-case caused the War' (that is in 1914).

Even Elliott O'Donnell never went as far over the top as this in his story of the case of Amen-Re. He concludes his account by describing a secret exorcism which took place in the First Egyptian Room on 2 January 1921. Two young men with extraordinary psychic powers were attracted there by a spirit message – they had heard nothing previously about the evil power of the mummy-case. One of them described the moment of exorcism:

I saw the troublesome spirit almost at once. It appeared on the breast of the lid, above the hands. It was like a mop, with a flat face in it, flat as a jellyfish. I called to Wyeth, 'Look out, there it is!' Wyeth didn't see it, but I felt, rather than saw, a flame-like substance passing from Wyeth towards the mummy case, and a minute afterwards everything was clear and natural.

They later explained to O'Donnell that powerful 'protecting curses' had been placed on the mummy-case to prevent the body from being

The mummy-case of Amen-Re (British Museum).

defiled. This had meant evoking a familiar spirit as sentinel. The act of exorcism dismissed the familiar and so brought an end to the evil that had been evoked so long ago.

What follows is an anti-climax after the story of Amen-Re yet it is a personal mystery which remains without explanation. In 1961 I was assisting a colleague to photograph a series of objects at the museum for an encyclopaedia of world art. One of the items was an African voodoo-mask, made of wood and dried grass. My colleague handled this to put it in place in front of the camera: immediately his hand began to bleed profusely yet there was no scratch to be seen and careful examination showed that nothing sharp was hidden in the mask. Fortunately the wound healed normally.

Another exhibit at the museum is the suit of golden armour from Bryn yr Ellyon (Hill of the Fairies) in Flintshire. This place was long reputed to be haunted by the ghost of a golden knight. In 1832 the site was excavated and the skeleton of a man wearing golden armour found. As Eric Maple says in *The Realm of Ghosts*:

> Strange that a ghost should have stood guard over a grave for fifteen hundred years, successfully defying medieval treasure hunters and modern robbers until the arrival of an iconoclastic age in which the terror of ancient demons had been superseded by the cold curiosity of the antiquarian.

The British Museum was originally housed in a seventeenth-century mansion, Montagu House, which was opened to the public in 1759. To the north of Montagu House were fields and meadows, one with the intriguing name – 'The Field of the Forty Footsteps'. Torrington Square, badly damaged by bombs in 1942 when two people were killed there, occupies much of it today. The story of how it came by its name was printed in the *Arminian Magazine* in 1781.

> That two Brothers quarrelled about a worthless woman, and according to the fashion of those days, fought with sword and pistol. The prints of their feet are about the depth of three inches, and nothing will vegetate, so much as to disfigure them. The number is only eighty three: but probably some are at present filled up. For I think, there were formerly more in the centre, where each unhappy combatant wounded the other to death. And a bank on which the first who fell, died, retains the form of his agonizing couch, by the curse of Barrenness, while grass flourishes all about it. Mr. *George Hall*, who was the Librarian of *Lincoln's-Inn*, first

shewed me those steps, twenty eight years ago, when, I think, they were not quite so deep as now. He remembered them about thirty years, and the man who first shewed them him, about thirty more; which goes back to the year 1692: but I suppose they originated in King *Charles* the Second's reign. My Mother well remembered their being plowed up, and corn sown to deface them about fifty years ago. But all was labour in vain; for the prints returned in a while to their pristine form; as probably will those that are now filled up.

The ghost of Charles Dickens was reported to have been seen in 1971 at 29 Doughty Street, the house where he once lived, which is now restored as a museum. He was seen to glide along the pavement outside by a gang of workmen on scaffolding – a short, slim figure in dark clothes with a stove-pipe hat. One of the workmen was so upset that he left the job there and then without collecting his wage-packet.

University College Hospital in Gower Street has a ghostly nurse known as Lizzie who worked there at the turn of the century. One of her patients was her fiancé whom she accidentally killed by giving him an overdose of morphine. It is said that whenever this drug is administered a strange nurse keeps watch over the proceedings, to make certain that the same mistake is not made twice.

A man with his head swathed in bandages used to haunt a tea-shop that once stood at the northern end of Gower Street. He is said to have originated in one of the small hotels of the area. A lady guest was startled out of her wits when the bandaged man appeared to her in her bedroom in the middle of the night. She described the bandages as being luminous, and how the figure faded into nothingness after a few fear-filled moments.

The ghost of one of its founders haunts University College: this is Jeremy Bentham (1748–1832), whose mummified body rests in a glass case at the college. He believed that the body should be preserved as a permanent memorial, and so, after dissection, this was the fate of his corpse. The lecture given at the time of dissection must have been memorable:

> There, on the dissecting-table lay the frame of that acute and benevolent man; before it stood the lecturer, pale as the corpse, yet self-possessed and reverent; around were seated most of the disciples and friends of the deceased. During the address there was a violent thunderstorm, which threw an indescribable awe over the

The preserved remains of Jeremy Bentham at University College
(University College).

whole scene. Every now and then the countenances of the dead and the living were lit up by the flashes of lightning; still the speaker proceeded, interrupted now and then by the thunder-crash, until at length it died away, and seemed to give up quiet possession to the lecturer's voice. In this address was given a brief but eloquent abstract of the life and writings of Jeremy Bentham.

After this the body was mummified, though not the head, the preservation of which proved unsatisfactory though it is still kept elsewhere. Bentham wears the white gloves he was seldom seen without, and grasps the walking-stick, called 'Dapple', which served him almost like a pet. As a philosopher he propounded the doctrine of Utilitarianism – that the aim of legislation should be to promote the greatest happiness for the greatest number. It is questionable whether this belief is compatible with the habits of a ghost; nevertheless the mummy occasionally leaves its case and wanders down the corridor to the library, 'Dapple' making a distinctive tapping noise *en route*.

The House in Berkeley Square

Number 50 Berkeley Square, has been the address of the famous antiquarian booksellers, Maggs Brothers, for many years. A hundred years ago, however, it had the unenviable reputation of being the most haunted house in London. George Canning, the Prime Minister, owned No. 50 until his death in 1827, and it was subsequently occupied by a Miss Curzon who lived until she was ninety, dying in 1859. The next lessee was a Mr Myers who appears to have been responsible for its sinister reputation.

When he took the lease of the house following the death of Miss Curzon, Mr Myers was expecting to be married shortly and furnished the house accordingly. At the last minute his wife-to-be, who he loved dearly, jilted him and the bitter disappointment of this undermined his reason and turned him into a recluse. He withdrew into a small room at the top of the building only opening the door to receive food from a manservant. At night, though, he would leave the squalor of his garret and wander through the once-grand rooms bearing a candle whose wan flame shed dim light upon the dusty, elegant furniture that had been bought to delight his bride. For many years he lived thus, becoming more and more eccentric, the house falling deeper into decay. In 1873 he was served a summons by the local council for failing to pay rates or taxes. He failed to answer this, but the magistrates dealt leniently with him, commenting that 'the house in question is known as "the haunted house" and has occasioned a good deal of speculation among the neighbours.'

This speculation appears to have made a nameless monster out of the activities of a miserly recluse, a being of another world responsible for a multitude of unspeakable, unsolved crimes. Its reputation became so bad that in 1879 the weekly magazine *Mayfair* took up the story. It is not known whether Mr Myers was still the tenant at this time.

Berkeley Square, especially in dull weather, is apt to inspire some of the ghostly feeling appropriate to its aristocratic character. Lying between the gayest of all the streets and the brightest of all the squares, this centre of Mayfair always seems oppressed into dullness by a sense of its own secret grandeur. But, as all the world knows, it is not a place where landlords are likely to find their

Berkeley Square in the 1880s (Guildhall Library).

property hangs long upon their hands; and therefore the most inattentive eyes cannot fail to be drawn by the aspect of one of the houses on the west side. The number is needless, for the house is unique, unmistakable, and alone in its outer desolation. If there be physiognomy in bricks and mortar, one would say that house has seen murder done. And yet it has been for so many years a familiar sight that none stop to look curiously at a valuable house left seemingly to decay, with windows caked and blackened by dust, full of silence and emptiness, and yet with no notice about it anywhere that it may be had for the renting. This is known as 'the haunted house in Berkeley Square'.

It appears that the house had an evil character for being badly haunted so long ago as when it was last lived in – that is to say, once upon a time. One day, a maidservant, newly arrived, was put to sleep in one of the upper rooms. An hour or two after the household was at rest, it was awakened by fearful screams from the new servant's room, and she was found standing in the middle of the floor, as rigid as a corpse, with hideously glaring eyes – she had suddenly become a hopeless and raving mad woman, who never found a lucid interval wherein to tell what had made her so. However, this, of itself, did not mean much, even when taken in connection with the house and with the room – women may go mad now and then without any ghostly dealings. The room was given up, but the house still remained occupied, and there seemed to be an end. But some little time afterwards, a guest arrived when the house had many visitors; and he, not unnaturally, laughing at such a skeleton in the cupboard, or being, perhaps, like many sceptics, inclined for a little experience in such adventures, eagerly volunteered for the room which all others were so shy of entering. It was arranged that if, after a certain time, he rang the bell of the room once, it was to be a sign that he found himself as comfortable as expected; but that if he rang it twice, some one should come up and see what was the matter. At the end of the given time the bell rang once only. But presently the same bell gave a frantic peal; and those who ran to his aid found the ghost-defier a corpse where the girl had gone mad before. And dead men tell no tales.

What had he or she seen, or felt, or heard, to kill the man on the spot, and to send the woman out of her mind? The general report into which these special cases have grown is that whoever has slept in that house (or room) has always been found mad, and has died before the tale could be told. We know not whether it was this house, or some other, which inspired the late Lord Lytton with the mystery of 'The House and the Brain'. Some go so far as to say that, in the next-door houses, nobody can sit with his back against the party wall without feeling an indescribably hideous thrill or shudder.

So much for legend. But the strangest part of the business remains to be told. In spite of the character of the house, some persons are occasionally found bold enough, or ignorant enough, to wish to become its tenants – but always in vain. A lady of high position lately made the attempt, and called at the house to make inquiries. It is popularly supposed that the house has no bodily inhabitants at all. But, after some delay, the door was opened by an old woman, who, holding the door in such a manner as to prevent any possibility of entrance, answered inquiries to this effect. The house was not to be let at all. She and her husband lived in it as caretakers. The landlord (unnamed by her) came once every six months; and then he would always lock the old couple up in one of the lower rooms, and went by himself into an upper room, which at other times was kept locked and of which he kept the key. And this was all that could be learned. Whether the upper room is *the* upper room is left to surmise, like what is done there; whether it is a chamber consecrated to magic by the rules of the black art, or whether it is used in some wiser or more innocent way.

We do not feel disposed to apologise either to the ghosts or to their landlord, whoever he may be, and whether a wizard or no, for intruding into their private affairs. These tales have been settling over the house for years, like the dust, encouraging all sorts of rumour and unwholesome superstition. . . . The best exorcism is publicity; and if the owner of the house in Berkeley Square does not really wish his property to run to waste, we have given him the best opportunity he can ask for of contradicting every word here written.

This appeal went unanswered, for *Mayfair* continued its crusade in two further editions. These were also unsuccessful. The reference to Bulwer Lytton's story 'The House and the Brain' is interesting. It was first published in *Blackwood's Magazine* in August 1859, and remains one of the most chilling horror stories ever written in the English language, rivalling those of Poe. While the article in *Mayfair* hinted at some of the stories circulating about the house, it left many unmentioned. One spoke of Lord Lyttelton, who spent a lonely vigil in the room on the top floor. He took with him two large-bore shotguns loaded with buckshot and silver sixpences. He believed that the latter would protect him from any evil forces attacking him, and in the event he fired one of the guns at something that seemed to throw itself at him out of the darkness. Morning light revealed a badly peppered floor but no other evidence, though he said that the 'something' dropped 'like a rocket' when shot. Another suggestion was that a gang of forgers put about the stories as a smokescreen to conceal their activities and explain the strange noises that emanated from counterfeiting coins.

When a Mr Bentley took the house with his two teen-age daughters, the younger girl at once noticed a strange musty smell in the house that she compared to that of the animals' cages at the Zoo. The fiancé of the elder girl, Captain Kentfield, came to stay at the house shortly after they moved in. The evening before his arrival a maid spent some time upstairs preparing him a room. The household was suddenly startled by hysterical screams coming from the room where she was working. They found her collapsed on the floor murmuring, 'Don't let *it* touch me.' These were the last words she spoke: she died in hospital the following morning.

Not dismayed by this tragedy, Captain Kentfield announced his intention of occupying the room regardless. He had only retired to it for about thirty minutes when terrible screams were again heard, followed by a pistol-shot. As before, the body was found on the floor, this time lifeless. There was no sign of the bullet that had been fired from the gun that he still clutched: he had died from shock, his face frozen into a frightful mask of terror.

One of the most widely known tales of the property was that of two sailors who, after a night on the town, saw the house standing empty and broke in to shelter until morning. Strangely, they chose a room on the top floor for this purpose. They were soon disturbed by violent bangs and crashes and then by the remorseless sound of footsteps approaching up the stairs. These reached the room where they sheltered, the door was opened, and a horrible shapeless object slid into the room. One of the sailors managed to bolt past it, and, terror-stricken, ran down the stairs and out into the street. Later he returned with a policeman to search the house, and though they found no trace of a ghost they later discovered the mutilated body of the other sailor, impaled on railings below the window of the haunted room, his neck broken and his features still reflecting the horror that he had escaped from, by jumping to his death.

A final explanation was suggested by Charles Harper in *Haunted Houses*, written in 1931. He believed that the house belonged to a Mr Du Pré, of Wilton Park, who kept his lunatic brother a prisoner in one of the attics. The poor man was so violent that no one was allowed to enter his room; he was fed through a small hole in the wall. His terrible groans and cries were often heard by neighbours and passers-by in the street. Harper writes that the house was eventually let on peculiar terms. The tenants paid £100 for the first year, £200 for the second, and £300 for the third. If the tenant failed to complete the three-year period he would forfeit a deposit of £1,000; a contract that would give credence to the most unlikely ghost.

Ghosts of the London Theatres

The belief that hauntings are a form of 'echo' of an emotional experience from a previous existence would go some way to explain the abundance of ghosts that haunt London theatres. After all, 'out of body' experiences are a part of the stock-in-trade of actors, and the psychic memories of their more intense performances must still reverberate from the walls of these places.

Many comedians seem to be susceptible to mental distress (Tony Hancock is one modern example), but it seldom becomes so acute as to lead to suicide. One of the greatest of all clowns – Dan Leno – eventually went mad and took his own life. In 1923, nineteen years after the death of Leno, another comedian, Stanley Lupino, saw the dead man's face reflected in his dressing-room mirror when he was playing in pantomime at the Theatre Royal, Drury Lane. The long-dead clown gave him helpful advice about his performance and afterwards Lupino found that his dressing-room was the one that Dan Leno had always used. Other actors have reported hearing a strange rhythmic drumming noise in this room, generally explained as being the sound of Leno rehearsing his famous clog-dancing routine.

In Richard Davis's book *I've Seen a Ghost*, Roy Hudd tells how he visited a friend's house in Ackerman Road, Brixton. On first seeing the house he recognised it from a recurring dream that he first experienced in childhood; one in which he explored the house, ending up in the cellar seeing himself reflected in mirrors that covered every wall. Hudd was able to go through the house describing each room before entering it. Of course this startled and intrigued his friends, and also his wife who had accompanied him. The house turned out to

(National Portrait Gallery)

have been the home of Dan Leno for several years, and a LCC plaque on the wall outside confirms this. Roy Hudd was so fascinated by this experience that he made a television programme on the great clown – showing his fantastic versatility as well as the torments that brought his death. Leno first appeared on the stage at the age of four as a contortionist. Later he became an incomparable raconteur and comic singer. He was the greatest of all pantomime 'dames'. His dance routines were also famous, and he would rehearse them in front of an array of mirrors. He was forty-four when he died. The programme was introduced with Roy Hudd's curious *dèja vu* episode and after it had been screened many people contacted him to tell of their meetings with Leno's ghost, many of which took place at the Theatre Royal, Drury Lane. All stressed the feeling of warmth and care that came from Leno, but Hudd was warned never to visit the grave of the clown, a warning which, says Richard Davis, he has taken care to heed.

Leno's ghost was also reputed to haunt Collins' Music Hall on Islington Green, demolished in 1963. Leno would attend rehearsals and auditions irritably snapping his fingers if he disapproved of a performance. The cleaning ladies grew so used to his 'presence' that they would work round him. A ghost was last seen in the theatre in 1960 when one walked through the walls of a cellar, but it seems that this was more likely that of the founder of the theatre, Sam Collins himself.

Returning to the West End and to the Theatre Royal, Drury Lane, we find the most famous of all Ghosts of the Theatre – the Man in Grey. No one in the profession would ever be displeased to see this figure, for he commonly appears before or during the run of a successful production. He wears a three-cornered hat, powdered wig, and grey riding-cloak. Appearances invariably take place during daytime – once before a full matinée audience. He always takes the same route along the back of the upper circle, starting from a room used as a bar on one side of the auditorium, vanishing through the wall on the opposite side. Nothing disrupts this routine, not even the fury of an air raid, for during the last war a fire-watcher saw the ghost when bombs were falling all around. However if you see him keep your curiosity in check, for if you attempt to approach him too closely – nearer than about forty feet – his features become hazy, his outline blurs, and he vanishes quickly.

During the last century some workmen were carrying out

Theatre Royal, Drury Lane.

alterations to the theatre on the Russell Street side where the walls are at their thickest. They came across a portion of wall that seemed to be hollow and when this was investigated it revealed a cavity occupied by a skeleton. Further examination showed that death was caused by a dagger that was still embedded between the ribs. Fragments of richly braided cloth were also found. Close to this cramped hiding-place the ghost begins his walk.

In one of his books on Drury Lane, Macqueen Pope (who claimed to have seen the ghost on numerous occasions) speculates that the Man in Grey was a wealthy yet naïve young man who made his first visit to the metropolis from the country during the reign of Queen Anne. In those days any of the public could wander backstage and so this handsome stranger, obviously with plenty of money to spend, proved attractive to one of the actresses. This inflamed the jealousy of a previous lover who stabbed the young buck and entombed the corpse in the small hole in the wall, where it lay undisturbed for 150 years. Although offers have been made to lay the ghost, these have always been refused by the management who recognise the value of the appearances which invariably herald a hit. Strangely the reinterment of the body found in the cavity (in a graveyard a short distance from the theatre) did not stop the Man in Grey from haunting the theatre subsequently. However it may be a reflection on the state of the English Theatre that he has not been seen in recent years. His appearances were most regular during the boom in the West End when the musicals of Ivor Novello and American successes such as *Oklahoma, South Pacific*, and *The King and I* were packing in the crowds. In the 1960s Harry Secombe and the cast of *The Four Musketeers* often saw the ghost, but few, if any, sightings have been reported since. Let us hope that the fortunes of theatreland revive so that the Man in Grey can once more enjoy his playgoing.

A less tranquil ghost at Drury Lane which is also less predictable in its perambulations, is that of the Irish actor Charles Macklin. In 1735, during a dispute about a wig with a fellow actor, Thomas Hallam, Macklin struck out with his stick and injured Hallam in the eye. The wound proved fatal, and as a result Macklin is said to stride across the front of the stage in eternal remorse. His is a grim and fearsome figure, most often seen before the start of a performance in the early evening.

Macqueen Pope tells, too, of a friendly spirit that occasionally helps newcomers to the stage to forget nerves and so improve their performances. It can even redirect them to a better position or show how their movements may be made more effective. If, as a performer, you feel unseen hands on your shoulders gently yet firmly pushing you around the stage, there is no need to be afraid – it is only the well-meaning yet nameless ghost of Drury Lane at work!

The Haymarket is London's second oldest theatre, after Drury Lane. It, too, has its ghosts, the one most regularly seen being that of John Buckstone, a comedian and dramatist who was Manager here between 1853 and 1878 when the Haymarket was enjoying its greatest period of prosperity. Buckstone was a well-liked man, who ran the theatre that he loved in exemplary fashion. Like the Man in Grey, he is only seen when the theatre is doing well. His appearances began a year after his death in 1880 when he was seen seated in the Royal Box where his place had been on occasions when royalty had visited the theatre in the past.

Donald Sinden saw his ghost when playing in *The Heiress* in 1949. As he passed Sir Ralph Richardson's dressing-room door he saw a figure at the window, dressed in a black frock-coat, peering intently at the street below. Believing it to be Sir Ralph he said 'Good evening!' but not receiving a reply continued down the stairs towards the stage. Half-way down he realised that Sir Ralph was actually on-

'How's the house tonight?' An early sketch of a theatrical manager.

stage at that moment, but returning to the dressing-room he found that the figure had disappeared. No other character in the production was 'free' at the time so it could only have been the ghost of Buckstone putting in one of his regular appearances.

Once, during a run of *The School for Scandal* the late Margaret Rutherford and her husband spent the night at the Haymarket as a rail strike prevented their return home. They slept in her dressing-room, which had an entrance directly on to the stage which had been bricked-up a long time before. Next to it was the wardrobe for the costumes, also used as a drinks cupboard. The actress dreamt that she went to this cupboard but was unable to close the door because of the full skirts of her eighteenth-century dress. As she attempted to do so she saw a man's hairy leg among them and then caught a glimpse of the face: it was John Buckstone, for she had once been shown his portrait in the National Portrait Gallery. The actress wrote of her experience in *Psychic News*, claiming that she had not known of Buckstone's association with the theatre until that time.

Two years later, in 1963, Buckstone was seen again. Although a harmless ghost, he seems to enjoy startling those who see him. This time the show was the two-man production *At the Drop of Another Hat*. In this the late Michael Flanders, seated in his wheelchair, appeared with Donald Swann at the piano. This report of Buckstone's manifestation was printed in *The Daily Telegraph:*

The Ghost Goes to S.W.1

A few days before Michael Flanders was appointed an O.B.E., Olga Bennett, assistant stage manager for 'At the Drop of Another Hat' at the Haymarket Theatre, noticed a man standing behind the entertainer's wheelchair while he was singing about London buses.

Naturally Miss Bennett was furious at this infringement of theatre rules until the figure moved to show that he was wearing a long black frock coat. He was obviously no stage hand.

No believer in ghosts, Miss Bennett forgot about the incident until she came into conversation with the authority on the Haymarket's history. Her description exactly fitted the ghost of J. B. Buckstone, manager of the theatre from 1852 to 1878.

Moving slightly away from the world of theatre – though (perhaps) remaining on the fringe of that of entertainment – the BBC has its share of ghosts. On the other side of Langham Place from its headquarters stands the Langham Hotel, which was a smart place to stay in Edwardian times but was later taken over by the BBC as an administration building. On the third floor a few bedrooms are preserved to serve their original purpose – and now accommodate announcers or other staff who have to stay overnight. The most infamous room is No. 333 where a ghost has been seen by several occupants. The announcer James Alexander Gordon had a disturbing night here soon after joining the 'Beeb' in 1973. As he had to introduce an early programme, he slept overnight at the Langham, arranging to be woken soon after first light. Well beforehand he awoke suddenly: on the far side of the room was a fluorescent ball, which, as he watched, began to take on a human shape which became more and more distinct. At length he could see that it wore formal evening wear of the Victorian era, complete with cloak and cravat. The figure remained translucent, and through him Gordon could still see the wash-basin. By this time the announcer was thoroughly alarmed. In a shaky voice he asked the ghost who he was and what he wanted, and as if in reply the wraith began to move, or rather float, towards him – two feet above the ground, its arms outstretched. Its eyes were fixed in a terrifying unblinking stare. Gordon did not wait for a confrontation but turned and fled from the room. He told the commissionaire of the incident in the lobby. He was most unsympathetic and refused to leave his post to investigate the matter. Thus Gordon had to return to the room alone in order to collect his clothes. The ghost was still there, but less menacing and less distinct than he had been before.

When he arrived at Broadcasting House Gordon told his colleague, Ray Moore of his encounter. Before he began to describe the figure in detail, Moore stopped him. He too had had a similar experience and his description of the ghost matched that of Gordon perfectly.* Many other people came forward with their own versions of this story when it was mentioned on television. One remarkable feature was that the figure only seems to appear during the month of October.

In Broadcasting House itself the ghostly figure of a butler was seen on a number of occasions. He carried a loaded tray before him and walked along the corridors with a stately tread, always in the early morning. His dignity might have been a little dented had he known that one engineer who saw him swore that he had a hole in the heel of one of his socks!

Few ghosts of the theatre are actively vindictive, but an exception appears to be the 'Strangler Jacket' which became notorious in 1948. The story began with the play *The Queen Came By* opening at the Embassy, Swiss Cottage, prior to its West End run. In the play Thora Hird played a Victorian seamstress. She found a short monkey-jacket she considered perfect for her part either in the wardrobe of the Embassy or on a barrow in a street market (accounts differ). This fitted her well initially but during the week that the play spent at Swiss Cottage she felt that it was becoming uncomfortably tight, and so it was let out before the West End opening at the Duke of York's Theatre. There it still felt tight and uncomfortable. When the understudy took over Miss Hird's part for one performance she also felt restricted in the garment and that night had a troubled dream in which the jacket was worn by a young woman in Victorian clothes. Other people in the company became interested in the sinister jacket and all experienced discomfort when they tried it on. One person found that she had been bruised on either side of her throat when she took it off as though someone had squeezed it attempting to strangle her. It was agreed that the jacket should be got rid of, but such was

*However, elsewhere Ray Moore said that the ghost was thickset, with cropped hair, who wore a jacket that buttoned up to the neck. He stood at the window of a room in the block opposite, on the fourth floor. This would give support to the theory that the ghost is that of a German officer who jumped to his death from a room on that floor shortly before the outbreak of the First World War.

the publicity that the story had attracted that it was agreed that a seance should be held first.

This was held at the theatre, and one of the mediums involved was able to describe a terrible incident. She saw a young girl struggling violently to escape from a man who had seized her and was attempting to push her head downwards into a butt of water. At last he was successful in this and carried the dripping corpse up some stairs to a shabby room where he stripped the clothes off the body (including the ill-famed jacket) before wrapping it in a blanket.

The jacket was later acquired by Americans who took it home with them to California. Several people who wore it there were afflicted with the same feeling of restricted terror, though there have been no recent reports of its whereabouts.

The Lyceum, in Wellington Street off the Strand, is a ballroom now – also famed for its beauty contests – yet a century ago it was a splendid venue for playgoers who came to see Irving or Ellen Terry perform in opulent Shakespearean productions. Only the portico survives of the old theatre which was the scene of a particularly grisly phenomenon in the 1880s.

A husband and wife were watching a performance from one of the boxes when, during the first interval, the woman glanced down into the stalls below and to her horror saw a lady sitting there with a man's severed head lying in her lap. Almost at the same moment the macabre object also caught the attention of her husband – and then the lights went down. They were unable to confirm their discovery at the next interval as the woman's lap was discreetly covered by her shawl. At the end of the play the lady left the theatre abruptly, pursued by the two onlookers, who were unable to approach her closely because of the post-theatre crowds in which she was soon lost. The incident lay dormant in the man's mind for years, only to be awakened when on a visit to a great house in Yorkshire he was confronted by the portrait of the man whose face he had last seen in the woman's lap at the Lyceum. When he asked about the fate of the man shown in the picture, he was told that he had been beheaded by the orders of Cromwell, and that his family had owned the land on which the original Lyceum had been built in 1772.*

A sad figure used to haunt the Coliseum in St Martin's Lane. On 3 October 1918 a young subaltern was killed in one of the last engagements of the First World War. At the precise moment of his death he was seen to walk down the gangway of the circle at the

*The Lyceum was built on part of the garden of Exeter House. The first Duke of Exeter was executed in 1400 for conspiring against Henry IV. Later the title of Marquess of Exeter came to the Courtenay family. Henry Courtenay, the first Marquess, was executed in 1538, but later holders of

Coliseum and take a seat in the second row. Friends of his saw him at the theatre and learnt of his death a few days later. He had spent his last hours in England at the Coliseum, perhaps watching the great Lillie Langtry who often performed there. The ghost was seen several times subsequently, but its appearances gradually became sporadic and now seem to have ceased altogether. At the same theatre David Hughes has claimed to have been encouraged by the gruff voice of the late Sir John Barbirolli while singing in *Madam Butterfly*.

There used to be scores of strip clubs in Soho; now only a few survive, one of the last being the Gargoyle Club in Dean Street. The club is on the top floor of an old building reputed to have been the home of Nell Gwynne. Most people who have seen the ghost at the Gargoyle identify the figure that they have seen as Charles II's buxom mistress. She wears a high-waisted dress, a large hat covered with a profusion of flowers, and a perfume of gardenias so powerful that it lingers in the room long after the ghost has disappeared (usually by way of the lift shaft).

The old Royalty Theatre used to stand next door to the Gargoyle but was severely damaged by bombs in the Second World War. Now the site is occupied by an office-block. It was a small theatre famous for staging the premières of many famous plays – *Trial by Jury, Ghosts, Charley's Aunt, Juno and the Paycock* among them. It dated from 1840 when it was built as a school for acting, though one of the ghosts appeared to belong to an earlier time, being dressed in white in the style of the reign of Queen Anne. The skeleton of a woman dressed in a similar costume was found when the site was being cleared for the Royalty. Possibly this lady is also responsible for haunting the neighbouring strip club. The Royalty also had the ghost of a sweet old lady who was seen by audience and players alike. She had a nod and a smile for most of those who encountered her but would disconcert them by suddenly vanishing.

The St James's always had the reputation for being an unlucky theatre. It existed from 1835 until 1957, standing just outside the periphery of the main galaxy of West End theatres in King Street, St James's. It was haunted by an eighteenth-century actress (who had stayed at Nerot's Hotel – the previous building on the site) and by a kindly ghost whose unseen hands would help on actors with their costumes or brush dust off their shoulders just prior to their call. He (or she) frequented one particular dressing-room. Of more interest, however, is its association with the ghost of Oscar Wilde whose

the title appear to have led lives which ended naturally. Perhaps it was a distant relative who incurred the wrath of Cromwell, or was it the head of Henry Courtenay which was seen in the lap of the mysterious woman at the theatre?

'thoughts after death' were given to sitters at a seance here in 1923. An eerie hand appeared to the two actors and an actress who made up the circle, its fingers clutched a pen, and when asked its identity it wrote 'Pity Oscar Wilde'.

This wittiest of dramatists, who died in 1900 – disgraced and persecuted – had earlier produced automatic writing for a seance organised by the Society for Psychical Research. On the first occasion he was contacted he wrote: 'I am Oscar Wilde. I have come back to let the world know that I am not dead. Death is the most boring thing in Life – except marriage or dining with a schoolmaster.'

Much more was transmitted through the magic pen – this time held by all those making up the circle, and Wilde's friends were able to ask questions, the answers to which convinced them of the identity of the writer. The pen wrote movingly of a ghost's existence:

You know that we are a sort of amphibian, who has a foot in either world, but belongs properly to neither. We live in the twilight of existence. In eternal twilight I move, but I know that in the world there is day and night, seed-time and harvest and red sunset must follow the apple-green dawn. Already the may is creeping like a white mist over lane and hedgerow, and year after year the hawthorn bears blood-red fruit after the white death of its may. . . .

Now the mere memory of the beauty of the world is an exquisite pain. I was one of those for whom the physical world existed. I worshipped at the shrine of things seen. There was not a blood-stripe on a tulip, or a curve on a shell, or a tone of the sea but had for me its meaning and mystery and appeal to the imagination. Others might sip the pale lees of the cup of thought, but for me the red wine of life! Pity Oscar Wilde!

Another poet/dramatist whose spirit has returned to earth is Dylan Thomas. He has been seen in the tiny Bush Theatre, once a BBC rehearsal-room on an upper floor of the Shepherd's Bush Hotel. On one occasion he was seen by several actors and technicians after a late rehearsal standing silently at the back of the auditorium. The hotel was a favourite drinking-ground of Thomas when he worked with the BBC.

Returning towards the West End, the Gaumont Cinema at Notting Hill Gate has a ghost, which the staff nicknamed 'Flora'. The cinema was originally the Coronet Theatre and the ghost is said to be the spirit of a cashier who was caught fiddling the box-office receipts in

Oscar Wilde (National Portrait Gallery).

the 1900s. When confronted with the evidence of her misdemeanour by the Manager she ran from his office, climbed the stairs to the 'Gods', and threw herself to her death from the balcony. A report in the *Kensington Post* in 1969 tells how staff meetings were so disturbed by the ghost when they were held in a room in the upper, disused, part of the building, that they had to be transferred to an office in a more-frequented part. Footsteps came from the stairs leading to the sealed-off Gods, and occasionally a pair of small brown shoes were seen, climbing the stairs by themselves. The haunting usually occurs during Christmas week.

The phantom of William Terriss, a famous leading man of the 1890s, also prefers to haunt in winter. He visits Covent Garden Underground Station as well as the Adelphi Theatre where he was appearing at the time of his violent death. An account of an appearance of his ghost was printed in the *Sunday Dispatch* on 15 January 1956:

Who is the ghost of Covent Garden Underground Station? Some people believe the station is haunted by a Victorian actor.

A four-page report has been sent to the London Transport Executive divisional headquarters. And this question has been put to officials:

Is the statuesque figure wearing white gloves and seen by members of the station staff, the spectre of William Terriss, the actor stabbed to death at the Adelphi Theatre by a maniac 59 years ago?

One member of the staff, Station Man Victor Locker, a West African, who believes he saw a ghost, cannot bear to work at the station. His application for a transfer to another station was granted immediately.

Just after midnight last November the last passenger had left the platform. Foreman Collector Jack Hayden saw a tall distinguished-looking man go into the exit.

'Catch that man coming up the emergency stairs, Bill,' he phoned to the booking clerk. *But no-one was there.*

On November 24th, at 12.40 p.m. Jack Hayden sat in the staff mess-room with the door open.

He told me: 'I saw a tall man wearing a grey suit, funny old collar and white gloves, looking at me from the ante-room.

'I said: "Looking for the cloakroom, sir?" The thing disappeared. No-one in the passage, not a sound of footsteps.'

William Terriss with his mistress and leading lady, Jessie Milward, in whose arms he died (Mander & Mitchenson Theatre Collection).

Four days later, at about midday, Hayden and Station Woman Rose Ring were in the mess-room when they heard a scream. Locker stumbled in grey with fright: 'A man, he was standing there . . . it pressed down on my head . . . it vanished,' he said.

Hayden rang headquarters in Leicester Square: 'We have a ghost here,' he said.

Foreman Eric Davey, a spiritualist, was sent down and held a seance in the ante-room. A reluctant Locker shouted: 'Mr Davey, Mr Davey, it's on you.'

Davey told me: 'I got the name Ter . . . something. That evening somebody suggested Terriss.' Pictures of Terriss were found that resembled a psychic sketch made by Davey. Both Locker and Hayden said: 'That's him.'

William Terriss was a well-liked, generous man of the theatre. However in the cast of the thriller *Secret Service* in which he played the lead was a young man named Richard Archer Prince who had a minor role. Prince had an immense jealousy of Terriss, and with every performance his hatred grew as he thought how much better he could play the hero. At last his passion could be leashed no longer. In the afternoon he went out and bought a dagger. In the early evening of 16 December 1897 he stabbed Terriss as he unlocked the stage door of the Adelphi in Maiden Lane. The actor died in the arms of his leading lady, whispering 'I will be back.' Prince was found guilty of murder but insane and spent the rest of his days in Broadmoor, the institution for the criminally insane, dying there in 1937, aged seventy-one.

The first sighting of the ghost of Terriss occurred in 1928 when a stranger to London, who knew nothing of the murder, encountered a strange figure in Maiden Lane dressed in grey clothes fashioned in turn-of-the-century style. This figure suddenly vanished, convincing the stranger that he had seen a ghost. When he was shown a photograph of Terriss he confirmed that this was the man whom he had seen. In the same year a leading comedy actress of the day ('June') was upset by a terrifying experience in her dressing-room. Resting between performances on a chaise-longue, she was startled by it beginning to shake and lurch, as though someone was kicking it from underneath. She looked beneath it, discovering no cause for its violent action, but when she lay down again the shaking began again and she felt light blows on her arms. Then they were tightly gripped and she saw a greenish light above the dressing-table mirror. There were then two taps that seemed to come from behind the mirror and then the strange light vanished. Later the actress learnt that her dressing-room had been that of Terriss's leading lady, Jessie Milward, and he always gave two taps with his cane as he passed its door. She carried bruises on her arms for some days after her experience.

More recently, in 1962, the greenish light was seen again, this time by two workmen alone in the auditorium at night. They thought it took the shape of a body as it floated across the stage. Soon afterwards an electrician saw the ghost clearly enough to say that it wore a grey suit. It parted the curtains noiselessly, walked across the stage and down the steps into the stalls. Then it climbed the aisle to the back of the theatre, crossing over to the opposite side at the last row of seats, its progress marked by the mysterious tipping of seats right across the theatre.

Theatres to the east of the West End also have their ghostly moments. Sadler's Wells takes its name from the medieval well discovered in Thomas Sadler's grounds in 1683. He exploited the iron-rich waters that even in the Middle Ages had been famous for their miraculous or medicinal powers. Part of the 'development' of the spa was devoted to entertainment, and a Musick House was built which by 1718 was known as Sadler's Wells. The legendary Joseph Grimaldi – often hailed as the greatest of all clowns – was a regular performer here from 1781 (when he was three) until his farewell performance in 1828. He is supposed to have been seen in one of the boxes, his long, white-panned face and glassy eyes a ghastly spectacle, especially when the occupants of the box are unaware of the companion seated behind them. He died in 1837 and his macabre last request was obeyed – his head was cut from his body before burial.

The final ghost from the troupe of theatricals haunts the Theatre Royal at Stratford – a Victorian theatre dating from 1884. The Fredericks family (who were great theatre-builders in the East End of London) took over in 1888 and it remained in their hands until 1957. The most famous of its managers was the kindly Fred Fredericks, and it is supposed to be his tubby, brown-suited figure that returns late each night to make sure that his initials remain on the proscenium arch that spans the stage. There is a tradition that if these are removed or even painted over disaster will overtake the Theatre Royal.

West London

Taking Greater London in its loosest sense, it may be said that it extends as far as the tentacles of the underground system spread, and as there are a couple of excellent stories located close to the terminus of the Piccadilly Line, that is the premise used in this chapter.

West Drayton

In 1885 the Reverend F. G. Lee's *Glimpses in the Twilight* was published. It included the following story of West Drayton, worthy of any Gothic horror film:

THE SPECTRAL BIRD AT WEST DRAYTON.

In the middle of the last century, *circa* 1749, owing to several remarkable circumstances which had then recently occurred, a conviction became almost universal among the inhabitants of the village, that the vaults under the church of West Drayton, near Uxbridge, were haunted. Strange noises were heard in and about the sacred building, and the sexton of that day, a person utterly devoid of superstition, was on inquiry and examination compelled to admit that certain unaccountable occurrences in regard to the vault had taken place. There are, it is said, three large vaults under the chancel – in the chief of which, towards its eastern part, the ancient and noble family of Paget find their last resting-place. Two other vaults are situated near the west end of the choir, one of the De Burghs, a more ancient family still. From each of these, the most remarkable knockings were sometimes heard, commonly on Friday evenings as was said; and many curious people from the village used to come together to listen to them. They were never either explained or explained away. Some people affirmed that one person had secretly murdered another, then committed suicide, and that

West Drayton Church (Guildhall Library).

both the bodies had been buried side by side in the same grave. Others maintained that three persons from an adjacent mansion-house in company had gone to look through a grating in the side of the foundation of the church – for the ventilation of the vault, and from which screams and noises were heard constantly, and had there seen a very large black raven perched on one of the coffins. This strange bird was seen more than once by the then parish clerk pecking from within at the grating, and furiously fluttering about within the enclosed vault. On another occasion it was seen by other people in the body of the church itself. The wife of the parish clerk and her daughter often saw it. The local bell-ringers, who all professed to deny its existence and appearance, one evening, however, came together to ring a peal, when they were told by a youth that the big raven was flying about inside the chancel. Coming together into the church with sticks and stones and a lantern, four men and two boys found it fluttering about amongst the rafters. They gave chase to it, flinging at it, shouting at and endeavouring to catch it. Driven hither and thither for some time, and twice or thrice beaten with a stick, so that one of its wings seemed to have been thus broken and made to droop, the bird fell down wounded with expanded wings, screaming and fluttering into the eastern part of the chancel, when two of the men on rushing towards it to secure it, and driving it into a corner, vaulted over the communion-rails, and violently proceeded to seize it. As the account stands, it at once sank wounded and exhausted on to the floor, and as they believed in their certain grasp, but all of a moment – vanished!

The following footnote appears to the Reverend F. G. Lee's text:

Mrs de Burgh, the wife of Mr R. L. de Burgh, sometime Vicar of West Drayton, writes thus to me:

July 16, 1883.

Your question has aroused recollections of often hearing sounds in Drayton Church like the strong fluttering of a large bird. It was many years ago; and I had quite forgotten it until I got your note. I can remember feeling persuaded that a bird must have got into the family vault, and in going outside to look into it through the iron bars to try if anything could be seen there, the sounds were then always in the chancel in the same place. This is all I am afraid I can remember about it. I have not even thought of it for years past.

JULIA DE BURGH.

A Mrs White, whose relations (gentleman-farmers in the village) lived at West Drayton from 1782 to 1818, tells me through a friend that thereabouts 'the country folks always believed that the Spectral Bird which haunted Drayton Church was the restless and miserable spirit of a murderer who had committed suicide, and who, through family influence, instead of being put into a pit or hole, with a stake through his body at the cross-road by Harmondsworth, as was the sentence by law, had been buried in consecrated ground on the north side of the churchyard.'

A lady and her sister – as I am informed (1878) – who on one Saturday afternoon in 1869 had gone into Drayton church to place some vases of flowers upon the communion-table, on coming out, each saw a great Black Bird perched upon one of the pews – which they believed must have escaped from the Zoological Gardens or some menagerie.

A gentleman who is well informed, thus writes:

The thoroughly sceptical tone of the newspapers is such that persons would be held up to scorn and ridicule who might have the hardihood to maintain the reality of any supernatural appearance or intervention. Though I *know* that Drayton Church is haunted by the spirit of a murderer, who appears as a very large raven, I do not add particulars and do not give name.

216

Ickenham, Twickenham, Cranford and Egham

The second station down the line from Uxbridge is Ickenham. In 1951 an electrician working on the platform in the early hours of the morning was startled by a middle-aged woman wearing a red scarf who stood watching him as he worked. When she had caught his attention she gestured that he should follow her, and led him across the station and down one of the stairways. Just before she reached the last step she vanished completely. This ghost has been seen by several London Transport workers over the years, and is supposed to be that of a woman who fell from the platform on to the live rail and was electrocuted long ago.

The churchyard of St Mary's, Twickenham, used to be haunted by the ghost of the famous satirist, Alexander Pope, who was buried there. In 1830 his skull was stolen from the grave (probably for the collection of the famous phrenologist, Johann Spurzheim) and subsequently his unmistakable hunched figure was seen hobbling around the church, talking and shouting to himself between terrible bouts of coughing. Although the apparition has not been seen recently, the uneven sound of a cripple's footsteps has been heard inside the church.

The Berkeley Arms at Cranford is a popular hotel with business-men using Heathrow. Before the invention of the aeroplane this was a part of Cranford Park, the setting for the imposing seat of the Fitzhardinge Berkeleys, Cranford House. Only a small part of this survives – a portion of the stable-block, but it was here, in the stable-yard, that the famous sporting squire encountered what he took to be a trespasser. Slapping his riding-whip against his boot, he demanded to know the stranger's business, whereupon the intruder disappeared into thin air. His sons once came across a strange kitchen-maid late at night. When they spoke to her she glided behind a firescreen and no trace of her could be found.

Most writers who deal with ghosts are very wary of mentioning haunted houses by name. This rises out of a celebrated case in the early years of this century which concerned a house at Egham, called 'Hillside'. It was then described as a 'modern Villa' and had been rented in 1903 by Stephen Phillips, a well-known dramatist of his day. He only occupied it for a short time, moving to a nearby hotel.

He complained that he was constantly disturbed by inexplicable happenings and noises, the worst of which sounded like a child being strangled. His daughter had seen the stooped figure of an old man, and no servant could be persuaded to stay in the place. Locals spoke of a child having been strangled there by an old farmer many years before. Thus the writer had had to give up the lease, and forfeited the deposit he had paid. The *Daily Express* first carried an account of the haunting in 1904. The agents for the owner brought an action for libel against the newspaper that was settled out of court for £200. In 1906, just as the house was recovering its respectability, the *Daily Mail* resurrected the story. Thus another action was brought – the estate agent maintaining that it had become impossible to let or sell the house at anything like its true value. This time the case came to court and the jury found for the agents, awarding them £90 damages. In *Haunted Houses* published in 1931, Charles Harper says that, at the time of writing, 'Hillside' was occupied by a policeman who lived there rent-free as caretaker. He believed the noises to be made by rats. In the same book Harper quotes a case in 1911 when a landlord sued a tenant of a house in Cathles Road, Balham, for non-payment of rent. The defendant said that the house was so troubled by ghosts as to be uninhabitable, and he had to move out soon after taking the property for a year. The judge was unimpressed by this argument, as are most modern housing authorities when tenants complain of ghostly disturbance or poltergeist activity and demand to be moved to different, invariably better, accommodation.

Alexander Pope (National Portrait Gallery).

Hampton Court and Richmond

Hampton Court Palace truly deserves a chapter to itself, it is so well haunted. Its builder, Cardinal Wolsey, has only been seen once, at a Son et Lumière performance in 1966, but other famous figures have appeared frequently over the centuries. Two of the wives of Henry VIII revisit rooms where they lived and suffered. Catherine Howard, Henry's fifth wife, was a girl of twenty when she died. She found the King sexually repulsive and foolishly directed her efforts elsewhere. When she heard that she had been condemned for these extra-marital activities she ran through the long passages of the palace pursued by guards until she came to the door of the chapel where Henry was attending Mass. She beat at the doors with her fists, screaming for mercy, while guards tried to restrain her, but her husband gave no sign of hearing her cries and she was soon dragged away. She was the only one of the wives who refused to accept her fate with dignity, struggling piteously until the final downward swing of the headsman's axe. Her wild cries still echo through the galleries, and her fists may be heard desperately beating against the door of the chapel.

The ghost of Jane Seymour has also been seen at the palace. Her intrigues against Anne Boleyn, her former mistress, were eventually successful but she died in childbirth just a year after becoming Queen. Twelve hundred Masses were ordered to be said for her soul, but even so her spirit remained restless, and she still walks, clad in white and bearing a lighted taper, up the stairs and through the Silver Stick Gallery.

The most frequently seen ghost of the palace has been identified as Mrs Sibell Penn, nurse to King Edward VI. She was devoted to the young, sickly King, and when he died at the age of sixteen suffered grief as deeply as any mother. Mrs Penn died of smallpox in 1562 and was laid to rest in the old church at Hampton Court, but her tomb may now be seen in the porch of the present building. It was the removal of her tomb that caused Mrs Penn to walk, for there were no accounts of anyone seeing her prior to 1821 when the old church was pulled down. Theo Brown, an authority on ghosts and folklore (and the author of *Devon Ghosts* in this series), sent me the following account of a meeting with this ghost:

This was told me in 1960, by the Reverend J. G. M. Scott, MA, the well-known bell-ringing expert:

Hampton Court Palace (Department of the Environment).

'A great-aunt of mine who died last year at the age of 96, lived in Hampton Court Palace, in a Grace and Favour house in Tennis Court Lane. Soon after she and her sister went there, they were puzzled by hearing from time to time a noise "like someone winding up an old-fashioned Waterbury Watch", which was sometimes accompanied by the sound of a woman's voice, though they could never make out more than the occasional word. It was only on enquiring from the Palace officials that they discovered that this was Mistress Penn's spinning wheel. My great-aunt (she was about four feet ten inches tall with a presence like a duchess) later saw Mrs. Penn. "I was woken up in the night," she said, "by someone bending over my bed and looking into my face. 'What do you want?' I said. 'You must go away. What do you mean by coming into my bedroom?' . . . and she said 'I want a home . . . I want a home.' So I said, 'Well, I'm sorry, you can't have one here; this is my bedroom and you must go away.' And she did, but when I thought about it in the morning I really felt quite ashamed of myself, because we had a spare room upstairs, and she could have had that."

The wives of Henry VIII.   221

Death on the block (British Library).

'I may say that I am quite sure that Aunt Edith knew almost as soon as she saw her that the figure was a ghost; and if you find it hard to believe that a lady of 90 could talk to a ghost with such authority and sang-froid . . . well, you never knew my Great Aunt Edith. I am sure this story is true, and I am sure that if Aunt Edith had thought of it at the time she would have given Mrs. Penn her spare room with great pleasure, out of sheer kindness.

'Mrs Penn, as you very likely know, was the nurse of Edward VI; I have read somewhere of her waking someone up by peering into his face, but this time it was a gardener having a quiet sleep during working hours, and not being Aunt Edith he was never the same man again.

'Aunt Edith saw her again, once, walking down Tennis Court Lane, wearing a tall grey head-dress. She is the best authenticated of the Hampton Court ghosts.'

Soon after the first sighting of the ghost of Mrs Penn the 'click-clack' of a spinning-wheel was heard, accompanied by the grumpy mutterings of an old woman. These sounds seemed to come from the wall of a large room in the south-west wing, and on closer examination it was found that this concealed a room that had been hidden for centuries. In it was found a spinning-wheel, the oak flooring beneath the treadle worn away by constant use.

Another account of this ghost is given in Mrs Stirling's *Merry Wives of Battersea*:

After wandering about at Hampton Court one afternoon I went on the terrace and rested there. It was a very hot day of brilliant sunshine, and as I watched the crowd pass to and fro along the pathway in front of me, I saw a wounded soldier in a hospital suit of blue coming along on crutches. I was gazing at him compassionately, when my attention was diverted to a woman approaching who was wearing an unusual old-fashioned dress with a picturesque cap of unwonted design. Concluding she was some foreigner in national costume, or else a nurse in some peculiar uniform, I was watching her idly, when, to my utter astonishment, *I saw her overtake and pass like an unsubstantial mist right through the crippled soldier*, who meanwhile remained unconscious of what was happening.

Dumbfounded at what I had seen, I sprang up and, scarcely knowing what I did, rushed up to a policeman who was near, exclaiming: 'Constable – I have seen a ghost!'

'Well, ma'am,' was the stolid reply, 'we often sees odd things hereabouts. What was she like?'

I explained – thankful that the man did not think me a lunatic; but he listened to my description sympathetically. 'Oh, we often

Queen Elizabeth I.

sees *her*,' he said at the conclusion, 'they say she was nurse to Edward VI.'

In 1907 another policeman reported a different haunting. His story was told in Charles Harper's *Haunted Houses*:

'On this particular night,' he said, 'I went on duty at the east front of the Palace at ten o'clock, and had to remain there until six o'clock next morning. I was quite alone, and was standing close to the main gates, looking towards the Home Park, when suddenly I became conscious of a group of figures moving towards me along what is known as the Ditton Walk. It is a most unusual thing to see anyone in the gardens at that time of night, but I thought it probable that some of the residents in the Palace had been to a party at Ditton and were returning on foot. The party consisted of two gentlemen in evening dress and seven or nine ladies. There were no sounds except what resembled the rustling of dresses. When they reached a point about a dozen yards from me I turned round and opened the gates to let them in. The party, however, altered their course, and headed in the direction of the Flower Pot Gates, to the north of the gardens. At the same time there was a sudden movement amongst the group; they fell into processional order, two deep, with the gentlemen at the head. Then, to my utter amazement, the whole crowd of them vanished; melted, as it seemed to me, into the air. All this happened within nine yards of where I was standing, in the centre of the broad gravel walk in front of the Palace. I rushed to the spot, looked up and down, but could see nothing or hear nothing to explain the mystery.'

Few policemen go on record as having seen a supernatural occurrence (though they are better placed than most to experience one) so that this report seems to have a special authenticity.

Henry VIII's daughter, Queen Elizabeth, died in the old Palace of Richmond at three in the morning of 24 March 1603. For days she had lain motionless on her deathbed, in a deep coma. Yet during this time servants and noblemen swore that they came across her walking vigorously through other rooms and passages in the palace, even as she lay dying upstairs.

Ham House stands just outside the boundaries of Richmond Park. This beautiful Jacobean mansion was haunted by the ghost of the wicked Duchess of Lauderdale. The story is that a little girl, six years old, woke up in the middle of the night to see an old woman scratching at the wall with her fingernails close to the fireplace. When the child sat up in bed the woman turned to look at her, and so horrible was the look on her face that the child screamed and hid beneath the bedclothes. People ran in to the room, and the girl emerged once she had been reassured that the old woman had gone. She told her story and the wall was closely examined at the place where she had seen the crone's fingers scratching. Beneath the plaster was a hollow space in which were hidden papers which proved that Elizabeth, Countess of Dysart, had murdered her husband in that room in order to marry the Duke of Lauderdale, favourite of Charles II and scourge of the Scots.

Chiswick

Barbara Palmer, Duchess of Cleveland, was also a favourite of Charles II for several years until he met Nell Gwynne. A great beauty as a young woman, in later life she grew to an enormous size and died from dropsy at her home, Walpole House, in Chiswick Mall. The ponderous sound of her footsteps is sometimes heard on the stairs there, and occasionally her grotesque figure is seen silhouetted against the great windows, her arms upflung, as she laments her lost beauty. Her sad, puffy face is also seen pressed against the window-glass of Chiswick House (built fifty years after her death), especially on stormy, moonlit nights. There is another strange phenomenon here – the smell of bacon and eggs that often pervades the rooms, though no cooking is taking place at the time anywhere in the house.

The Duchess of Cleveland (National Portrait Gallery).

Chiswick House.

It is said to be caused by 'the ghost of one of the mad cooks' though no one seems able to explain this intriguing solution further.

Not far away is Chiswick Warehouse – a vast furniture repository that for more than a century has been an unsightly landmark. No one knows what it is on the second floor of the building that so many workers find disturbing, but few like to work there alone. The most common complaint is the unnatural chill that strikes the face as this floor is entered, and the strange miasmic shapes that lurk there.

A ghost known as Percy haunts the Old Burlington pub in Church Street, Chiswick. This is supposed to date from Tudor times and was popular with the famous highwayman Dick Turpin. The modern police station at Chiswick occupies the site of Linden House, the scene of a violent murder in 1792 when Thomas Wainwright attacked his mother-in-law, Mrs Abercrombie, with a meat cleaver. Subsequently the site was used for a Fire Station where the ghost of Mrs Abercrombie would occasionally make an appearance in the basement, and it may be this ghostly lady who has made mysterious appearances on the third floor of the new police station.

Brentford and Ealing

Drinking the health of the Devil was a dangerous practice in the seventeenth century, and when Thompson, a waterman, tempted providence in this way in Mrs Phillpots's alehouse in September 1661, he must have had some idea of what to expect. A ballad commemorated his rash act, and the synopsis below the title summarises the incident perfectly:

Terrible News from BRAINFORD:
Or,
A perfect and true Relation of one *Thompson* a Waterman, and two more of that Function, being drinking in excess at *Brainford*, at the House of one Mrs. *Phillpots*, Thursday night, *September 12*, began a Health to the Devil, and another to his Dam; at which falling dead against the Table: With the Devils appearing in the Room visible, the Burial of the sinful Wretch; his Corps seeming heavy at first, but the Coffin afterward as light, as if there had been nothing in it.

Boston Manor House at Brentford is a fine Tudor/Jacobean building said to be haunted by a Lady Boston who was killed by her husband when he found her *in flagrante delicto* with another man. He was successful in keeping her death secret, burying her body in the park. Her ladyship glides shadow-like from the back of the house along a path leading to a great cypress tree, where she disappears. A lady in white, who drowned herself in the lake after an unhappy love-affair, also haunts the lawns at the back of the house.

In *Our Haunted Kingdom* Andrew Green tells of extraordinary events at a house (now demolished) at Ealing: 16 Montpelier Road. The building's unhappy history began in 1887 when Anne Hinchfield threw herself to her death from the top of its seventy-foot-high tower. She was twelve years old. In 1934 Mr Green's mother, a nurse, attended a sad sequel to the story. A nursemaid had thrown her young charge from the same tower and then jumped after her. While waiting for the police doctor to finish his examination of the bodies, Mrs Green had walked into the back garden and seen footprints appear on the wet grass in front of her. They stopped at a garden seat which moved slightly, as though someone had sat down on it.

After this the house stood empty for ten years 'but by then twenty suicides and the murder had occurred – all from the top of the tower'

228

16 Montpelier Road – the haunted house at Ealing (Mary Evans Picture Library).

(presumably Mr Green means the child's murder by the nursemaid). In the latter part of the war the property was requisitioned by the Government. In September 1944 Mr Green visited it with his father. In his book the author speaks of unseen hands helping him up the ladder to the top of the tower. When he was at the parapet he received a compelling mental urge 'to have a look in the garden. Walk over the parapet, it's only twelve inches to the lawn. You won't hurt yourself.' Fortunately it was at this instant that his father arrived at the top of the tower, and he grabbed his son by the scruff and so prevented another 'suicide'.

Subsequently the house was converted into flats, but maintained a sinister reputation, suffering specially from mysterious gas leaks which officials were always unsuccessful in tracing. New flats have occupied the site since 1970 but, again according to Mr Green, their occupants are still occasionally troubled by 'unusual noises'.

Hammersmith

Of all the London 'villages' Hammersmith has, over the years, suffered the most from ghosts. It has also attracted a number of bogus ghosts, and one such hoaxer caused the death of an innocent passer-by in 1804.

During the latter part of the previous year the inhabitants of Hammersmith had been greatly troubled by a white-cloaked figure which would jump out at them from ill-lit corners. One such incident caused a female victim, heavily pregnant with her second child, to be so shocked that she died within two days. On another occasion a wagon carrying sixteen passengers was ambushed by the 'ghost'. The driver abandoned his eight-horse team and his passengers 'precipitately', and only good fortune prevented disaster when the horses bolted. Little wonder, then, that the people of Hammersmith were indignant about these events. One of them, Francis Smith, decided to take the law into his own hands. An old history of Hammersmith tells the story:

On the night of Tuesday, January —, Francis Smith, an exciseman, who lodged at Mr Oakley's adjoining the White Hart, in Hammersmith, being at that house the same evening, and we may suppose, warm over his liquor, wrought himself up to the resolution of going in quest of the ghost. Unhappily supposing something more substantial than a mere airy form, he loaded a gun, and sallied out with William Girdler, the watchman of that part of Hammersmith, who had previously agreed upon a password, whereby they might distinguish each other, which was – 'Who comes there?' 'A friend.' 'Advance, friend.' Girdler then continued upon his regular beat, while Smith, that evening, went down Black Lion-lane. The circumstances that immediately followed, we cannot exhibit in a clearer point of view, than that of the ensuing evidence given before the Coroner, and upon the trial.

It appeared before the Coroner, that Smith took his station in Black Lion-lane, one of the places where the ghost used to make his escape when hard-pressed by his pursuers. He had not long been in waiting before he fancied he saw the wished-for object. A figure dressed in white (that is, Thomas Millwood, the plasterer, in a white jacket and trowsers)* approaching, Smith fired, and the mistaken object fell to the ground. Millwood was then on his way to

230

*The working-dress of that trade.

The Hammersmith 'Ghost'.

a house in the neighbourhood, where his wife was at work, to fetch her home, which his sister also relates upon the trial:

She said her brother was about 23 years of age, and was a plasterer by trade. On the evening of Tuesday last, he was at the house of his father, in Black Lion-lane, with whom the witness resides. He left the house between ten and eleven o'clock, and the witness being almost immediately struck with a presentiment that some accident would befall him, she accordingly went to the door and stood on some bricks, in order to look out for him. She then

231

heard a voice say, 'D———n you, who are you? Stand else I'll shoot you!' and the report of a gun immediately succeeded. Her brother was perfectly sober. The neighbourhood had for about two months been disturbed with the report of a ghost; but she did not believe, nor had ever heard, that her brother had assumed such an appearance.

Mr John Lock, wine merchant, in Black Lion-lane, Hammersmith, said, that as he was returning home from the Plough and Harrow, on the evening of Tuesday last, about half past 10 o'clock, in company with Mr Geo. Stow, he was accosted by Francis Smith, one of his Majesty's officers of excise, who asked to speak with him. Upon going aside, Smith informed him that he had shot a man, whom he believed to be the ghost. The witness informed Mr. Stow of the circumstances, and they accompanied Smith to the place. They found the deceased lying in a cross lane leading from Beaver-lane to Black Lion-lane, upon his back, apparently dead. The wound was under his left under jaw, and the skin of his face was exceedingly black. Smith did not appear sensible that he had done anything wrong, till the witness warned him of the consequences of such a step. He then seemed much affected, and said, that he had spoken twice, but had received no answer, and that the night was very dark.

William Girdler, a watchman, said, that he had a slight acquaintance with the deceased. That the neighbourhood had been much alarmed for two months past, with the rumour of a ghost walking through Black Lion-lane. That he went his rounds as usual on Tuesday evening last. That he had appointed to meet with Francis Smith, in order to go in search of the ghost. They had exchanged a watch-word, which they were to use. When the witness came near Mr. Stow's house he heard the report of a gun, and a few minutes afterwards, as he was going to the White Hart public-house, he met a young woman, who told him that he was wanted. Having gone on a little way, he met Smith, and asked him what intelligence? Smith answered very bad. They then met Mr. Stow, and went to the place where the deceased lay. Smith said that he would deliver himself up; that he had spoken to the deceased twice before he fired, but he would give him no answer.

The Coroner summed up the evidence with great ability and humanity, when the Jury, after some deliberation, returned a verdict of *Wilful Murder*. A warrant was then made out, and Smith committed to Newgate.

At his trial at the Old Bailey the evidence heard by the Coroner was repeated, and after instruction by the Judge – the Lord Chief Baron – they returned with a verdict of manslaughter. This was not acceptable to the Judge, who told them severely that if a man killed another with malice in his heart, then that was murder, even if he mistakenly killed the wrong man. Thus, without retiring again, the jury amended their verdict to one of guilty (but recommended mercy) and Smith was accordingly sentenced to be hanged on the following Monday, and his body given to the surgeons for dissection. However, by seven o'clock on the evening of the trial a stay of execution had been obtained, and Smith was later sentenced to spend one year in prison.

Meanwhile in Hammersmith the fate of the unfortunate Millwood had had a salutary effect on the 'ghost', for friends or relatives were instrumental in bringing him to justice. *The Times* of 6 January 1804 reported:

> The *real Hammersmith Ghost* has, it is said, been discovered. The lamented sacrifice of poor *Milwood*, the bricklayer, had such a powerful effect, that last Thursday evening an information was lodged before a Magistrate against one GRAHAM, a shoemaker, who has a wife and three children, for going out at night wrapped in a blanket, with a design to *represent a Ghost!* Graham was consequently taken into custody, and examined before the said Magistrate as to the cause of his assuming such an appearance, said, that he had done it in order to be revenged on the impertinence of *his Apprentices*, who had terrified his children by telling them stories of ghosts. He expected to check them of this disagreeable bent of their minds to the prejudice of his children, by presenting them, as they passed homewards, a figure of a ghost, which, it seems, he managed very successfully.

An amusing postscript to this story comes from the *Sunday Herald* of 22 January 1837:

> At the Kensington petty sessions on Tuesday, a bald-pated, grey-headed, old man, named James Graham, the individual who caused such excitement in the neighbourhood of Hammersmith some years since by enacting the part of a ghost, and during the pursuit of whom a man was unfortunately shot, was charged with another man named Joseph Mitchell, before Messrs. Codd and Barlow, the

sitting magistrates, with having been drunk and disorderly, on Saturday night, at Hammersmith.

Police constable Dowling stated, that between twelve and one o'clock on Saturday night, while he was conveying a disorderly prostitute to the station-house, the prisoners interfered and created such a disturbance that they were obliged to be taken into custody. They were first requested to go home quietly, but they declared that they would go where they pleased, and cursed and swore very much. They had both evidently been drinking.

His ghostship, in his defence, addressed the bench in a whining voice, as follows:— Sirs, on Saturday evening I went to the pawnbroker's to fetch home my best coat; for, as I always go two or three times on the Lord's day to a place of worship, I like to go respectable. You have heard I am charged with swearing. Now, as I am a worshipper of the true God, the great Jehovah, is it probable I would do so? I am a quiet spirit; and I associate, to quote the language of David, with 'the excellent of the earth, in whom I delight.' I am not a frequenter of low public-houses, but went to the Hammersmith coffee-house, and had half a pint of warm ale. While there my companion came in, and asked me to have a glass of ale; I said, 'Thank ye, but your's is fourpenny, and mine sixpenny.' We, however, had three pints of ale together, and when we came out the streets were in a very quiet state. Sirs, there is usually more than a hundred persons in the streets of Hammersmith at that time on a Saturday night, but then they were very quiet, more so than I have seen for years. I suppose it was owing to the working people having so little work, and consequently little money to spend. Well, Sirs, as we were going home we met a tender female between two policemen, who were conducting her to the station-house. I said to my companion, 'What a pity a delicate woman should be locked up on such a cold night.' The policeman said that if I interfered he would lock me up too. I immediately exclaimed, 'Lock me up! Impossible! I never violated the laws of my country. I never injured man nor mortal.' I then went to the station house. Now, Sirs, could it be possible I could be drunk? I'm a man that never will drink spirits, and, therefore was not drunk; I was just going home to my poor old woman, and to a warm bed, but they put me instead into what they call a cell, with boards for bed, and a block of wood for my pillow, by which I yesterday was prevented from what has been a blessing to me, the worship of my great Creator, the great God. I

234

am not an ignorant man, Sirs, I can give you a description of the Great God in language of—

Mr. Codd: Stop, I cannot take my ideas of God from the description of a man who frequents public-houses until twelve o'clock on Saturday nights. – Inspector Mullins, and policeman Ayres, T167, corroborated the evidence of Dowling when taken into custody. – His ghostship was fined 5s., and Mitchell 1s., or 14 days in the House of Correction.

The murder of Millwood and the arrest of Graham failed to put a stop to the bogus ghosts of Hammersmith. In 1824 another visitation was bothering the ever-vulnerable citizens – this time the ghost was far from being harmless, as the following report from a local journal relates:

THE HAMMERSMITH MONSTER

Such has been this personage's conduct of late, that he has now got the name of 'Monster,' instead of the comparatively harmless one of the 'new' Hammersmith Ghost. Not content with frightening women in lampless lanes, a sufficiently cowardly and cruel proceeding, he now rarely quits the terrified objects who may happen to come in his way without scratching or seriously wounding them. The indignation that has been hence produced amongst the inhabitants may be imagined, but it is hardly possible to conceive how much alarm is occasioned amongst the females in the neighbourhood. Several women have been so alarmed as to be seriously ill with fits, &c, for many days afterwards; others have been scratched or torn in the face, as if with hooks; and all are no little alarmed to go out after dark, except along the main road, even with protectors. . . . Suspicion has been directed to a crazy sort of person, who ostentatiously amuses himself with chalking on the gates and doors about Hammersmith divers gloomy sentences, such as 'Be ye ready!' 'Prepare to die!' 'Your end is near!' 'Ye are all lost sinners', &c. only he is said to be an aged person, and the 'Monster' has much activity. Many sums have been offered for the Monster's apprehension, especially by persons on the Upper Mall, that being a favourite haunt, and several stout persons are regularly on the look-out.

Within eight weeks this ghost was caught. He was 'a respectable-looking young man' named John Benjamin, a farmer and hay salesman from Harrow. He was committed for trial at the Sessions but unhappily there is no cutting to tell of his fate there. Eight peaceful years elapsed before another ghost arose – this time his antics appear to have had a sexual motivation:

RESUSCITATION OF THE HAMMERSMITH GHOST. – It is in the recollection of most of our readers that about eight years since much excitement was created by a report that a ghost had appeared to a number of persons in the neighbourhood of Hammersmith, Fulham, &c, several of whom, more particularly females, against whom he appeared to have a great animosity, had been much frightened and ill-treated by him. After continuing his freaks for some time, he became so troublesome that the parochial authorities adopted measures for his apprehension, and after watching for him for some nights he was taken in one of the lanes attired in full ghostly costume, and was sent by the magistrates to the House of Correction to undergo a little wholesome discipline for his pranks. Since that time nothing has been heard of his ghostship until about six weeks ago, when he re-appeared in a lane at North End, and it is reported that he has been seen subsequently in Webb's-lane, Hammersmith, and Acton, but the principal scene of his adventures is stated to be the mud huts in Chiswick-lane, and that the servant of a Mr. Scott was attacked by him there, his assaults, as before, being directed against females. On Saturday night last it was currently reported that he had been taken by the police at Acton, attired in a large white dress, with long nails or claws, by which he was enabled to scale walls and hedges for the purpose of making himself scarce when requisite; and that when brought to the station-house he proved to be a celebrated captain of sporting notoriety. Several of the inhabitants attended the Hammersmith, &c., petty sessions on Monday, in the hope of obtaining an audience of the spiritual *incognito*, when it was found that the statement of his apprehension was premature. Another report states him to be dressed in armour, and that he has laid a wager that he will strip the clothes off a certain number of females in a given time, and that he has now only one more to strip to win the bet. It is to be hoped that the police will put a stop to the pranks of his ghostship previous to his completing his task, and that he may receive a proper reward for his exertions.

The theory concerning the wager is interesting in that a similar explanation was put forward for the anti-social activities of Spring-Heel Jack, whose startling appearances were to terrorise Londoners south of the river four years or so later.

Although there are no accounts of this ghost being captured, it seems that for one reason or another his troublesome antics ceased (perhaps he moved to Barnes or Blackheath) and apart from the report of a ghost met with in St Peter's Square in the mid 1850s, the remainder of the century appears to have been free of ghosts.

In fact local interest in Hammersmith ghosts was only rekindled a hundred years later when in July 1955 the *West London Observer* carried an article stating that the Hammersmith ghost appears every fifty years in St Paul's churchyard when the moon is full. An aged local resident told the reporter that he had seen the ghost on its last appearance in 1905, 'wearing a white winding sheet, its eyes flaming'. The *Observer* had calculated that the following Wednesday night would be the date of its next visitation, and its intrepid reporter intended to sit up and wait for it in the churchyard.

Four hundred spectators also turned up, enough to put off any but the most brazen ghost. Hoaxers, having avoided the police who had sealed off the churchyard, entertained the crowd briefly, but most left after the clock struck midnight, no ghost having appeared. The reporter and a few hardy souls remained, however. They had remembered that British Summer Time made the appointed time an hour later, and were rewarded by the sight of a figure draped in brilliant white, that had no legs, and seemed to float from the church porch to a tomb that stood apart, dedicated to members of the Fenn and Colvill families who died between 1792 and 1848. While the reporter hurried to another, better, vantage point, other watchers saw the ghost float on to the tomb and then vanish inside it. Four other people watching from a window overlooking the churchyard confirmed this story, and added that they noticed a strange wind blow through the trees which heralded the arrival of the ghost. All this was in marked contrast with scenes at the churchyard earlier when police, who had locked the gates, were kept busy chasing away ghostly impersonators, mainly 'Teddy boys in white shirts'. Presumably the next scheduled appearance of the ghost is in 2005.

The most likely ghost to haunt Hammersmith would seem to me to be Sir Nicholas Crispe, a local tycoon who died in 1665 having just been made a baronet. He lived at Crabtree House, a mansion also known as Great House and later as Brandenburg House when it was

Sir Nicholas Crispe (Guildhall Library).

238

the home of Queen Caroline after the death of George III. In his will Sir Nicholas directed that his heart should be placed in an urn in Hammersmith Chapel '. . . where for over 150 years it was the macabre custom to take it out on the anniversary of its interment and "fresh it with a glass of wine", a custom which only ceased when the heart became decayed, and was finally enclosed in a leaden case.' (*More Different than Others*, Angus Macnaghten, 1971). The chapel stood on the site of the present church where there is still a monument to Crispe.

Hammersmith also had a very famous haunted house. This was Beavor Lodge, the home of the artist Sir William Richmond, and later of his son, Sir Arthur. Unfortunately the lodge was pulled down after IBM bought the property in 1928. It was an eighteenth-century house, plain in style, yet with pleasing proportions and a garden that ran down to the Thames. This was reached by crossing Beavor Lane (then known as Green Lane) and entering by a small gate in the wall. The house was built by Samuel Beavor (or Bevor) who died in 1761, and there is nothing in its subsequent history to account for its motley array of ghosts. Most famous of these (because she was seen so frequently) was the Grey Lady. Two theories conflicted in explaining her presence. One said that coiners once occupied the property, and when a woman accidentally discovered them at their work they killed her by sewing her up in a sack and throwing her into the Thames. Another explanation was given at a seance held to solve the haunting. The sitters were told that the ghost was the spirit of a nun who secretly had a baby. To avoid disgrace she killed the child, burying its body in a meadow opposite the lodge.

Sir William Richmond, his wife, and their children took up residence in the lodge in the early 1870s.

Almost immediately all the members of the household complained of hearing noises in the lower part of the house – windows would be violently shaken every night between two and four o'clock, and steps were heard apparently going about the house. *I myself frequently had a door opened for me before entering a room,* as if a hand had hastily turned the handle and thrown it open. Then, occasionally, we used to hear sounds of someone sobbing and sighing, *deep, long sighs at all times of the day.* I used to hear these sounds in my bedroom, and on the little staircase leading to it; my husband used to hear them in the dining-room beneath. Sometimes

I would hear the sound of stitching in the room out of my bedroom, as if some hard and very coarse work were being done, and then the sound of something being dragged across the floor. I got to have a feeling which was most uncomfortable at times of being *watched*.

When Mrs Richmond had these experiences she had not heard the story of the coiners who sewed the poor woman into the sack.

The first sight of the Grey Lady was in October 1875, when Mrs Richmond was reading to three of her children in the dining-room. She rang for the parlour-maid and on hearing the door open, looked up to see a strange female figure, dressed in a grey diaphanous material, who walked up to the table, behind the children. For a long moment Mrs Richmond stared at her, then the woman turned towards the door and, as she moved towards it, seemed to dissolve away into nothing. Within the next eight weeks two of the servants saw the figure, on separate occasions, without knowing of their mistress's experience. One was so upset that she gave up her post at Beavor Lodge. The following year the Richmonds' six-year-old daughter, who slept in a small room adjoining that of her parents, awoke screaming. They ran to her at once and she told them that she had just seen 'a wicked-looking old grey woman' at the end of the bed, who had stood looking at her with evil, hateful eyes – '. . . then suddenly she went down through the floor with a loud noise.' Again, the little girl had not been told of any supernatural happening in the house.

The experiences were now growing to be more substantial – Mrs Richmond even had her hair pulled by the ghost – yet her husband remained sceptical even though his wife wrote of them to the Psychical Research Society. Then he, too, was drawn into the web of haunting.

One autumn day he was alone in the house, and had settled in his favourite chair by the fire, his collie, Nelson, by his side fast asleep. The dog woke suddenly, growling, and as he did so the handle of the door shook, but the door itself remained closed – yet a woman stood on the threshold of the room. She was dressed in the habit of a nun, her face concealed by a veil. The dog cowered at the feet of his master, shaking with fear, until after a few moments the figure disappeared as suddenly and mysteriously as it had come, dissolving into the atmosphere.

The Grey Lady was also often seen in the garden where she particularly favoured a seat beneath a pear tree. Once she was seen at the same time by two different people (one a bishop) from separate vantage points some distance apart. They were able to compare notes and the descriptions tallied exactly.

Apart from the activities of the Grey Lady, family, guests, and staff were sometimes disturbed by a noisy gathering known by the Richmonds as the 'Roystering Beavorites'. Occupants of the bedrooms would be troubled by the sounds of loud voices in the early hours of the morning. There would be the slamming of carriage doors, etc., as though a boisterous party was breaking up, though on occasion the roistering would continue for two or three hours. Often such a disturbance presaged the appearance of the Grey Lady within a week or so. Investigation in daylight never revealed anything amiss downstairs, and the noises always ceased abruptly if anyone left his or her room to investigate.

The Grey Lady was finally put to rest after the seance when she had explained the reasons for her spirit being earthbound. After prayers were offered for the peace of her soul the household was left in peace: though on his deathbed in 1921 Sir William Richmond pointed to a shadowy part of the room and painfully gasped '*There stands the Grey Lady.*'

Two further stories of the Richmond family are of interest. One of the favourite models of the Pre-Raphaelites was a young Italian, Gaetano Meo, who had the striking good looks of the Classical Greeks. He, too, became an artist of talent, and in later life used to recall the strange incident that he experienced on first visiting Beavor Lodge:

Do you believe in ghosts? I do not! and yet I once had a strange experience for which I cannot account. Eccolo! I went to sit to Mr Richmond for the first time. Now when there are two doors to a house, I always choose the humbler one, so I went round to the back door and rang the bell. Almost instantly the door was opened, and there stood before me a very pretty, dark-haired lady, who welcomed me graciously, and to my surprise addressed me in faultless Italian.

'Why do you come to this door?' she asked in that language; 'go round to the other one.' And I went.

Afterwards I explained to Mr Richmond why I had come to the front door, and I asked him who was the pretty lady who had spoken to me in such perfect Italian. He looked perplexed, and said

Geo Phoenix
1893

he could think of no one in the house answering my description; his wife was out, and no one else knew my native language. Enquiries were made, but the mystery could not be solved.

I never saw the lady again or discovered who she could have been; but some time after I saw a painting of Mr Richmond's first wife who died so soon after her marriage. *And there I recognised the face of the pretty lady who had first welcomed me to Beavor Lodge!* (Quoted in *The Richmond Papers*, ed. A. M. W. Stirling, 1927.)

Finally, and from the same source, there is another story connected with the Pre-Raphaelites. In 1896 Sir William was on a tour of Italy, staying in the Etruscan town of Volterra. There he had a dream startling for its lucidity. He dreamt that he was in St Paul's Cathedral attending the funeral of his great friend Millais.

. . . But instead of one coffin there were two, which were placed respectively on either side of the pavement which led down into the crypt. The committal prayer was about to be said, when from one of the coffins issued forth the dead man – but not the Millais Richmond had left in London, broken by illness and suffering; this was the Millais of forty years before, the Sir Galahad who had enchained Richmond's boyish fancy – Millais in the splendour of his early manhood, in the full tide of his buoyant, beautiful youth. Towering beside the coffin, he stood erect before the crowd, he laughed, and tossing his shapely head he cried in forcible, characteristic speech: 'I'll be damned if you bury me! Bury the other – the old chap! *I* am immortal. *I* am not dead at all. I live, and shall live for ever!'

The friends assembled for the interment remonstrated with him, but the Youth, standing firm and defiant, held his ground. '*I am not dead*,' he persisted, '*and never shall be!*'

Further pressure, however, prevailed, and at last the splendid young fellow, palpitating with life, went back into his box, to be lowered into his grave in company with the quiescent 'old chap' in the other coffin!

The dream was so powerful that Richmond was determined to travel back to England as quickly as possible, and in fact had made all preparations for departure when a letter arrived telling him that Millais had died in London a few days previously. He was still able to hurry back in time to attend his friend's funeral in St Paul's.

Sir William Richmond, 1842–1921 (National Portrait Gallery).   243

Chelsea and Kensington

Chelsea's reputation as a Bohemian quarter is reflected in the character of its ghosts, though there do not seem to be as many here as might be expected. Cheyne Walk is said to be haunted by the ghost of a bear (seen, too, at the Tower of London) which seems likely, since in the sixteenth century there was an arena here where the vicious sport of bear-baiting was promoted. One of the most beautiful of the riverside houses here has an excellent selection of ghosts on offer. The bear is occasionally seen in the garden, and a grotesque figure 'something like a Dutch doll' was once seen leaning from an upstairs window by several house guests. A dog that was with them showed signs of utmost terror, until the frightening object suddenly disappeared. Quite frequently a gathering in one of the rooms would hear the sound of something limp and heavy being dragged across the floor – in the very room where they stood. The sound made all talking and laughing stop abruptly. Nothing was ever seen to account for the noise. On one notable occasion the owner of the house rudely dashed from the room where he was in conversation with a visitor. Returning apologetically he said that he had suddenly had a vision of a woman lying on the chesterfield in the room, her throat gashed open. Apparently a particularly messy murder had been committed in the house many years before.

There is another animal ghost in Glebe Place, close by. The eccentric Dr Phene lived in a large house here; he was so devoted to his horse (which had once saved his life) that he had it buried within sight of his house when it died. After his death many people claimed to have seen the ghost of a man on horseback in the area between Cheyne Walk and King's Road (to the west of Oakley Street). When Dr Phene's property was redeveloped the skeleton of a horse was discovered in the garden. A nursemaid who was burnt to death on the top floor in 1912 is said to haunt a house in Milbourne Grove.

The Richmond family lived in a remarkably well-haunted house in Hammersmith and seem to have been particularly sensitive to the supernatural. In Mrs Stirling's *Life's Little Day* the following story is told, in the words of Sir William Richmond's grandmother:

> My mother died when we lived in the City. My father immediately left the house and took another in Chelsea at the back of which was

Cheyne Walk, Chelsea (Guildhall Library).

a large and neglected garden. Pleased at the liberty we thus gained, we City children delighted in that garden for games and pastimes, and we had with us in our romps a Newfoundland dog of a breed which had just been imported.

One day we were engaged in playing 'catch who catch can'. There were four of us – my eldest brother, I, and two others. My eldest brother, running first, came to some worn stone steps amidst the bushes which descended apparently into a kind of hole. I followed. Suddenly we stopped short. There at the bottom of the steps stood our mother, dressed in a blue silk gown with white spots. Saying nothing, but standing there in the attitude of warning my brother back, her appearance struck terror into us, and we retreated immediately.

Upon our returning to the house, we at once related the fact that we had seen our mother in the garden. Our father grew very angry, and sent us supperless to bed for what he considered was obviously a monstrous lie.

A few days afterwards the Newfoundland dog was missing: search was made for him in the garden, and by and by it was found that he must have made his way down these same steps where we had intended to go, he must have trodden upon some rotten planks which were at the bottom, and so fallen into a deep well which was concealed there, and been drowned.

In the same book Mrs Stirling tells an equally remarkable story of George Eliot who came to live in Chelsea after her marriage and died there in 1880.

Respecting George Eliot, William De Morgan told me the following story which he heard from Mrs. Katherine Macquoid, whose works of fiction began to appear in 1859, and who lived to be a nonagenarian. For many years Mrs. Macquoid occupied a house in Chelsea, and when George Eliot married Mr. Cross and came to settle in the same neighbourhood, Mrs. Macquoid told her husband that she intended to call upon the new resident. 'But,' she informed De Morgan, 'before I had an opportunity of doing so, a curious thing happened. One night I woke suddenly and saw the figure of George Eliot standing between the bed and the wall. The apparition was distinct and unmistakable. I heard a voice giving me a message and then the phantom vanished. Next morning I could remember nothing of the message except "sixty-one", which I feared meant I should die at the age of sixty-one. When I saw my son, however, that day, he told me that George Eliot was dead. She had died about the time I saw the apparition, and at the age of sixty-one.'

An Irish friend, Harry MacDowell, of Celbridge, County Kildare, has provided an authentic Chelsea ghost story. It is best told in his own words:

We moved into a newly-built house in Elystan Street, Chelsea, in 1960. It stood on a bombed site where there had been a tombstone-maker's yard before the War. One night, having gone to bed on the second floor, I found I'd left my book in the dining-room so I went down to get it. When I returned to the bedroom Joan, my wife, said 'Well, were they there?' I was quite unaware that for about four years she, too, had often entered the ground-floor dining-room (which occupied the entire width of the house at the back) and been aware of a crowd of poorly dressed people milling about in a sort of foggy atmosphere. The house was built on a gateway because when I first saw it – half-built – the pavement outside had not been altered and one could see where the kerb curved in. Afterwards I looked for books on the area in Chelsea Library and I remember one which said that the street was part of a very rough area in the 1820s (or perhaps a little later) and that a policeman had been strung up by the mob on a lamp-post.

An interesting feature of this account is that the haunting had come fresh to Harry, yet Joan knew that he had experienced it without him mentioning it. I have been unable to discover if later owners of the house were also troubled by this unusual milling mob of ghosts.

The foreboding of death features in a story of Kensington that dates from December 1913, and is told in Charles Harper's *Haunted Houses*. As the Vicar of one of the churches there was leaving the building after choir practice, he was stopped by an agitated lady who begged him to accompany her to a house near by in Montpelier Square. She told him that someone was dying there who was concerned about the state of his soul and needed to consult a man of God before he died. Thus he walked with her to a waiting cab which drove them a short way to an imposing town-house. The lady hustled the Vicar out of the cab and he ran up the steps of the house and rang the bell. The door was opened at once by a butler. What followed is described by Charles Harper:

'Does Mr.—— live here?'

'Yes, sir.'

'I hear he is seriously ill and has sent for me.'

The butler seemed astonished almost beyond words. He expostulated that his master was not ill, that as a matter of fact he was in the best of health.

'But this lady——,' exclaimed the Vicar, as he turned round, and then an expression of blank astonishment came over him.

The taxicab and the lady had completely disappeared.

But they can do that, however, without any supernatural implications.

The butler looked on the clergyman as either a madman or a practical joker, and was about to slam the door when his master came along the passage and inquired what it was all about.

'Are you Mr. ——?' asked the clergyman. 'I heard that you were seriously ill, that you were concerned about your soul, and that you had sent for me.'

He described the lady who had brought him, and the 'dying' man said he could not identify her; that he had no such friend or acquaintance. They discussed this matter on the doorstep for a few moments, and then the clergyman was invited to come inside.

'It is very strange,' said Mr. ——, 'that you should have been sent on such an errand in such a mysterious way. As a matter of fact, though I am perfectly well, I have been troubled lately about the state of my soul, and I have been seriously contemplating calling upon you to discuss the matter with you. Now that you are here let us brush aside this strange incident, and if you will give me the time, we will discuss what has been on my conscience.'

The clergyman stayed for an hour or so, and it was then arranged that his new acquaintance should come to the church the next morning and they would continue their discussion after service. He did not appear at the church, and the vicar, very much interested, called to see what was the matter. He was met at the door by the butler, *who told him that his master had died ten minutes after he left the house on the previous evening.*

They went upstairs to the bedroom where the dead man lay, and on a table in the middle of the room stood a portrait of the lady who had brought the clergyman in the cab from the church.

'Who is that?' asked the astonished clergyman.

'That, sir,' replied the butler, 'is my master's wife *who died fifteen years ago.*'

Kensington Palace was the birthplace of Queen Victoria and remains a Royal Residence. Several of our monarchs died here, among them George II. He was a reluctant King, unhappy at being forced to live away from his native Hanover. However Kensington Palace was his favourite English home and he spent his last days here, fretfully watching the weather-vane above the entrance. He was waiting for the wind to change so that news from Germany could reach him, muttering in broken English 'Vhy tondt dey com?' It is these words, and his pained, wan face, that are occasionally heard and seen at the palace. He died just before his messengers arrived in England with the long-overdue dispatches.

The almost complete destruction of Holland House in 1940 was a grievous blow to the architectural heritage of London. This was one

248

Holland House (Guildhall Library).

of the most spectacular of Jacobean mansions: built for Sir Walter Cope in 1607, it was inherited by his daughter who married Sir Henry Rich, first Earl of Holland, in 1622. He added to the house and employed the most talented artists and craftsmen of his day to decorate the interior. In the Civil War he supported the Royalists, and was captured at St Neots. After a spell of imprisonment in Warwick Castle he was brought to trial and beheaded in 1649 in Palace Yard. His execution gave the Earl the opportunity to make a last gesture of defiance against his dour enemies. 'He lived like a knave, and died like a fool. He appeared on the scaffold dressed in a white satin waistcoat, and a white satin cap with silver lace. After some divine conference with a clergyman and an affectionate leave-taking with a friend, he turned to the executioner and said, "Here, my friend, let my clothes and my body alone: there is ten pounds for thee – that is better than my clothes, I am sure of it. And when you take up my head, do not take off my cap."' (From Clarendon's *History of the Rebellion*.) Rich nevertheless died bravely, and the headsman succeeded in taking his head from his body with one blow.

It was the Earl's ghost that used to haunt the magnificent Gilt Room – the principal reception room on the first floor of the house. 'Its first lord . . . issues forth at midnight from behind a secret door, and walks slowly through the scenes of former triumphs with his head in his hand. To add to this mystery, there is a tale of three spots of blood on one side of the recess whence he issues – three spots which

can never be effaced.' (From *The History of Holland House* by the Princess Marie Lichtenstein.) Thus the headless Earl is the archetypal ghost of the English mansion.

The later history of Holland House was hardly less interesting. It was frequented by painters, poets, and statesmen, among them Byron, Scott and Macaulay. In the grounds was an avenue poetically known as Nightingale Lane, and this was the scene of another ghostly encounter, which also occurred to a member of the Rich family. The diarist John Aubrey wrote of this 'spiritual experience' in his *Miscellanies* of 1696:

> The beautiful Lady Diana Rich, daughter to the Earl of Holland, as she was walking in her father's garden at Kensington, to take the air before dinner, about eleven o'clock, being then very well, met her own apparition, habit and everything, as in a looking-glass. About a month after she died of small-pox. And 'tis said that her sister, the Lady Isabella Thinne, saw the like of herself also before she died. This account I had from a person of honour.
>
> A third sister, Mary, was married to the Earl of Breadalbane, we are informed, and it has been recorded that she also, not long after her marriage, had some such warning of her approaching dissolution.

Part of the east wing of the house survived the bombing and this has been restored as a Youth Hostel. A party of Ghanaian students staying there in July 1965 believed they saw the Earl walking in the park late one night, head in hand.

From the mansions and palaces of the district we turn to ghosts of more humble backgrounds. In *Canadian Homes*, January 1961, it was reported that 51 Peel Street, close to Holland Park, was troubled by the sounds of ghostly footsteps. The house was described as being tiny and charming, typical of the area, and the Canadian couple had often heard inexplicable sounds such as footsteps during the ten years or so that they had lived there, as had many of their visitors. Apparently two workmen were killed when they fell from the roof during the construction of the house.

The phantom bus that haunts North Kensington between the Cambridge Gardens and Chesterton Road junctions on St Mark's Road is one of the strangest of London ghosts, even though it seems to have lain dormant for almost fifty years. Its presence was acknowledged after the death of a young motorist in June 1934. He

A London General omnibus. 251

suffered a terrible death when his car, for no apparent reason, swerved off the road, hit a lamp-post, and burst into flames. A reason for the accident was put forward at the inquest by several witnesses, who spoke of their own encounters with the ghost bus. It always appeared on the same stretch of road, usually at the junction of Cambridge Gardens with St Mark's Road. It was always a No. 7 operated by the London General Omnibus Company. Thus it carried the word 'General' on its side: the LGOC became the London Passenger Transport Board in 1933, and by June 1934 nearly all of its fleet bore the 'London Transport' lettering. Incidents involving the bus always occurred at the same time, 1.15 a.m., a strange hour for a No. 7 to be about. Witnesses came forward to tell how the bus tore down the middle of the road towards them, and how they desperately swung their vehicles off the road to avoid it. When they looked back no bus was ever seen. After the inquest even more people came forward with their own experiences, while others put forward rational explanations (it was a late staff bus, or an apparition caused by reflections, etc.). However it would seem to be a difficult tale to tell policemen today, as they lean on the window of an erratically driven car, breathalysers at the ready. . . .

Finally, a mention of London's best-known haunted pub – the Grenadier, behind Hyde Park Corner in Wilton Road. As befits its locality, it is a smart, ultra-respectable place today, but in the early nineteenth century it was much less respectable. Its best rooms served as a mess for officers from barracks close by, while the other ranks were allowed to drink below, in the cellars. The ghost is supposed to be that of a young subaltern who was caught cheating at cards. He was so badly beaten by his fellow players that he died in the cellars, where he had staggered to avoid further punishment. His spirit still haunts the Grenadier to remind the landlord and his customers of this former patron's brutal demise. The ghost always appears in September and manifests itself in a number of different ways; sometimes it is a figure glimpsed roaming through rooms supposed to be empty, sometimes as a mischievous poltergeist moving things for the hell of it. On one occasion it was seen by a Chief Superintendent from Scotland Yard. The landlord of the time told the story to the *Chelsea News*: 'We saw puffs of smoke without a cigarette. The Superintendent put his hand up to where the smoke was coming from and he pulled it away when he felt the heat of the cigarette. But there was nothing there.'

South London

Blackfriars and Southwark

The doyen of ghost-book writers, Elliott O'Donnell, collected the story of the ghost of a pig-faced lady which used to haunt a house in Markham Square, Chelsea. The story may have had its origins in an obscure pamphlet in the British Library printed in 1641 – *A Certain Relation of the Hog-faced Gentlewoman*:

> The pig-faced lady, whose name is Tamakin Skinker, was born at Wirkham on the Rhine, in 1618. Some people assume she is English-born, being a native of Windsor on the Thames. All the limbs and lineaments on her body is well featured and proportioned, only her face, which is the ornament and beauty of all the rest, has the nose of a hog or swine; which is not only a stain and blemish, but a deformed ugliness making all the rest loathsome, contemptible, and odious to all that look upon her. Her language is only the hoggish Dutch 'ough, ough', or the French 'owee, owee'. Forty thousand pounds is the sum offered to the man who will consent to marry her. Her person is most delicately formed; and of the greatest symmetry. Her Manners are, in general, simple and unoffending, but when she is in want of food, she articulates, certainly something like the sound of pigs when eating, which may perhaps be a little disagreeable. Miss Skinker is always dressed well. She is now in London looking for a husband. She lives in Blackfriars or Covent Garden. The doubt between the two places is lest the multitude of people who would flock to see her, might, in their eagerness, pull the house down in which she resides.

The poor creature's life must have been a nightmare, so it is small wonder that she returned to haunt the house where she lived, and from *Phantoms of the Theatre* by Raymond Lamont Brown it seems that her home was in Blackfriars. He tells how an actor, William Barrett, lived in a house (now demolished) in Blackfriars. He had taken it because of the cheap rent – no one else seemed to want to live there. This is Barrett's story, as related in Mr Brown's book:

'One night' said the actor to friends at Covent Garden one day, 'as we were about to retire and had reached the foot of the staircase leading to our bedroom, my wife and I heard footsteps on the

landing above us. Both my wife and I were aghast. 'Oh, no, we've got burglars!' I gasped. But no. A rustling of a lady's gown followed. Then the air seemed to go chilly and cold. Death seemed to be hovering about in its most terrible form. The footsteps became clearer, and there appeared before our eyes. at the top of the stairs, a lady in an old-fashioned dress – I should say probably early seventeenth century. Then she began to descend the stairs. Strange to say, she had the head of a pig, an ugly, repulsive pig – small eyes and snout complete. Well, down this horrible creature came – moving toward us. My wife screamed and then fainted. I managed to catch her as she fell. Looking up, my wife still in my arms, I observed with great pleasure that the terrible thing had vanished.'

Southwark Cathedral is a friendly church in every sense. As a photographer, I frequently have to work alone in churches and many induce a feeling of great unease, as though someone is standing, unseen, just behind you. Southwark has never inspired such a fear, yet an unaccountable happening was experienced by myself and a colleague while we were working there.

We had been photographing the interior of the cathedral for a guidebook. As daylight faded we packed up our lights and cameras and put them away in a vestry overnight. The door of the vestry was locked, and so was the church itself; no functions were being held there that night.

When the film was processed we found that the frame between the last picture of the afternoon and the first of the morning had been exposed, though not by us. It showed a fantastic array of colourful, seemingly meaningless, squiggles, amid symmetrical patterns like the ones made swinging a torch from a string in front of the lens in a dark-room. We were certain that these had not been made accidentally (the shutter having been open while the camera was being carried, for example) and so felt that a supernatural explanation was possible. We showed the transparency to several people at the church who were as intrigued as we were, and it was eventually sent to the then Bishop of Southwark, Mervyn Stockwood, who has a great interest in psychical research. Unfortunately the picture was lost in transit, and we have never been able to repeat the incident as an experiment.

The Bishop's House at Southwark was haunted by the ghost of an old Polish woman who had died there. Her melancholy ghost depressed the staff (though not the Bishop who found it easy to tolerate her) so that in the end a service of exorcism was held. The ghost has not been heard of since.

Southwark has always been one of the most colourful parts of London with a strong character of its own. The pubs around Borough Market still testify to this. Its character seems to have been just as earthy in earlier days, judging from the accounts which came out of the Borough then, like this *Full and True Relation of the Appearing of a dreadful Ghost* which was published in 1690:

It so happened, that one *J. Dyer,* a Joyner, reputed to be a Man of much Honesty and Integrity, industrious and laborious in his Calling, marrying some years since to a Woman, by whom he had divers Children; in process of time, her Peevishness and turbulent Temper created some Mis-understanding between them, and Cavils with the Neighbours, and what contributed the more to the Latter, was their keeping a Publick House at the time in *Deadmans-Place* in *Southwark.* The Husband, it seems, perceiving her much given to love Strife and Contention, laboured to restrain her by all manner of ways, but those availed not, till Death, that tames the most Headstrong, stept in, and took her out of the World. And now the good Man, upon this Alteration in his Family, promised himself a more comfortable Life than what he had enjoyed during his Marriage, but it proved otherwise, for she who disturbed him in her Life-time, was resolved to disquiet him after her Death: It seems she was discontented upon her Death-Bed, and the Cause, amongst other things, was, because her Husband lent Money without her Consent, which she feared would be lost.

Long her Body had not been buried, but the House was disquieted in the Night time with unusual Noise, which by degrees increased, to the Terror of those that were in it, or lived near it; but this not sufficing, she one Night appearing to him in a threatning Shape, with a flaming and dreadful Countenance, whilst he was trembling at so horrid a Sight, and praying for Mercy and Protection from God, he received a mighty Blow on the Arm with a Pot, which has rendered that Arm lame, if not useless.

Ever since, at other times, there were other Shapes and Disturbances, so that terrified with such unusual Disorder, he left that House as a Place haunted by evil Spirits; and leaving his Children, till he could settle again, with some of the Neighbours, their Houses were likewise terrified with Noises and disturbances,

256

insomuch that they were forced to send them away, and then the Disturbance ceased, as also it did in the other House after the Removal.

This person, after the aforesaid Removal, settled in *Rochester-Yard,* distant from the former Dwelling, thinking there to be quiet; but it was not his Luck, for there the Noise and Disturbance began again in a more fearful Manner, to almost distracting him; for instead of one Spirit, it is said there came three, two of them in Ruffs, and all in threatning Postures, with Flame and Fury.

This wearied him in a manner out of his Life, as not knowing whether to fly from such a Pestilence, yet resolved to try once more, and being advised to get farther off, he took a Conveniency in *Winchester-Yard*, near St. *Mary Overies Stairs*, where he now is; but this was not a sufficient Flight from the pursuing Spirit, here again the revengeful Ghost found him with Terror and Amazement, growing more and more desperate, for on *Sunday* Night last, being the second of *March*, as he was in his Bed, he was violently seized by a strong Hand, and very barbarously used, though he at that time could discern no certain Shape; and so far proceeded this malicious Spirit to destroy him, that his Breath was stop'd till he was almost stifled, but it appeared after a hard Strugling, he was freed, though left in a very sad Condition. He says he felt a perfect hand, but for a time such Terror seized him, that he made no further Search, praising God that the Spirit had no Power over his Life, though it has brought him almost to the Gates of Death.

Many hundred of People have been to see him, to satisfie their Curiosity by enquiry, and we hear some Ministers have been Consulted to give him Spiritual Consolation, and bear up his Spirits, Least this great Affliction should Craze his Wits.

Another delightful story from Southwark deserves mention, though it hardly involves anything ghostly. This is the synopsis of the ballad from its title-page:

A *WARNING* For all as such desire to Sleep upon the GRASS: By the Example of *Mary Dudson* Maid-servant to Mr. *Phillips* a Gardener, dwelling in *Kent street*, in the Borough of *Southwark*: Being a most strange, but true Relation how she was found in a Dead-sleep in the Garden, but no ordinary Noise could awake her. As also how an Adder entered into her body, the manner of her long Sickness, with a brief Discovery of the Cause at length by her

The Ghost of Mr. Powel.

strange and most miraculous Vomiting up of about fourteen young Adders, and one old Adder, on *August* 14, 1664, about fourteen Inches in length, the Maid is yet living. The like to this hath not been known in this Age.

The ballad follows, after which:

> *Those that desire to be satisfied of the Truth more at large, may repair to this wofull Wight, a Spectacle of Gods mercy, and an object of true Charity, being a constant Laborer in her health: It is hard to say whether she will live or die. She lyeth over against the sign of the* Ship *in* Kent-street *in the Borough of* Southwark. *This Relation the Author had from her own mouth.**

A final seventeenth-century ghost famous through pamphlet and ballad, was that of Mr Powel, a baker who lived close to the Falcon inn, Bankside. His spirit was still restless five months after his death: so much so that it had driven his son and all but one of the servants from the house. This was Joan, a housemaid, who bravely ignored all the provocations of the ghost until it confronted her in the garden:

> ... towards the Evening, going into the Garden, under a Pear-Tree, she espied her old Master standing up, with his Fists knit close together, his Eyes half sunk in his Head, his Face extraordinary Black, and in the same Cloaths he used to wear when he was alive.
>
> This sudden Apparition, did very much amaze and startle her, putting her into a great trembling, quivering, and shaking; since which time, she hath been very ill, and on *Monday* last lay dangerous sick in the Borough, having left the Dwelling-house of her old Master, situated near the *Faulcon* at the *Banck-side*: But the troubled Spirit remains there still, and the House is as much haunted as formerly; notwithstanding some Artists (by some called Conjurers) remain there day and night, using all possible means they can to lay this troubled Spirit, and are continually reading and making of Circles, burning of Wax Candles, and *Juniper*-wood; but as yet all proves unfeasible; only thus far they effected their work, That some few nights ago, having made a great Circle in the Garden, the Spirit of Master *Powel* appeared, to whom one of them

---

*From *The Daily Telegraph*, 13 March 1982: A young woman who underwent surgery for severe stomach pains had a six-foot snake in her intestines, the Syrian daily *Al Baath* reported yesterday. Surgeons were unable to remove the reptile.

Doctors reportedly speculated that the woman, Khadija el Reefi, 25, from the town of Aleppo, drank well water polluted with snake eggs as a child. Surgery in Syria to remove the snake was unsuccessful, and Khadija was sent to Spain for a second operation which also failed to remove the snake despite using anaesthesia on it.

The newspaper said the snake 'cheeped' like a chicken when it was hungry.
It claimed Khadija and people near her could hear the snake sounds.

The Falcon Inn, Bankside (Guildhall Library).

said: *We conjure thee to depart to thy place of Rest.* He answered, Wo be to those that were the cause of my coming hither.

The rest (being eight in number) kept close to their Books, and fain would have brought him into the Circle, but could not; whereupon one of them said, *The Son of God appeared to destroy the works of the Devil:* which caused him to vanish away like a flash of Fire, hitting one of them upon the Leg, who hath lain lame ever since, and left such a scent of Brimstone in the Garden, that all the *Juniper*-wood they could burn for many hours together, could not take away that Sulphurous smell. Many there hath been to enquire of the Truth hereof, who are very well satisfied therein, and some of the Gentlemen (before specified) still remain in the House, to allay the Spirit, if they can; for it is conjectured, there hath been much Money hid, either in the Garden or about the House, which as yet cannot be discovered.

Unfortunately it is not known whether the 'Conjurers' (or the Ghost?) were successful in finding the cache of treasure.

260

East to Woolwich

Bermondsey's ghosts have a delight in haunting pubs. The Horns, in Crucifix Lane, beneath the railway arches at the approach to London Bridge Station, used to be troubled by the heart-rending sobs of a little girl. Since the misery of the ghost was upsetting both the landlord's family and the staff, an exorcist was brought in who was able to explain that two ghosts were present in the pub, an old lady and the unhappy girl. The latter had apparently been very ill, as had her mother. Both mother and child died, apart from each other and away from the Horns, but the ghost of the little girl returned to the pub, as that was where she remembered being with her mother. The exorcist was able to lay the unhappy spirit, but not that of the harmless old lady, who apparently continues to bang on the walls and move the furniture.

The Anchor Tap in Horselydown Lane used to have a ghost named 'Charlie'. He was never seen, but was a mischievous ghost fond of hiding things in the most unlikely places. Another unseen ghost was reported at the Thomas à Becket in the Old Kent Road. Here there used to be a standing wager of a fiver which was won by anybody brave enough to spend five minutes alone in a room on the top floor. The landlord usually kept the money as quaking customers retreated to the bar after spending a minute or so upstairs.

The King's Arms, at Peckham Rye, looks an unlikely pub to be haunted. It is an angular modern building which has colourful umbrellas shading pavement tables in summer. The previous pub on the site was completely destroyed by a direct hit from a bomb in 1940, eleven people being killed. It is this tragedy that is said to account for the haunting of the modern pub. Staff have told of hearing old wartime songs being sung here by a ghostly choir accompanied by a jangly piano ('Lilli Marlene' being a particular favourite). Footsteps also come from a room kept locked and empty, and the shape of a woman wearing the fashion of the early 1940s has also been seen.

Camberwell only seems to have two ghosts. The spirit of an old clergyman, dressed in the clerical style of yesteryear, was often seen in Churchyard Passage, by St Giles's Church. Although there were reports of its having been seen in the 1970s, the ethereal intensity of the ghostly priest seems to be diminishing, and it is apparently difficult now definitely to identify the figure as being that of a clergyman. The long-demolished music hall at Camberwell, the

Greenwich Hospital (Guildhall Library).

Palace, used to have a dressing-room visited by the ghost of a lion-tamer mauled to death on-stage in 1902.

The Greenwich approach to the Blackwall Tunnel is haunted by a motor-cyclist, in full leather gear, who was killed there in an accident in 1972. Another story that originated in October of the same year also concerned a motor-cyclist. He stopped to give a male hitch-hiker a lift on his pillion, and drove through the tunnel, shouting a conversation to his passenger *en route*, in the course of which the latter told him where he lived. When he emerged on the northern side of the river he turned again to shout a remark to the hitch-hiker, only to find that he had vanished. Panic-stricken he drove back through the tunnel and then returned to Blackwall without finding the least trace of his missing passenger. The next day he visited the address he had been given to be told that from his description the boy who had ridden on his pillion had been dead for some years. Similar stories come from other parts of the country, including one from the A13 London – Southend road where in 1968 a young girl was picked up by a motor-cyclist at the Wickford Roundabout. Thereafter details of the story are identical to the one related above.

A celebrated photograph, supposedly of a ghost, was taken in the

Queen's House at Greenwich in 1966. The shrouded figure appeared on the Tulip Staircase and the photographer, a Canadian clergyman, was certain that there could only be a supernatural explanation for the mysterious figure in his Kodachrome transparency. However, reading Peter Underwood's detailed account of the incident in *A Host of Hauntings*, I, as a professional photographer for the past twenty-five years, am unconvinced. The photographer claimed that the camera was hand-held, and the exposure time was from four to six seconds, yet it was said to be possible to identify a ring the figure was wearing on one of its fingers. The photograph had been taken from a low level: 'it was necessary to crouch down at the side of the doorway and tilt the camera upwards'. Anyone who could hold a camera in such an awkward position and get a sharp picture from an exposure of four seconds would have supernatural powers himself. Most amateurs know the difficulty of retaining sharpness at a twenty-fifth of a second, let alone for a time a hundred times longer!

The Queen Anne block at the Royal Naval Staff College is said to be haunted by the ghost of Admiral Byng, who was imprisoned here before being executed for treason in 1757. This manifests itself in a variety of ways – mysterious footsteps, a 'filmy' figure, as well as a sinister shrouded presence, which vanishes when addressed. Admiral Byng was confined in a small top-floor room in the south-east pavilion. He was unjustly sentenced to death at a court martial in Portsmouth, and shot on board the *Monarque* on 14 March 1757.

The ghost of a wealthy eighteenth-century resident of Greenwich haunts Trafalgar Road in spectacular style. Lord John Angerstein is collected from the Ship and Billet Inn by a coach drawn by four headless horses which drives him to his former home which stood on Vanbrugh Hill.

Another haunted pub is the Fort Tavern, Sandy Hill Road, Woolwich. Here a strange vague figure has been seen on two occasions, but the most usual form of haunting is the sound of heavy footsteps which have disturbed landlords and their families over many years.

A White Lady used to haunt the Paragon district of Blackheath. She was the ghost of a maidservant, Annie Hawkins, who drowned herself in a nearby pond after an unhappy love-affair. A better-known ghost frequents a library at Blackheath located in a house called 'St John's', in the park of the same name close to Shooters Hill. The house was formerly a vicarage, the childhood home of Elsie Marshall.

Death of Adm.l Byng.

(Mary Evans Picture Library).

Her father became Vicar of St John's in 1874, when Elsie was five years of age. As soon as she was old enough, Elsie joined the Church of England Zernana Society as a missionary and in 1892 she sailed for China to take up a position in a remote province. On 1 August 1895, a gang of bandits who called themselves the 'Vegetarians' attacked the mission and killed everyone they found there, including poor Elsie. Her spirit made its way back to the house where she had been so happy as a child, and today the library staff cheerfully accept her presence, knowing that the strange occurrences they experience there (such as all the lights coming on when the building is empty, or an unseen body brushing past them at the door) may be put down to the ghost of Elsie.

Hare and Billet Road also leads off Shooters Hill, and here a darkly dressed Victorian lady is supposed to await her married lover. When he failed to turn up at the rendezvous she hanged herself from a branch of the great elm that stood by the road. She only appears on misty autumn evenings, and was last reported in 1971.

Shooters Hill itself has always had an evil reputation. Two hundred or so years ago it was frequented both by highwaymen and smugglers, and many people met violent deaths here. The bodies of executed highwaymen were often left hanging from a gibbet here, their skeletal remains intended to warn off their fellows. Another White Lady used to haunt the cross-roads where Well Hall Road meets the Hill. In 1844 a lady's skeleton was unearthed about fifty yards from this cross-roads: it seemed as though she had been brutally murdered; carefully braided golden hair still adhered to a savage wound at the back of her head. Her ghost restlessly wandered about this stretch of road for many years, giving heart-rending cries of terror or despair, though she has not been seen recently. Her identity was never discovered and she was buried in the nearby churchyard.

Close by is Charlton village where the beautiful mansion of Charlton House has a wonderful variety of ghosts on offer. Most famous is that of Sir William Langhorne, a wealthy merchant trading with India, who lived in the house, designed by Inigo Jones, until his death at the age of eighty-five in 1714. His great sorrow was that he was unable to beget an heir to his fortune, though he was twice married. Thus his ghost pursues living ladies that catch his fancy: on occasion it has even been accused of rape! Perhaps the ghost is not quite so active now as it was formerly since recent overnight guests have only complained of 'presences' in the bedrooms. Wardens of

Charlton House (Mansell Collection).

Charlton House (now a Community Centre) speak of a spot on the first landing of the staircase where an uncanny chill strikes. Eric Maple pointed out that a carved devil's head was on the banister of the staircase and looked directly towards the corner from where the mysterious draught came. The north wing of the house was bombed during the war and, in the course of rebuilding, workmen discovered the body of a baby boy in one of the chimneys, mummified by years of smoke and heat. The ghost of a servant-girl has been seen wandering through the grounds, and she carries a baby in her arms.

It is said that dreadful memories of the Lewisham train disaster of 1957 are stirred by ghostly voices heard at three in the morning close to Chiesman's Store, Lewisham. Strangely, they seem to emanate from mid-air – 'very mournful, eerie, and disturbing'.

The Lady of Lee was an eighteenth-century lady-in-waiting to Lady Dacre who was murdered when she was alone in the great house. Subsequently her spirit used to return to a gatekeeper's lodge at the end of the long drive that led to the house. A cottage in Brandram Road, Lee, now stands on the site of the old lodge, and the ghost, wearing a mop-cap, bodice, and long flowing dress has been seen there in this century. Pentland Manor House, Old Road, Lee (a hostel for the girls from Goldsmiths' College) is haunted by the ghost of a long-dead seaman, Robert Smith, who was killed in a naval engagement during the Napoleonic Wars. Two of the students at Pentland House who shared a room were afraid to spend the night alone there because of the attentions of this ghost.

The ruins of Lesness Abbey at Catford are supposed to be haunted (though the ghost has never actually been seen) and so is the junction of Bromley Road and Southend Lane (Bellingham). Here the ghost of Alice Grant still lingers; she was killed on 2 September 1898, when she was knocked off her bicycle by a brewer's dray. Alice was returning home having spent the day with her friend Jessie in the countryside of Kent. Her ghost is seen at dusk, wearing a white blouse with leg-of-mutton sleeves and a long, black skirt, looking for the friend with whom she had spent her last, happy, day alive.

In May 1971, the *Kentish Independent* carried reports of a ghostly RAF pilot who had begun to haunt a butcher's shop at Tavy Bridge, Thamesmead. This was immediately linked to the wreckage of a Spitfire which had recently been found near by when excavations were being made to construct a children's paddling-pool. Scepticism never succeeded in totally discrediting this ghost, as the following account from the *Eltham Times* of 22 January 1976 shows:

The Ghostly figure of a RAF World War II fighter pilot has been seen walking along Tavy Bridge, Thamesmead, on dark and moonless nights according to local stories.

One theory circulating in the area is of a pilot whose Spitfire was shot down during the Battle of Britain in the latter months of 1940, crashing on the marshes near Woolwich. Another is that the ghost is of a pilot who crashed in February of the same year. unfortunately no-one seems to know exactly where the Spitfire crashed and who was flying it. Now two new theories have been advanced. The first comes from Mr. J. Boult of Grove Road, Belvedere who claims that remains of a fighter were found when excavations were being carried out near Southmere lake, Thamesmead, in 1971.

And the second comes from the Battle of Britain Museum at Chilham Castle, Gravesend, where a spokesman said two Spitfire wings, one from Woolwich and another from an unspecified place in the marshes, are on display.

He corroborated Mr. Boult's claim that the fighters were found in 1971 and suggested that the machine which crashed in February 1940 was involved in some kind of experimental flight.

What is clear is that the Thamesmead ghost is hardly likely to be a result of the fighter that came down near Woolwich – and the mystery surrounding the other Spitfire seems to have a suitably enigmatic background for a ghost.

However the GLC have claimed that no aircraft was ever found in Thamesmead, and as nobody can definitely say that either fighter was found there, the mystery remains unsolved.

St Thomas's Hospital

St Thomas's Hospital stands on a wonderful riverside site opposite the Palace of Westminster. Nearly all of the Victorian building has disappeared, to be replaced by modern glass and concrete structures, but Block Eight of the old hospital survives, and this is the haunt of the famous Grey Lady.

She is grey because this was the colour chosen by Florence Nightingale for the uniform of her nurses in the Crimea (she subsequently founded her School for Nursing at St Thomas's). There is no question that the ghost is that of a nurse of yesteryear (the grey uniform was changed to blue in the early 1920s) – what is disputed is the cause of the haunting. It is variously suggested that it is the ghost of a nurse:

> who was over-sensitive to a Sister's sharp tongue; on being severely reprimanded she ran off and threw herself to her death from the top-floor balcony; or
> who killed herself after administering the wrong dose of a drug to a patient, thus causing his death; or
> who died of smallpox on the top floor of Block Eight.

This last reason is the oldest, and was used to explain the presence of the Grey Lady on the top floor of Block Eight in the 1880s. The next written account of her dates from 1929 when Mr Edwin Frewer, later the Superintendent of Works at St Thomas's, encountered the ghost soon after taking up a post at the hospital:

> First there was the feeling, the clammy sensation that made me stop abruptly. It was like driving suddenly into a fog.
>
> Then this figure of a nurse came walking down the middle of the corridor. She was dressed in very old-fashioned uniform with a long skirt, and her face was distraught. The whole scene was incredibly vivid but there was a kind of haze around the nurse that separated her from her surroundings.
>
> There was a look of horror in her eyes. I can still feel the shock that made me stop stock still. I was aware that this was a very real woman, of about thirty, who was desperately seeking release from torment.

St Thomas's Hospital (Guildhall Library).

His colleague with whom he was walking turned and asked him what was the matter. . . .

'Just look at this nurse!' I said. He looked but said he saw nothing. As I pointed to her she just disappeared. I was quite new to the hospital and could not have had any pre-conceived picture of this nurse, nor of the tragedy attached to her. The memory of her face, with its look of horror, remains with me after all these years.

On a bright April morning in 1937 Dr Anwyl-Davies saw the Grey Lady in the same corridor as Mr Frewer. He raised his hat and greeted her. When she glided past him without seeming to notice his presence he turned to look after her, and saw her outline turn transparent, and then she disappeared. The doctor was so struck by this experience that eleven years later he wrote of it in the *Journal of the Society for Psychical Research* and he remained convinced that he had seen a ghost for the rest of his life.

The next appearance of the Grey Lady was probably the most dramatic. It occurred in November 1943, when London was suffering under a double burden of conventional night-time bombing raids, plus the attentions of the new flying-bombs which struck in daylight hours, and brought a new terror to the civilian population. St Thomas's suffered badly from both forms of aerial bombardment, and

Mr Charles Bide was responsible for salvaging any items of value from the debris. He had laboriously climbed to the top floor of Block Eight (part of the staircase had collapsed) and was alone there piling undamaged furniture, etc. in a safe, dry place until it could be taken down. Having lifted a painting from the wall he noticed a mirror hanging next to it, miraculously uncracked. As he reached to take it down he saw the Grey Lady reflected in it, standing behind him.

What held me were the eyes. This apparition *knew* that I could see it. The eyes were just like a cat that's been locked out all night, and got cold and nobody wants it, unloved and uncared for. . . . They were terrible eyes and held mine, it seemed like ages. The intense cold . . . the cold that came from her was twenty times colder than the actual cold outside, and the hair on the back of my head went right up.

Mr Bide described the smell that accompanied the apparition – like the sweet smell that comes when you pull moss or grass up from between flagstones – and how suddenly the spell was broken, and he was able to hurry from the scene, down the broken staircase.

Many years later he half-regretted his flight from the ghost:

. . . I think, that if I could have only stood my ground, this person was trying to tell me something. I wish I'd held my ground, but I'm afraid I was too much of a coward, and I never stopped. But an awful feeling, the feeling she brought with her of depression . . . you know what depressions are like, don't you? . . . well this depression that she brought with her was twenty times worse than that. An *awful* feeling . . . a *terrible* feeling of loneliness and depression.

(Extracts from an interview Mr Bide gave to Nick McIver on 24 August 1979, contained in the files of the Society for Psychical Research.)

Although none of those mentioned thus far came to any harm after seeing the Grey Lady, a more sinister aspect to her appearances was reported by Peter Underwood in *Haunted London*. He describes how five patients saw the Grey Lady on separate occasions between 1956 and 1959. All died within a few days of her appearance. (Evidence of this usually came about when patients spoke of the kind nurse dressed in grey who had tended to their needs: of course no such nurse worked on the wards.)

Westwards from Lambeth to Barnes

Lambeth Palace has been the residence of the archbishops of Canterbury for seven centuries. The oldest part of the fabric is contained in the walls of the crypt, built on five levels, the earliest part dating from the thirteenth century. Many human skeletons have been unearthed here, some from secret burials of victims who succumbed to tortures applied here. Not surprisingly, the palace and its environs are well haunted. The ghost of Anne Boleyn may be seen making her last journey, by boat, from the palace to the headsman's block at the Tower of London. She left Lambeth from the Water Tower, and her spectral barge has been seen on the adjacent stretch of river. Anne's voice has been heard, too, by the door to the Undercroft where she was tried for adultery before Archbishop Cranmer. Her sobbing pleas and piteous moans cease when the startled passerby stops to listen.

The Lollards Prison still reverberates with the cosmic echoes of those who suffered here for their faith centuries ago. Many people find themselves unable to climb the spiral staircase that leads up to the chamber. Some of the inscriptions scratched on the walls of the prison speak of the agonies of the inmates. A haunted door sometimes opens easily; on other occasions it mysteriously locks itself. One man had reason to thank whatever supernatural agency causes this phenomenon. During the Second World War he was on the roof firewatching when he was called down to the duty-room. However, he was stopped by the haunted door which had locked itself. While he was waiting at the door a bomb dropped directly on the duty-room: had the door allowed him to pass he would certainly have been killed.

The Elephant and Castle Underground Station (Northern and Bakerloo Lines) is haunted by the sound of running footsteps. These are frequently heard by maintenance staff working there after services have stopped, especially on wintry nights. When the Victoria Line was being built it was necessary to make a new tunnel beneath the Thames close to Vauxhall Bridge. The navvies who excavated this in 1968 firmly believed in the ghost many of them met in the dark gloom. Irishmen working on the project called him 'The Quare Feller' and one described him as being at least seven feet tall, with outstretched, menacing, hands and arms. They believed that they had disturbed one of the Plague pits of 1665.

271

Battersea has its ghosts: the Old Swan pub was rebuilt in 1969 though the smugglers' tunnels which lead from its cellars to the neighbouring Parish Church survive. The original pub was flourishing in the twelfth century – popular with the watermen who rowed passengers up and down the Thames, the most important of London's thoroughfares in medieval and Tudor times. The ghost at the Old Swan has not appeared at the rebuilt pub.

Close by is Old Battersea House, built by Wren as a Dower House for Viscount Bolingbroke. This was the home of Mrs Stirling, a prolific writer who is the source of many excellent ghost stories. She died shortly before her hundredth birthday in August 1965. Mrs Stirling always enjoyed telling visitors about the ghosts who frequented her home, though she had to admit that she had never seen any of them herself. However she had a great friend who was particularly perceptive of them. One day she suddenly stopped Mrs Stirling from sitting in a fifteenth-century Italian armchair and when she was asked why she had done this replied that a man was sitting there already. He had a tiny pointed beard, a great Elizabethan ruff round his neck, and held a rapier in his hand – and the old lady had been about to sit in his lap!

On another occasion, in 1943, the same lady was left in the hall while other tea-time guests went upstairs with Mrs Stirling to look at a painting. When they returned their hostess noticed that her friend was looking preoccupied and later asked her whether anything was the matter. She replied:

'I was waiting for you alone in the hall, when I glanced up and saw a man looking over the banisters on the upper landing. To my surprise he was wearing a plumed hat, a gay coat with, what particularly struck me, some remarkable odd-shaped diamond buttons, and jack-boots which I could see through the balustrades of the landing. As I gazed in surprise at this figure, he turned and came slowly downstairs towards me. While he approached, I distinctly heard his sword strike against the oak stairs with every step he trod, but when he reached me he took no notice of my presence. He brushed rudely against me as he passed, and, without apology, walked on through the swing doors opposite and disappeared.'

'Was he like anyone you can recall?' I asked.

'If it was no one in fancy dress,' she said, 'he was exactly like a picture I have seen of the great Duke of Marlborough – *yes, and I recognised the very odd arrangement of the eight buttons on his coat, two and two each side.* But the Duke was never in your house.'

'On the contrary,' I explained, 'tradition says he was constantly here. He was a great friend of Lord Bolingbroke.'

She looked at me thoughtfully. 'It *was* the Duke,' she said conclusively, 'and he shoved me because I am a relation!'

This story is told in *The Merry Wives of Battersea*, by A. M. W. Stirling, published in 1956. The strength of character of the old lady is well illustrated by her attitude to another friend, the late Queen Mary, who often used to call at Old Battersea House. She was adept at admiring antiques in the houses she visited in the expectation that she would be offered the piece as a gift. On every occasion that she called upon Mrs Stirling the Queen commented on the beautiful colour of the blue plates made by her brother-in-law, William de Morgan. Each time Mrs Stirling agreed on the great beauty of the colouring, adding that it was her favourite colour, too. The Queen always departed without the articles on which she had set her sights: these must have been the only occasions when this technique of adding to her own collection failed.

The files of the Society for Psychical Research provide a story from Wandsworth. It is contained in a letter from the proprietor of a fish restaurant in Wandsworth Road, dated December 1962:

Dear Sirs,   523 Wandsworth Road

I respectfully bring to your notice a phenomena that has occured at the above address, and trust that it may be of sufficient interest for your investigation, which I would welcome.

In April of this year, I opened a Fish Restaurant here. The business potential was very good, and the weekly turnover increased rapidly over the first four months.

In the last six or seven weeks of that period, a large black and beautiful dog was seen to pass from the rear rooms of the premises, through the Shop, and out into the street, from whence it would turn right, and lope away up the main road and out of sight. This 'visitation' occured six or seven times, always between 6 and 6.30 p.m., and when we were sitting at a table, in the then empty shop, and with the rear door locked. On one occasion he brushed solidly against my wife's leg, and on each appearance was seen by three of us clearly.

Then the 'visitations' ceased, and from that time until the present, my business has fallen into a sharp decline, and quite out of character with the potential previously referred to.

The extent of this is really alarming, as well as unaccountable, and I am now inclined to connect this with the 'visitations'. With this in mind, I seek your good offices, in which I repose much faith. I am reasonably free for interview at any time convenient to yourselves, and would thank you in anticipation of your early and favourable reaction.

Yours faithfully,

p.p. R. Shekerzade

A.B. Butcher (Mr.)

The file also contains a handwritten note by G. W. Lambert, a former President of the Society, explaining the satisfactory outcome of the incident:

Mr Butcher (for Mr Shekerzade) phoned 11 December 1962 – he said that they had ascertained that a former owner of the restaurant used to bring a black dog there. It was run over at a cross-roads nearby and killed, so the one seen by Mr and Mrs S. must have been its ghost. He also said that since the SPR representative had called there had been a great improvement in the custom at the restaurant, which was now at a satisfactory level.

Wandsworth Prison is haunted by a sad ghost named Annie. A cutting from the *Wandsworth Borough News* describes her activities, somewhat flippantly, perhaps:

Prisons are not without their ghosts, and our local detention centre – Wandsworth Prison – has its own spectre inmate.

She is known as 'Wandsworth Annie' and has been seen by prisoners and officers alike, often walking along the high vaulted corridors in this grim Victorian edifice.

Annie is believed to be the ghost of a middle-aged woman who had died in the prison some twenty years after it was opened as a house of correction for men and women, and the haunting habit, if it can be described thus, is a shabby grey dress. But she is a passive figure and confines herself to the occasional walk along the corridors, with no moans, shrieks, or clanking of chains.

A letter to the Editor of the same newspaper describes another

Ranelagh (Guildhall Library).

local ghost – the White Lady of Ranelagh. Long ago, it seems, a fair
lady was with her lover in the grounds of Old Ranelagh when they
were interrupted by a jealous suitor who stabbed his rival in the back.
On nights with a full moon '. . . the assassin madly rides his horse up
the drive, past the old gatekeeper's lodge, and out into the Lower
Richmond Road, and later, slowly and mournfully, walks a lady
wringing her hands, weeping, and crying the name of the murdered
man "Paul, Paul".'

Clapham and Stockwell

Turning to the east again, the Plough Inn on Clapham Common was so well haunted in 1970 that the landlord eventually lost his job for taking too much interest in the ghost, which was, apparently, bad for trade. The Plough is a very old pub, and its top floors had long had the reputation of being haunted by a ghost named Sarah. After the arrival of the new landlord the appearances of Sarah increased suddenly, frightening the resident staff considerably. She was seen standing by an open window dressed in white, her long black hair blown by the breeze. Then she vanished abruptly. The departure of the landlord whose interest in Sarah was displeasing to the owners of the pub brought a respite from the haunting. Another mystery of the Plough was its secret room, opened up in 1970. Previously the window of this room was occasionally seen to be open, yet, for some reason unknown, the door to the room had been bricked up for many years.

In 1772 Stockwell was still a 'retired village' – yet events early in that year had given it a notoriety that rivalled Cock Lane's during the heyday of the 'ghost' there. The story was told in an 'authentic, Candid, and Circumstantial Narrative' published with the blessing of those then being troubled by the ghost. They included:

Mrs Golding, an elderly lady of independent fortune at whose house in Stockwell the transactions began.

Mrs Pain, her niece, who had been married for several years to Mr Pain, a farmer, of Brixton Causeway [*imagine a farm at Brixton today!*].

Ann Robinson, Mrs Golding's maid, a young woman, about twenty years old, who had lived with her but one week and three days.

I shall not take up any more of the reader's attention from the narrative, but begin as follows.

On *Monday, January* the 6th, 1772, about ten o'clock in the forenoon, as Mrs. *Golding* was in her parlour, she heard the china and glasses in the back kitchen tumble down and break; her maid came to her and told her the stone plates were falling from the shelf; Mrs. *Golding* went into the kitchen and saw them broke. Presently after, a row of plates from the next shelf fell down likewise, while she was there, and nobody near them; this astonished her much, and while she was thinking about it, other things in different places

Stockwell village (Guildhall Library).

began to tumble about, some of them breaking, attended with violent noises all over the house; a clock tumbled down and the case broke; a lanthorn that hung on the staircase was thrown down and the glass broke to pieces; an earthen pan of salted beef broke to pieces and the beef fell about, all this increased her surprise, and brought several persons about her, among whom was Mr. *Rowlidge*, a carpenter, who gave it as his opinion that the foundation was giving way and that the house was tumbling down, occasioned by the too great weight of an additional room erected above: so ready are we to discover natural causes for every thing! But no such thing happened as the reader will find, for whatever was the cause, that cause ceased almost as soon as Mrs. *Golding* and her maid left any place, and followed them wherever they went. Mrs. *Golding* run into Mr *Gresham's* house, a gentleman living next door to her, where she fainted.

The key factor, as the writer of the pamphlet emphasised above, is that as long as Mrs Golding and her maid were together, in any house, the troubles continued. Meanwhile kindly neighbours were moving to safety the breakables which remained intact at Mrs Golding's house. At this time Ann Robinson was upstairs in the house 'and when called upon several times to come down, for fear of the dangerous situation she was thought to be in, she answered very coolly, and after some time came down as deliberately, without any seeming fearful apprehensions'.

Mrs Pain was sent for from Brixton as the neighbours believed her aunt to be dead, but by the time she arrived at Mr Gresham's house Mrs Golding had recovered, though she remained very faint. A surgeon was called in from Clapham to bleed her, and about this time bedlam broke out again, now in Mr Gresham's house.

> The glasses and china which stood on the side-board, began to tumble about and fall down, and broke both the glasses to pieces. Mr. *Saville* and others being asked to drink a glass of wine or rum, both the bottles broke in pieces before they were uncorked.
>
> Mrs. *Golding's* surprize and fear increasing, she did not know what to do or where to go; wherever she and her maid were, these strange destructive circumstances followed her, and how to help or free herself from them, was not in her power or any other person's present: her mind was one confused chaos, lost to herself and every thing about her, drove from her own home, and afraid there would be none other to receive her; at last she left Mr. *Gresham's* and went to Mr. *Mayling's*, a gentleman at the next door, where she staid about three quartures of an hour, during which time nothing happened. Her maid staid at Mr. *Gresham's*, to help put up what few things remained unbroke of her mistress's, in a back apartment, when a jar of pickles that stood upon a table, turned upside down, then a jar of rasberry jam broke to pieces, next two mahogany waiters and a quadrille-box likewise broke in pieces.

Mrs Golding was taken to her niece's house at Brixton, accompanied by Ann. For most of the afternoon all was peaceful. The maid was sent back to Stockwell to see whether the disturbance continued there. On her return she reported that nothing untoward had occurred since they had left. However trouble broke out at Brixton soon afterwards:

> But about eight o'clock in the evening a fresh scene began, the first thing that happened, was, a whole row of pewter dishes, except one,

fell from off a shelf to the middle of the floor, rolled about a little while, then settled, and what is almost beyond belief, as soon as they were quiet, turned upside down; they were then put on the dresser, and went through the same a second time: next fell a whole row of pewter plates from off the second shelf over the dresser to the ground, and being taken up and put on the dresser one in another, they were thrown down again.

The next thing was two eggs that were upon one of the pewter shelves, one of them flew off, crossed the kitchen, struck a cat on the head, and then broke to pieces.

Things went from bad to worse until there were few articles left intact in the farmhouse.

All the family were eye witnesses to these circumstances as well as other persons, some of whom were so alarmed and shocked, that they could not bear to stay, and was happy in getting away, though the unhappy family were left in the midst of their distresses. Most of the genteel families around, were continually sending to enquire after them, and whether all was over or not. Is it not surprising that some among them had not the inclination and resolution to try to unravel this most intricate affair, at a time when it would have been in their power to have done so; there certainly was sufficient time for so doing, as the whole from first to last continued upwards of twenty hours.

At all the times of action, Mrs. Golding's Servant was walking backwards and forwards, either in the kitchen or parlour, or wherever some of the family happened to be. Nor could they get her to sit down five minutes together, except at one time for about half an hour towards the morning, when the family were at prayers in the parlour; then all was quiet; but in the midst of the greatest confusion, she was as much composed as at any other time, and with uncommon coolness of temper advised her mistress not to be alarmed or uneasy, as she said these things could not be helped. Thus she argued as if they were common occurrences which must happen in every family.

This advice surprised and startled her mistress, almost as much as the circumstances that occasioned it. For how can we suppose that a girl of about twenty years old, (an age when female timidity is too often assisted by superstition) could remain in the midst of such calamitous circumstances (except they proceeded from causes best known to herself) and not be struck with the same terror as every other person was who was present. These reflections led Mr. Pain, and at the end of the transactions, likewise Mrs. Golding, to think that she was not altogether so unconcerned as she appeared to be. But hitherto, the whole remains mysterious and unravelled.

The chaos continued through the night. The children had to be taken to the barn for safety, and none of the household was able to rest. By five in the morning even the furniture was tumbling about, and it was decided to abandon the house to the ghost. They went across the road to the house of Richard Fowler, who had been at Mr Pain's during the evening, but had been so terrified that he had soon returned home. The same scene began here all over again: a fire was almost started when a lighted lantern was upset and oil spilled across the room

. . . the maid then desired Richard Fowler not to let her mistress remain there, as she said, wherever she was, the same things would follow. In consequence of this advice, and fearing greater losses to himself, he desired she would quit his house; but first begged her to consider within herself, for her own and public sake, whether or not she had not been guilty of some atrocious crime, for which providence was determined to pursue her on this side the grave, for he could not help thinking, she was the object that was to be made an example to posterity, by the all seeing eye of providence, for crimes which but too often none but that providence can penetrate, and by such means as these bring to light.

To the poor old lady this sanctimonious advice must have seemed like the last straw. Worn out and in despair, she returned to her own house at Stockwell with her niece's husband and the maid. Soon after they entered the house the troubles began anew 'upon the remains that were left':

A nine gallon cask of beer, that was in the cellar, the door being open, and no person near it, turned upside down.

A pail of water that stood on the floor, boiled like a pot.

A box of candles fell from a shelf in the kitchen to the floor, they rolled out, but none were broke.

A round mahogany table overset in the parlour.

Mr. Pain then desired Mrs. Golding to send her maid for his wife to come to them, when she was gone all was quiet; upon her return she was immediately discharged, and no disturbances have happened since; this was between six and seven o'clock on Tuesday morning.

At Mrs. Golding's were broke the quantity of three pails full of glass, china, &c.

At Mrs. Pain's they filled two pails.

Thus ends the narrative; a true, circumstantial, and faithful account of which I have laid before the public; for so doing, I hope to escape its censure; I have neither exaggerated or diminished one circumstance to my knowledge; and have endeavoured as much as possible, throughout the whole, to state only the facts, without presuming to obtrude my opinion on them. If I have in part hinted any thing that may appear unfavourable to the girl, it proceeded not from a determination to charge her with the cause, right or wrong, but only from a strict adherence to truth, most sincerely wishing this extraordinary affair may be unravelled.

The above narrative, is absolutely and strictly true, in witness whereof we have set our hands this eleventh day of January, 1772,

MARY GOLDING.
JOHN PAIN.
MARY PAIN.
RICHARD FOWLER.
SARAH FOWLER.
MARY MARTIN.

It was probably assumed at the time that the poltergeist was a disturbed spirit unwittingly harboured by the girl. Throughout history this sort of activity seems to be generated by some form of psychic energy present in adolescence. Many, many years later, however, the true story was published. Ann Robinson confessed the truth of the matter to a clergyman, the Reverend Brayfield. She wished to have the house empty so that she could entertain her lover there. Walford's *Old and New London* explains the mechanics of her trickery:

> She placed the china on the shelves in such a manner that it fell on the slightest motion; and she attached horse-hair to other articles, so that she could jerk them down from an adjoining room without being perceived by any one. She was exceedingly dextrous at this sort of work, and would have proved a formidable rival to many a juggler by profession.

Bibliography

Abbot, G.	*Ghosts of the Tower of London*, 1980
Aubrey, John	*Anecdotes*
	Miscellanies, 1696
Bailey, James Blake (editor)	*Diary of a Resurrectionist*, 1896
Bovet, Richard	*Pandaemonium*, 1684
Braddock, Joseph	*Haunted Houses*, 1956
Brown, Raymond Lamont	*Phantoms of the Sea*
	Phantoms of the Theatre, 1978
Davis, Richard	*I've seen a Ghost*, 1979
Emslie, J. P.	See *London Studies*, No. 1, 1974
Farson, Daniel	*Hamlyn Book of Ghosts*
Grant, Douglas	*The Cock Lane Ghost*, 1965
Green, Andrew	*Our Haunted Kingdom*, 1975
Haining, Peter	*The Mystery and Horrible Murders of Sweeney Todd*, 1979
Hallam, J.	*Ghosts of London*, 1975
Harper, Charles	*Haunted Houses*, 1907, 1931
Hopkins, Thurston	*Ghosts over England*
Howitt, W.	*Northern Heights of London*
Hutton, Luke	*The Black Dogge of Newgate*, 1638
Ingram, J. H.	*The Haunted Houses and Family Traditions of Great Britain*, 1884
Jarvis, T. M.	*Accredited Ghost Stories*, 1823
Knapp and Baldwin	*New Newgate Calendar*
Lambert, G. W.	'Geography of London Ghosts', from *Proceedings of the Society for Psychical Research*, No. 720
Larwood, J.	*Story of the London Parks*, 1872
Lee, F. G.	*Glimpses of the Supernatural*, 1875
	Sights and Shadows, 1894
Lichtenstein, Princess Marie	*The History of Holland House*
Linebaugh, P.	*Albion's Fatal Tree*, 1975
Maple, Eric	*The Realm of Ghosts*, 1964
	Supernatural England, 1977

O'Donnell, Elliot	*Haunted Houses of London*, 1909
	More Haunted Houses of London, 1920
Palmer, Samuel	*History of St Pancras*, 1870
Pope, W. J. M.	*Ghosts and Greasepaint*, 1951
	Haymarket Theatre, 1948
	Theatre Royal, Drury Lane, 1945
Prickett, E.	*History of Highgate*
Rollins, H. E.	*The Pack of Autolycus*, 1931
Shute, Nerina	*London Villages*, 1973
'Spectre Stricken'	*Ghostly Visitors*, 1882
Stirling, A. M. W.	*Ghosts Vivisected*, 1957
	The Merry Wives of Battersea, 1956
	The Richmond Papers, 1927
Underwood, Peter	*Haunted London*, 1973
	A Host of Hauntings, 1973
Walford, E.	*Old and New London*
Welby, H.	*Mysteries of Life*, 1861
	Signs before Death, 1875

Journals
Arminian Magazine, 1781
Gentleman's Magazine, various issues
Medical & Physical Journal, The (Royal College of Surgeons) Volume IX
The News – a Miscellany of Fortean Curiosities, January 1976
Notes & Queries, various issues
The Terrific Register, 1825

Index